WORK & FAMILY

Toby L. Parcel
Daniel B. Cornfield
Editors

WORK & FAMILY

Research Informing Policy

Sage Publications, Inc.
International Educational and Professional Publisher
Thousand Oaks ▪ London ▪ New Delhi

For information:

Sage Publications, Inc.
2455 Teller Road
Thousand Oaks, California 91320
E-mail: order@sagepub.com

Sage Publications Ltd.
6 Bonhill Street
London EC2A 4PU
United Kingdom

Sage Publications India Pvt. Ltd.
M-32 Market
Greater Kailash I
New Delhi 110 048 India

Printed in the United States of America

Library of Congress Cataloging-in-Publication Data

Main entry under title:

Work and Family: Research informing policy/edited by Toby L. Parcel
  and Daniel B. Cornfield.
        p.   cm.
    Includes bibliographical references and index.
    ISBN 0-7619-1307-6 (cloth: alk.paper)
    ISBN 0-7619-1308-4 (pbk.: alk. paper)
      1. Work and family. 2. Women—Employment. 3. Work and family—
  United States. 4. Women—Employment—United States. I. Parcel, Toby L.
  II. Cornfield, Daniel B.
      HD904.25 .W686 1999
      306.3′6—dc21   99-050414

This book is printed on acid-free paper.

00   01   02   03   04   05   06   7   6   5   4   3   2   1

Acquisition Editor:	Peter Labella
Editorial Assistant:	Renee Piernot
Production Editor:	Sanford Robinson
Editorial Assistant:	Nevair Kabakian
Typesetter:	Marion Warren
Indexer:	Cristina Haley
Cover Designer:	Ravi Balasuriya

Contents

Introduction

I ssues at the nexus of work and family continue to claim the attention of scholars, policymakers, and citizens. Most adults engage in paid work. At various points in their lives, most adults also simultaneously bear primary responsibility for children and other family members (Coltrane, 1996; Hochschild, 1997; Parcel & Menaghan, 1994). Sociologists have responded to this reality by devoting increasing attention to issues regarding work and family. In particular, sociology has pointed to social inequalities associated with work-family imbalance. Some of these inequalities are based on gender, as women often shoulder a disproportionate part of the burden in both caring for family members as well as participating in paid employment. Additional inequalities may fall according to race and class cleavages, with members of racial minorities and less economically advantaged groups less able to balance work and family demands simultaneously. Sociology's commitment to rigorous empiricism, both quantitative and qualitative, is an important foundation for uncovering these differences and for suggesting mechanisms to achieve resolution.

This volume contains some of the best chapters addressing these questions that researchers in our field are producing. An important foundation for this volume was the Special Issue of *Work and Occupations* published in November 1996, titled "Work and Family: Research Informing Policy," edited by Toby L. Parcel and published by Sage Publications. Subsequent to that, Parcel and Daniel Cornfield worked together to solicit and shape additional chapters that complemented and enhanced the themes raised in that journal issue. This volume represents the cumulative results of those efforts.

Why are issues of work and family so central to our thinking at the close of the 20th century? These issues have always been important, but social changes in the institutions of both work and the family have interacted to increase their salience for adults in many societies (see Parcel & Menaghan, 1994, Spain & Bianchi, 1996, and Blau & Ehrenberg, 1997, for useful overviews). Sharp expansion of white-collar work as well as the advent of the information age have increased the numbers of jobs for which women are likely to be hired. Complementary decreases in the importance of manual, agricultural, and production work, traditionally dominated by men, complete the picture. Barriers to women's participation in many professions employing men have been reduced, thus increasing the opportunity for some women to participate in high-paying employment. At the same time, men's wage increases have slowed relative to the gains that they experienced in the 1960s; both the actual and perceived costs of establishing a household and raising a family have risen. In addition, levels of women's education have risen steadily over time, to the point where women are more likely than men to graduate from high school and where college attendance rates for women come close to those of men. Changes in norms regarding the traditional gender roles have allowed some women to make educational and employment choices that have involved greater duration of employment after marriage and after childbearing, even when their children are young. With both greater investment of women's human capital and increased opportunities for female employment, it is not surprising that in 1996, close to 62.7% of mothers with children under 6 worked outside the home (U.S. Bureau of the Census, 1997).

At the same time, family structure has also changed. Spain and Bianchi (1996) use data from several U.S. Censuses and other federal sources to trace important changes occurring in patterns of childbearing, marriage, and living arrangements for cohorts of women born between the early 20th century and the 1970s. They find that age at first marriage has risen, and adults spend smaller proportions of their lives married, primarily owing to increased rates of divorce, although these rates have declined slightly in recent years. Trends toward later marriage (as well as delay of remarriage) have contributed to growth in single-parent families. In 1994, female-headed households constituted 27% of all households (U.S. Bureau of the Census, 1995, p. xvii). Childbearing outside of marriage has increased so that by 1993, 31% of births were to unmarried women; close to one quarter of White women's births and more than two thirds of births to Black women were outside of marriage (Ventura, 1995).

But with these changes have come intense debates regarding attendant costs to families and society. There is divergent opinion about whether maternal work has greater costs than benefits, and whether individual families may benefit from maternal earnings at the expense of their children's long-term well-being and the well-being of society. Of course, few question the necessity of paternal work or wonder, for example, whether paternal overtime might be deleterious to child development. The assumption is that paternal work is normative, whereas maternal work is defined as at least a potential problem. Several of the chapters in this volume argue that paternal and maternal work should be treated more evenhandedly, and this is a welcome innovation that we explore more thoroughly later.

Two elements emerge from these debates. The first is the issue of how *time* underlies much of the concern regarding the simultaneity of balancing work and family. The second concerns how social policies as well as choices families make interact either to assist or to hinder the challenges of managing work and family obligations. We begin by considering the several ways in which time is relevant to work-family nexus. We then comment on related literature and show how our chapters suggest the relevance of social policy to the daily lives of families who face competing demands at home and at work.

TIME

The most obvious way in which time is relevant to work and family is in the sense of the daily "juggling act" that arises as families try to balance simultaneously the demands of paid employment and family life. This interpretation of time gives rise to numerous questions regarding strategies that families might employ in order to reduce the time pressures that having "two jobs" necessarily entails (Hochschild, 1989). For some families, having (typically) mothers engage in part-time work helps to reduce the overload from dealing with both work and family. We know, however, that this option, so popular in Great Britain and Germany, appears less frequently in the United States. As noted above, even mothers with young children are quite likely to work full-time. Other strategies that families employ to balance work and family obligations include, in two-parent households, having the adults work during different hours of the day or different days of the week; even women in female-headed households may work nonstandard hours in order both to care for children and to maintain household income. As implied above, the issue of whether it is necessarily the mother who must bear the burden of the daily juggling act is an important one. Given average earnings differentials between men and women, some families will make the decision that maternal part-time work is a rational choice. Traditional sex role attitudes reinforce this choice. In other families, however, maternal pay may be nearly equal to or exceed spouses' pay. In these cases, having mothers engage in part-time work may not be optimal for all concerned.

The concept of the life course is the second way in which the notion of time influences our thinking about work and family. Thinking about the life course directs us to take a longitudinal as opposed to cross-sectional look at the family. When one parent engages in part-time work "while the children are young," implicit in this statement is the realization that the family may opt for a different decision as the children grow older. Usually it is the mother who withdraws from the labor force while children are young, with the expectation that she will return at some point in the future. Thus, these families at least implicitly acknowledge the reality of the life course, suggesting that paid employment is more or less feasible at certain points given other obligations.

The rationale may be that when the family is in its early stages, a high proportion of parental time needs to be invested in the home in order to promote child well-being and to reduce conflicts between caring for young children and pursuing paid employment. As children grow older and require less direct care, income demands to pay for college and to fund adult retirement may suggest that a greater ratio of parental time be invested in paid work relative to unpaid time in the home. Thus, the life course influences parental time allocation in two ways. First, the needs of children suggest changes in parental time allocation as children mature. Second, adult needs to provide support for themselves after retirement may reinforce decisions to shift adult time from home to paid employment as the life course proceeds prior to retirement. This model does not address the reality of adults caring for elderly parents as well as working. Nor does it address what happens to the "sandwich generation," those adults who simultaneously care for both children at home and elderly parents, as well as pursue paid employment. However, acknowledging this complication merely reinforces the importance of the life course as an organizing framework for thinking about work and family.

Finally, historical events, which necessarily unfold over time, can be relevant to family well-being. Viewing the family in historical perspective also encourages us to take a longitudinal view. In addition, however, it requires that we acknowledge that macrolevel historical events can influence the ways in which work and family play out in the lives of citizens. The reason that issues of work and family are at the forefront of our thinking today is that we are in a historical period where investments in human capital, job availability, and decline in traditional sex roles produce conflicts between work and family requirements for many adults. Such conflicts were less common earlier in the 20th century, although there has been variation in the extent of this conflict and accommodations to it. For example, during World War II when women took over many jobs at home to support the war effort, company-run day care centers were more common than in the 1950s when women were explicitly discouraged from working outside the home. And taking a historical view is different from using the life course as an organizing device. Families in many generations go through the same sets of life cycle demands and opportunities. Differences in historical circumstances can alter how these same life stages are experienced (see Elder, 1974; Elder, Modell, & Parke, 1993).

RELEVANT PRIOR RESEARCH

This volume is not the first to identify the themes of the life cycle or the work-family balance as relevant to thinking about work and family. However, in order for our volume to build upon these prior works in a useful way, we identify a few of the most central contributions to this discussion here. Indeed, the issue of time is one around which several authors have organized their thinking. In a well publicized work, *The Time Bind,* Arlie Hochschild (1997) argues that for many families, work has become "home" and home has become "work." She uses a qualitative case study to show that many adults look forward to work because of the valuable interactions with other adults that it provides, and that a high proportion of the overtime hours these adults work are actually voluntary, as adults seek the positive social reinforcements provided by other adults with compatible responsibilities and orientations. At the same time, these commitments demand energy that might otherwise be devoted to family life. For these reasons, the tasks that need to be completed at home begin to be viewed more as work than anything else; adults see these tasks, often involving caring for children, as less socially rewarding than the work tasks associated with employment. Hochschild argues that these trends are disadvantageous to children, and recommends that parents spend less time at work and more time at home. Kerry Daly (1996) is also concerned about the hurried pace of life in North American culture. He argues that we need to examine the time that families spend together and the social forces that impact its duration and allocation. Placing his arguments in historical perspective and framing them with sensitivity to various family forms, Daly advocates both public support and private initiative in achieving a pace of life consistent with an appropriate quantity and quality of family time. Finally, John Robinson and Geoffrey Godbey (1997) rely on data produced over three decades using the "time diary" strategy that asks respondents to fill in diaries on a daily basis so that researchers might understand in detail how they allocate time. They find that Americans work less at home and in the workplace than they perceive, and that they have more leisure time available than they realize. They also detect trends in gender equalization in time use, and offer cross-cultural comparisons based on analogous research abroad. They advocate that Americans make better use of the considerable leisure they do have, including reducing the amount of time watching television.

SOCIAL POLICY

The second issue derived from these debates concerns how public and private policies might alleviate or exacerbate pressures that parents experience to manage work and family simultaneously. As dual-earner households become more common, both citizens and policymakers question whether policies at work are supporting the duality of their obligations, and/or whether governments should be doing more to help families engaged in both paid employment and family care. Currently, the major federal government policies that address work-family accommodation specifically are the Family and Medical Leave Act of 1993, the tax credit for child care and household maintenance expenses, and recent legislation involving welfare reform. For some workers these laws are supplemented with policies of private employers who may provide child care referrals or subsidies, flextime, or cafeteria plans allowing spouses to pick and choose a combination of benefits that will optimize family well-being. Of course, individual households develop strategies to manage their particular circumstances involving work and family obligations. Single-parent households have fewer options from which to select strategies to achieve work-family equilibrium.

In this volume, we have asked the authors to consider what implications their findings may have for policies that employers and governments might adopt. In doing so, we take seriously a responsibility that findings from social science be usefully applied to suggesting how society might be improved. The authors' recommendations involve actions by governments or businesses, as well as strategies that families might employ to manage the juggling act with less stress. In reality, it is combinations of both formal policies and private strategies that will enable families to care for one another and engage in paid employment to provide the financial means of support.

WHAT HAVE WE LEARNED ABOUT POLICY?

Several policy themes appear repeatedly across the chapters. One major theme concerns the importance of child care as a major form of support for families with employed mothers. Heike Trappe shows how state-supported child care was an important asset to mothers' managing both work and family obligations in the German Democratic Republic, although she does not believe that the demise of this care will portend a wholesale trend in mothers withdrawing from the labor force. Sandra Hofferth shows that having child care available at the work site is one benefit that will encourage mothers to return to work promptly after childbirth. Amy Cox and Harriet Presser suggest that, given the tendency for significant numbers of working mothers to work evening, night, and weekend shifts, child care is needed during these nonstandard hours. Given that these jobs may be disproportionately the ones that welfare-leavers will take, such child care could be important to the success of welfare transition.

Several chapters point to the importance of education about work-family during most stages of the life course. Roberta Iversen and Naomi Farber suggest that promoting social capital development through families, schools, and social agencies is most likely to encourage norm formation supportive of work values. Monica Johnson and Jeylan Mortimer advocate public schools as good contexts for encouraging adolescents to think through the duality of the work and family roles most adults face, and suggest that this time in the life course is important, because attitudes held during adolescence influence critical work and family choices in young adulthood. Integrating thinking about family into "career days" may encourage better planning for their futures.

Several other studies speak directly to the importance of policies that encourage work-family balance, with particular attention to issues of time management as central to this task. Jerry Jacobs and Kathleen Gerson point to bifurcation in work hours and job opportunities along occupational lines. Professionals and managers often face pressures to work extensive overtime hours but have the advantage of earning sufficient incomes to enable material support of the family. Workers in lower status occupations have lower hourly wages, and are often given opportunities for only part-time employment. Thus, they have more time to care for family members, but may not generate sufficient earnings to provide adequate financial support. They advocate social conditions that would ease this bifurcation. Both Hofferth and Parcel, Nickoll, and Dufur stress the importance of part-time work for parents at different stages in the life course. Hofferth views it as an inducement to encourage mothers to return to work promptly after childbirth, and Parcel et al. suggest that having part-time work available both to mothers and to fathers might be helpful in encouraging children's verbal facility. Joanne Sandberg and Daniel Cornfield caution that the passage of the Family and Medical Leave Act, a gender-neutral law allowing employees in some firms unpaid leaves to care for new or ill family members, has not prompted gender-neutral behavior among leave-takers. Rather, traditional gender roles influence leave-takers' decisions to terminate leaves.

This summary has certainly not exhausted the policy implications found in these chapters. It has suggested, however, that it is possible for theoretically and conceptually driven sociological research to yield interesting and important implications for social policy. It also suggests that there are common themes in policy inference derived across research undertaken with different methods and based on different data sources. We hope that these chapters provide not only important input into vital debates regarding work and family, but also encouragement to other social scientists to use their research both to inform theory as well as to suggest avenues for social betterment.

VOLUME ORGANIZATION

Our volume is divided into three major parts. In Part I, "Setting the Stage," the chapters examine the macro historical context in which families make choices regarding the balance of work and family obligations. The first chapter, "Work and Family in Women's Lives in the German Democratic Republic," by Heike Trappe, allows us to consider how societal variation in work-family policy influences adult socioeconomic well-being. The second chapter, "Public Opinion and Congressional Action on Work, Family, and Gender, 1945-1990" by Paul Burstein and Susan Wierzbicki, paints a fascinating portrait of how social policy in the area of work, family, and gender has evolved in the United States during the post–World War II period.

Part II, "The Juggling Act," addresses the demands parents experience as they attempt to manage both day-to-day responsibilities for work and family as well as changes in work and family responsibilities that occur over the life course. Four chapters identify strategies that families can pursue to manage these responsibilities. Jerry A. Jacobs and Kathleen Gerson, in "Do Americans Feel Overworked? Comparing Ideal and Actual Working Time," wonder whether adults would like to work more or less than they currently do work. They argue that both men and women desire jobs that allow them to provide adequate material support for families, but also work hours that accommodate family responsibilities. Amy G. Cox and Harriet B. Presser, in "Nonstandard Employment Schedules Among American Mothers: The Relevance of Marital Status," look into usage of nonstandard employment schedules by married and nonmarried mothers; their data suggest that working nonstandard hours is an important option for many families, and they chart the determinants of this choice. Sandra L. Hofferth, in "Effects of Public and Private Policies on Working After Childbirth," is concerned with how women balance work and family obligations following childbirth. She explores use of part-time work as a mechanism to meet new and ongoing responsibilities. In a related chapter, "Returning to Work: The Impact of Gender, Family, and Work on Terminating a Family or Medical Leave," Joanne C. Sandberg and Daniel B. Cornfield investigate gender differences in the reasons for working parents' terminating a family or medical leave; they find that gender underlies the determinants of these decisions, thus reinforcing the importance of considering gender explicitly in studying work-family connections and of encouraging more men to provide direct care for family members.

Part III, "Later in the Life Course," examines the implications of the work-family nexus for the well-being of both children and adolescents. Toby L. Parcel, Rebecca A. Nickoll, and Mikaela J. Dufur, in "The Effects of Parental Work and Maternal Nonemployment on Children's Reading and Math Achievement," find that the most important determinants of cognitive achievement among 9- to 12-year-olds are characteristics of parents and children themselves, with parental work characteristics playing moderating roles. Monica Kirkpatrick Johnson and Jeylan T. Mortimer, in "Work-Family Orientations and Attainments in the Early Life Course," study how young adults think they will manage both work and family responsibilities. They find that young women expect to make some compromises in order to "have it all" over the life course, but that young men are more likely to have traditional views regarding the advisability and feasibility of wives' combining work and family. Finally, Roberta Rehner Iversen and Naomi Farber address issues of intergenerational value transmission in their chapter, titled "Transmission of Family Values, Work and Welfare Among Poor Urban Black Women." They show that economic self-sufficiency is more likely when there are multiple mechanisms through which adolescents and young adults receive messages regarding the importance of education and work; concrete help in achieving economic self-sufficiency is also helpful.

REFERENCES

Blau, F. D., & Ehrenberg, R. G. (Eds.). (1997). *Gender and family issues in the workplace.* New York: Russell Sage.

Coltrane, S. (1996). *Family man: Fatherhood, housework, and gender equity.* New York: Oxford University Press.

Daly, K. J. (1996). *Families and time: Keeping pace in a hurried culture.* New York: Russell Sage.

Elder, G. H., Jr. (1974). *Children of the Great Depression: Social change in life experience.* Chicago: University of Chicago Press.

Elder, G. H., Jr., Modell, J., & Parke, R. D. (1993). Studying children in a changing world. In G. H. Elder, Jr., J. Modell, & R. D. Parke (Eds.), *Children in time and place: Developmental and historical insights* (pp. 3-22). New York: Cambridge University Press.

Hochschild, A. R. (1989). *The second shift.* New York: Avon Books.

Hochschild, A. R. (1997). *The time bind: When work becomes home and home becomes work.* New York: Henry Holt.

Parcel, T. L., & Menaghan, E. G. (1994). *Parents' jobs and children's lives.* New York: Aldine de Gruyter.

Robinson, J. P., & Godbey, G. (1997). *Time for life: The surprising ways Americans use their time.* University Park: Pennsylvania State University Press.

Spain, D., & Bianchi, S. M. (1996). *Balancing act: Motherhood, marriage, and management among American women.* New York: Russell Sage.

U.S. Bureau of the Census. (1995). Household and family characteristics: March 1994. *Current Population Survey,* Series P20, No. 483. Washington, DC: Government Printing Office.

U.S. Bureau of the Census. (1997). *Statistical abstract of the United States: 1997* (117th ed.). Washington, DC: Government Printing Office.

Ventura, S. J. (1995). Advance report on final natality statistics, 1993. *Monthly Vital Statistics Report, 44*(3), (Suppl.). Hyattsville, MD: National Center for Health Statistics.

PART I

Setting the Stage

H eike Trappe's work provides a fitting introduction by setting a comparative context to consider how women managed time across their lives in the German Democratic Republic (GDR). Trappe analyzes life histories of four birth cohorts of women born between 1929 and 1961 and living in East Germany in 1990. She addresses two key questions: How did women combine work and family responsibilities in the former GDR? What consequences did those strategies have for the careers of women from different generations? She documents that the more recent availability of state-supported child care changed how women dealt with work and family responsibilities. Whereas older cohorts tended to sequence work and child rearing, younger women tended to adopt both work and family roles simultaneously. Trappe speculates that with the unification of East and West Germany and the lack of continued state support for child care, women will diversify their strategies for combining work and family as opposed to withdrawing from the labor force. Among the older cohorts, child care availability also facilitated upward mobility in job qualifications. The findings suggest that state policy regarding child care support can have profound effects on the strategies that women and families use to combine work and family responsibilities. The chapter contributes to thinking about time in two ways. First, the historical period in which a family lives can have major effects on the choices the family makes for either sequencing or combining roles. In particular, although some may regard the socialist system as discouraging to individual initiative, in terms of providing support to those adults with both work and family responsibilities, it has some advantages. Second, the chapter clearly

1

shows how critical child care is to supporting choices of families who adopt major family and work roles simultaneously. Having state-supported child care was an important strategy for managing "the juggling act" in the former GDR.

The volume's second chapter takes a different approach to setting the stage for our discussion of work and family. Paul Burstein and Susan Wierzbicki discuss the evolution of social policy regarding the intersections of work, family, and gender. Their chapter divides into two parts. First, they develop a model of policy evolution. Based on prior research by Burstein and colleagues (Burstein & Bricher, 1997; Burstein, Bricher, & Einwohner, 1995), they identify the preconditions for congressional action to legislate policy change. Initially, a "difficult condition" must be defined as a "problem." For this to happen, people must think that something can be done about it; for the situation to become a public problem, people must think that the government should act. In addition, Congress must define the problem in a unified way, with the key elements being consensus regarding the harm that the problem is causing, as well as the causes of the problem itself. Regarding policy in the nexus of work, family, and gender, congressional committee members might identify a problem as causing harm if women fail to fulfill traditional roles, or alternatively, if there is unequal treatment by gender. Such harms might be a function of several causes, including decisions by organizations such as business or the government, the choices of individuals, or biological differences between men and women. With this myriad of possibilities that might influence whether and how problems are defined, it is clear that the evolution of a "difficult condition" into a "public problem" must be taken as a matter for investigation, not as a matter of assumption.

The second part of the chapter applies this model to legislation regarding work, family, and gender during the post–World War II period. Using public opinion data, these authors demonstrate that as the public moved to more egalitarian views regarding men's and women's roles at work and at home, Congress enacted laws requiring equal treatment at work and at least partial accommodation of working women's needs. Although the chapter does not claim to demonstrate causation, its theoretical framework makes a compelling case that at least partial causation is plausible. Taken together, both of these chapters sensitize us to how macro historical circumstances are important to influencing the choices of work and family that are made privately by individual households, and alert us as to the critical role that public opinion plays in shaping policies that societies adopt.

REFERENCES

Burstein, P., & Bricher, M. (1997). Problem definition and public policy: Congressional committees confront work, family, and gender, 1945-1990. *Social Forces, 76*(1), 135-168.

Burstein, P., Bricher, M. R., & Einwohner, R. L. (1995). Policy alternatives and political change: Work, family, and gender on the congressional agenda, 1945-1990. *American Sociological Review, 60*(1), 67-83.

REFERENCES

CHAPTER 1

Work and Family in Women's Lives in the German Democratic Republic

HEIKE TRAPPE

Even 10 years after the breakdown of the German Democratic Republic (GDR), social scientists still disagree over what consequences state social policies had on women's lives. High labor force participation and the combination of paid work and family responsibilities are, for some, proof of the achievement of gender equality and women's emancipation (Behrend, 1990; Bütow & Stecker, 1994; Meyer, 1991). This position is very close to the official argumentation of the German Democratic Republic's government and implies that social policies contributed to women's advancement. For others, the same empirical facts indicate a rigid policy that was aimed at integrating all women into the labor market and resulted in women's permanent "double burden" (Wendt, 1992). The idea that younger women with children would draw back from the labor market voluntarily after the unification—a scenario that has not come true yet—was based on this viewpoint.

I would like to argue that both views are deficient. They cannot cover the ambiguous consequences of social policies on women's lives as protection and restriction at the same time. Also, they imply a rather static perspective

AUTHOR'S NOTE: From "Work and Family in Women's Lives in the German Democratic Republic," by Heike Trappe, November 1996, *Work and Occupations, 23*(4), pp. 354-377. © Copyright 1996 Sage Publications, Inc.

that excludes changing societal conditions that shaped women's opportunity structures. It is well documented that the relationship between social policy and women's lives represents a complex phenomenon that has different features in different systems of social welfare (Lewis, 1993; Sainsbury, 1994). The former state socialist societies, with their specific mixture of public and private responsibility, add another example to the varying distinction of social policy regimes.

With respect to the relations between state policies and the ways in which women "choose" their strategies for balancing work and family, the GDR was an especially interesting case among the state socialist societies. Several developments, such as the extent of women's labor force participation and the provision of child care facilities for small children, were more pronounced here than anywhere else. The GDR was the only country that consistently pursued the idea of integrating almost all women into the labor force and, therefore, steadily increased the provision of child care. It is also important to take into account that the proclaimed emancipation of women and the creation of corresponding conditions has been part of an ongoing confrontation and competition with West Germany and was an important source of legitimacy for the GDR's government. The availability of inexpensive child care, together with free contraception and abortion rights—starting in the early 1970s—as well as supporting measures for women with children to facilitate the continuation of their work or schooling made for a certain degree of choice about whether and when to have children that was not the same in other state socialist countries. Therefore, it could be argued that the GDR went the furthest in balancing its policies toward women as producers and reproducers (Einhorn, 1993).

Another reason to analyze how women responded to the changing structural conditions for the combination of work and family demands is to learn more about the experiences that East German women of different generations bring into the unified Germany (Braun, Scott, & Alwin, 1994; Einhorn, 1993; Kolinsky, 1991). Because the former West Germany and the former East Germany share a common history and culture until just after World War II, the unique experiences of women in the GDR are very arguably due to the political and social arrangements in this society. To some extent, the two countries were at opposite ends of the spectrum in how they supported mothers of small children, with the aim in the East to keep women employed and in the West to discourage them from staying in the labor market. Thus the two countries provide a striking comparison of the effects of policies that attempt to help women reconcile employment and child rearing (Ostner, 1993; Trappe & Rosenfeld, 1996).

This chapter addresses two questions: How did women combine employment and family responsibilities in the former GDR?; and What consequences did those strategies used by women of different generations have for their occupational careers?

I analyzed life histories of four birth cohorts of women born between 1929 and 1961 and living in East Germany in 1990. The data were from a retrospective study conducted in East Germany, the East German Life History Study (EGLHS), carried out by the Max Planck Institute for Human Development and Education in Berlin (Huinink & Mayer, 1995).

I begin with a summary of sources for changes in women's lives during the history of the GDR. This gives a framework for interpreting later results in their sociohistorical contexts (Elder, 1993).

SOURCES FOR WOMEN'S CHANGING LIVES IN THE HISTORY OF THE GDR

The major cause of women's changing life-course patterns was the national economic need for their labor and therefore an unusually strong emphasis on the importance of women's employment, as well as the extension of educational opportunities to women following the GDR educational expansion. In addition, the official ideology was that women and men were equal in a socialist society, and as in some Western societies, there was a strong belief in employment as the key to the eradication of inequality between women and men (Friedan, 1963; Myrdal, 1941; Penrose, 1990). The government in the GDR was, as in all state socialist societies, officially committed to a policy of women's emancipation and gender equality. This goal would be achieved through legislation and social policy and by changing women's lives much more than men's (Einhorn, 1993). It was mainly in the power of the ruling socialist party (SED) to define gender equality and the ways to get there. The officially proclaimed prerequisites for gender equality changed in accordance with the society's political, economic, and demographic development.

In the early years of the GDR, there was a high demand for labor to rebuild a society destroyed by war and saddled with war debts to the Soviet Union. These specific historic circumstances, as well as the lack of male workers and the shortage of management caused by the war, made women's labor force participation and their education a crucial matter for the society's reconstruction. Germany's industrial tradition, the existence of a qualified workforce since the beginning of the twentieth century, and women's relatively high labor force participation during and before World War II made it easier to pursue such a strategy in the GDR than it was in other socialist countries (Heinen, 1990).

The demand for labor was further strengthened by the need to replace the dwindling labor force lost to extensive emigration to West Germany and West Berlin prior to 1961. Between 1949, when the GDR was founded, and 1961, when the wall was built, 2.7 million people, or 14% of the 1949 population, left the GDR because they experienced expropriation and loss of status, but also because of disappointing prospects with regard to their standard of living (Ulrich, 1990). During the 1950s, women's labor force participation became a question of survival for this society. Beginning in 1950, women had the right to decide about their employment by themselves and were juridically equal to men. The decision to be employed was supported by the individual need to earn one's living, as well as by economic and political circumstances. In this respect, the principle of "equal pay for equal work" was made part of the first constitution for the GDR in 1949. State policies tried in many ways—for instance, part-time work—to integrate unmarried women and, later, married ones into the labor force. These attempts were accompanied by an ongoing ideological devaluation of household work and housewives. The government set up a series of measures linked to the social security system, which had the effect of penalizing those people not in paid employment and which replaced the principle of the right to work with that of the obligation to work by the end of the 1950s. Beginning with the abolition of food supply stamps in 1958, families with only one income were clearly disadvantaged compared to double-earner families.

During the 1960s, new attempts were made to make the economy more efficient. A great emphasis was put on an accelerated development of the economy's scientific and technical level. This resulted in a sharp increase in the demand for skilled labor, including that of women. Women were considered to be equal to men not only when they worked, but also when they had similar educational qualifications. With this intention, many efforts were made to give women special opportunities to improve their qualifications, to develop a better understanding of technologies, and to get greater access to positions of higher responsibility. Those efforts included special promotions for the qualification and further education of women and were sometimes adapted to the living conditions of working mothers.[1] Young women, as well as young men, who started their work life after this period generally had a "qualified labor force entry" because of the combination of a state-controlled educational system and a well-structured occupational system (Huinink & Solga, 1994, p. 240). With the convergence of formal qualifications for women and men born in the GDR, the main goal of the qualification offensive addressed to women was achieved. Thus it lost its importance in the late 1970s.

Because women's family responsibilities seemed to be the principal obstacle to increasing their labor force participation and furthering their education, special policies were initiated that were aimed at helping women to be workers, mothers, and housewives. These policies began appearing in the 1960s and were intensified in the 1970s and 1980s. This new orientation came about within the context of decreasing fertility rates starting in the 1960s. The official understanding of gender equality changed from qualified employment to the reconciliation of work and maternity. In addition to providing inexpensive or free child care, the corresponding policies made it possible for women (but not men) to take paid leaves with a job-return guarantee after childbirth and during children's sickness and to reduce working hours while the children were small. The opportunity to use these policies or to work part-time in connection with childbirth was only open to women. One of the basic contradictions under state socialism was that women were defined as workers and mothers while there was no similar redefining of men's roles.

Thus it continued to be women who adjusted their employment situation during the childbearing years, which leads to the hypothesis that these adjustments have had serious consequences for women's occupational careers in each time period. Furthermore, changing societal conditions should affect the strategies women used to combine family responsibilities and employment in different ways. Generally, I expect that women who started to work before these social policies were initiated, and especially before public child care became widely available, tended to sequence their work and family roles. This means that these women had disrupted employment patterns: In connection with children's births, they interrupted their employment for longer periods often combined with part-time work. During the time they were out of the labor force, they cared for their children. On the other hand, younger women—who were born after the founding of the GDR and started their work life with higher qualifications after the social policies were adopted—are assumed to have combined childbearing and employment at the same time. These women should have shorter labor force interruptions for family reasons and less part-time work. Child care became a task of public institutions. In summary, women developed different strategies to deal with the difficult task of balancing family and work. These strategies were influenced by social policies, including public child care, and they affected women's occupational careers, as will be shown later, in different ways.

TABLE 1.1 Relative Labor Force Participation Until Age 35 (in percentages),
Median Age at Entry Into the Labor Force (in years), and
Qualification Required in the First Job (in percentages)

	Cohort			
	1929-1931	*1939-1941*	*1951-1953*	*1959-1961*
Relative labor force participation	74.1	81.6	86.4	83.0
Percentage in:				
Full-time work	66.4	71.5	72.4	72.2
Part-time work	7.7	10.1	14.0	10.8
Nonemployment:				
Employment disruption	22.9	15.8	11.7	15.2
Later schooling	3.0	2.6	1.9	1.8
Median age at entry into the labor force	16.2	17.3	19.0	19.1
Qualification required in the first job:				
None	72.3	24.0	11.2	14.5
Skilled worker	23.7	60.5	55.8	53.3
Technical college	2.3	10.3	20.7	23.0
Higher education	1.7	5.2	12.3	9.2

SOURCE: Author's calculations; East German Life History Study (Huinink & Mayer, 1995).
NOTE: Relative labor force participation is the proportion of time spent in employment between entry into the labor force and age 35. Cohort 1959-1961 is included in 1989, instead of at age 35.

DATA

To test these hypotheses, I analyzed work and family histories of 1,182 East German women born in the birth cohorts 1929-1931, 1939-1941, 1951-1953, and 1959-1961, and living in the former GDR in October 1990. These retrospective data were taken from the East German Life History Study (EGLHS), conducted by the Max Planck Institute of Human Development and Education in Berlin (principal investigators: Johannes Huinink and Karl Ulrich Mayer). It is one of the few surveys that allow comprehensive analyses of women's life histories under state socialist conditions. The cohorts for this project have been chosen to cover the different periods of the GDR's 40-year

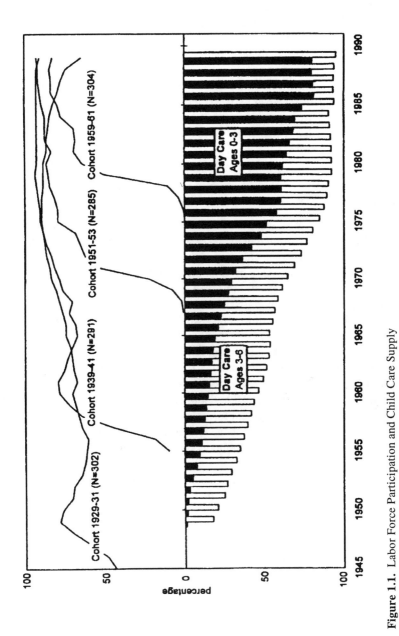

Figure 1.1. Labor Force Participation and Child Care Supply

SOURCE: East German Life History Study (Heinink & Mayer, 1995) and Statistisches Amt der DDR (1990, pp. 57, 62).

history. Face-to-face interviews were conducted with representative samples of women and men between September 1991 and September 1992 (for more detail, see Huinink & Mayer, 1995). The data used here were cut off at the end of 1989, when the first social and economic changes resulting from the collapse of the regime began to be felt. Such an approach seems to be necessary to exclude changes in women's strategies caused by the breakdown of the former system and the takeover by West German social policies, for example, increasing changes from part-time to full-time work or early returns to work after children's births, which were short-term strategies to secure employment.

ANALYTIC STRATEGIES

In a first step, I want to show how common paid employment and family responsibilities were for women in the GDR and whether their increased labor force participation was connected with delaying of family events or with an increasing number of women who remained childless. Women's rising engagement in paid work and their improved education are often thought to be related to a postponement of marriage and childbearing (Lesthaeghe, 1995). Then, I show how the quality of women's work in terms of their qualifications changed across the cohorts.

After that, I concentrate on the most important strategies women used to combine child rearing and employment. Here, the use of public child care, labor force disruptions, and part-time work are considered. It is important to note that this is not a comprehensive list of adjustments to family demands but a reduction of reality to typical forms.

To show the consequences of those strategies on women's occupational careers, I estimate logit regression models of upward mobility between the first job and the job held at age 35 or in 1989 (for the cohort 1959-1961). This age refers also to the previous steps. It has been chosen because the period up to age 35 includes the life stage with small children for most of the women. However, for women of the youngest cohort, this was not the case because their occupational careers can only be followed until the end of 1989 (age 28-30) to exclude occupational mobility changes caused by the *Wende*. Consequently, for these young women, it will not be possible to register all the consequences that strategies for adjustment to family responsibilities had for their chances to be upwardly mobile because the adjustment process had not

TABLE 1.2 Employment Disruptions in Women's Life Courses Until Age 35 (in percentages)

	Cohort			
	1929-1931	*1939-1941*	*1951-1953*	*1959-1961*
Never employed	1.0	—	—	—
Continuously employed	7.0	6.2	8.8	10.5
Employed with disruptions of 7 months or less	32.7	37.8	26.6	21.4
Employed with disruptions of at least 8 months: Family-related employment disruptions	51.0	53.6	61.1	66.8
Nonfamily-related employment disruptions	8.3	2.4	3.5	1.3
Women with family-related employment disruptions of at least 8 months:				
One disruption	66.5	65.8	58.3	57.1
Two disruptions	24.9	28.6	31.4	37.9
Three or more disruptions	8.6	5.6	10.3	5.0
Median duration of one family-related employment disruption (in years)	4.7	2.5	1.2	1.1
25% quartile	2.3	1.1	0.9	1.0
75% quartile	8.7	4.6	1.7	1.5

SOURCE: Author's calculations; East German Life History Study (Huinink & Mayer, 1995).
NOTE: Cohort 1959-1961 is included in 1989, instead of at age 35.

yet finished. Because of the stated reasons, results for this cohort must be interpreted with some caution.

VARIABLES AND MEASURES

Women's *labor force experience* is measured as labor force participation over the life course and as relative labor force participation. These two measures supplement each other in a useful way and follow the suggestions of Gornick (1992) and Hakim (1993). The first is the proportion of women who were employed among all women from age 15 to their age in 1989.[2] Because unemployment did not exist after the mid-1950s, female labor force participation includes only employed women. The relative labor force participation is the proportion of time spent in employment between entry into the labor force and age 35. This will be broken down further by the proportion of part-time and full-time work. *Part-time work* is defined as working fewer than 40 hours a week.[3] *Entry into the labor force* is considered as the first job lasting at least 6 months, to avoid jobs held during holidays or short periods. *Occupational qualification* at labor force entry is measured as a job characteristic, as qualifications required in the first job. This seems to be a better measure than educational qualification because it reflects the level at which women really worked. The following skill levels are distinguished: none, skilled worker, technical college, and higher education.[4]

The *use of public child care* is a variable based on the amount of time that children spent in public child care institutions. Children whose total duration in child care facilities until age 6 exceeded 2.5 years are considered to have been in institutional child care. A combined measure of number of children and child care arrangement is used in the logit regressions to depict *parental responsibility. Employment disruptions* in women's work histories are distinguished as family related and nonfamily related in accordance with the reasons women gave. Special attention was paid to those that were family related and had a length of at least 8 months. This duration has been defined so broadly because it should not include the obligatory pregnancy and childbirth leave that every woman had to take, which has been 26 weeks since 1976 (Trappe, 1995).

Finally, *different work time arrangements* in women's life course, such as only full-time work, only part-time work, and the change between full-time and part-time work, are considered as adjustments to family responsibilities.

Upward mobility is defined by moves between different levels of qualification required in a job. The individual position within the occupational structure of the GDR was strongly determined by the level of vocational training and occupational qualification. Formal qualification was an essential prerequisite to getting access to corresponding jobs (Mayer & Solga, 1994).

In the logit regression models, I include a variable that refers to the special political conditions in the GDR: *membership in the ruling socialist party* (SED) or in one of the linked parties. It can be assumed that overt system loyalty affected women's occupational careers independent of their strategies to

TABLE 1.3 Proportion of Women With Different Temporal Work Arrangements
Until Age 35 (in percentages)

		Cohort		
	1929-1931	*1939-1941*	*1951-1953*	*1959-1961*
Only full-time work	72.9	70.8	67.0	78.3
Only part-time work	4.7	3.4	6.7	7.2
Change between full- and part-time work	22.4	25.8	26.3	14.5
Ratio, labor force experience in part-time/full-time work	0.11	0.14	0.18	0.15

SOURCE: Author's calculations; East German Life History Study (Huinink & Mayer, 1995).
NOTE: Cohort 1959-1961 is included in 1989, instead of at age 35.

combine family and work (for men, see Huinink & Solga, 1994; for women
and men, see Solga, 1995).

WOMEN'S CHANGING LIFE COURSE PATTERNS

For women in the GDR, it was very common to form their own families. More
than 90% of women in all cohorts married at least once and had at least one
child. Consequently, the proportion of women who remained childless has
been very small. About 60% of all women had at least two children. The
number of children decreased on an average from 2 in the cohort 1929-1931
to 1.6 in the cohort 1959-1961. This decline has been caused mainly by an increasing renunciation of third and successive children. In combination with
low childlessness, this implies the near universality of the family with one or
two children.

The first marriage and the birth of the first child took place at an early age.
The median age at the first marriage decreased across cohorts from 22.5 years
(cohort 1929-1931) to 21.1 years (cohort 1951-1953) and increased slightly
again for women of the youngest cohort. The latter can be attributed to the increasing number of nonmarital unions. On the other hand, the median age at
the birth of the first child declined across all cohorts from 23.4 years to 22.0
years,[5] suggesting that more of these first children were borne by unmarried

women (cohort 1959-1961: 40%). Traditionally, all children were born at an early maternal age, predominantly before age 35. This has also been true for 95% of the children borne by women of the oldest cohort.

The early and extensive formation of families suggests that nearly all women had to find arrangements to combine child rearing and work or child rearing and vocational education.[6] This leads to the question of how women's employment changed across the cohorts.

As shown in Table 1.1 and Figure 1.1, the political efforts to integrate women into the labor force were quite successful, but this process included several steps. It is worth noting that women of the two earlier cohorts were already employed before the qualification offensive took place in the 1960s and before social policies to facilitate combining a job and motherhood became widely available in the 1970s. Contrary to widespread assumptions (e.g., Pischner & Giele, 1993), there existed in the GDR no simple relationship between social welfare policies and women's labor force participation. This can be seen in Figure 1.1, where the employment rates of women of the four cohorts are compared to the availability of child care facilities. The figures in the lower part are based on official statistical data (Statistisches Amt der DDR, 1990). The integration of women into the labor force in the 1950s and the 1960s occurred with few or no supporting measures. Women started to work primarily from individual economic need and because of economic pressure initiated by the state, as I have described earlier. When it became obvious that no further increase in women's labor force participation could be reached without improving the child care supply, the state took the initiative.

Women were already employed to a large extent before social policies were implemented, but their employment was not a long-term commitment. Consequently, the main effect of these policies was an increase in the amount of time that women spent in the labor force within the life stage with small children, from 74% in the oldest cohort to 86% in the cohort 1951-1953. In the two younger cohorts, men's labor force experience was only slightly higher than women's. Except among women of the oldest cohort, there were no significant differences in the extent of their employment by marital status, number of children, or education (Sørensen & Trappe, 1995). Women's rising engagement in paid work was caused by an increase in full-time as well as in part-time work, but full-time work was much more common (see Table 1.1). In this respect, Figure 1.1 indicates a considerable change in the shape of women's age-specific labor force participation curves. Women's employment in the two earlier cohorts decreased in the period when they formed their families and were living with small children and increased again afterward.

For women of the younger cohorts, this was not the case anymore. This pattern suggests that women in the two earlier cohorts interrupted their employment for longer periods of time when they had small children, whereas younger women tended to combine child rearing and employment. Table 1.1 shows that the amount of interruption to women's employment decreased considerably across cohorts. The next section will refer to this development in greater detail.

That women's employment became more continuous was connected to an increasing age at entry into the labor force. Women of the oldest cohort (1929-1931) started their work life on average at age 16 immediately after the end of World War II (see Table 1.1). So it is not surprising that about 3 of 4 women began to work in jobs that required no qualifications. This picture changed for the next cohort; about one quarter started to work in unqualified jobs. The two younger cohorts show patterns of dramatic change. These women entered the labor force on average at age 19 because they spent more time in vocational education. The exceedingly high proportion of women who started to work in jobs that required the qualification of a skilled worker or a technical college degree indicates that the political attempts to improve women's qualifications were, in fact, successful. Compared to men, women of the two younger cohorts were no longer disadvantaged in getting an educational qualification, but the process of women's higher qualification was accompanied by an increasing sex segregation of occupations (Sørensen & Trappe, 1995).

Summarizing these results, the most important change in women's employment patterns was the transition from disrupted employment and less-qualified occupations to steady employment and more-qualified positions. This change was highly influenced by state policies. In contrast to the situation in some Western societies, the increase of women's labor force participation in the GDR and the improvement of their qualifications was not connected to a delay of childbearing or an increasing proportion of women remaining childless. Consequently, nearly all women had to deal with the challenging task of combining family responsibilities and employment.

ADJUSTMENTS TO FAMILY RESPONSIBILITIES

As already indicated in Figure 1.1, the supply of child care facilities changed remarkably during the existence of the GDR. Although public child care, especially for small children, was still rare in the 1950s and 1960s, it was greatly extended in the later periods.[7] How did this development influence

TABLE 1.4 Logit Regression of Upward Mobility in Required Qualification Between First Job and Job at Age 35

| | Dependent Variable = Upward Mobility Between First Job and Job at Age 35 | | | | | |
| | Women in Cohorts 1929-1931 and 1939-1941 | | | Women in Cohorts 1951-1953 and 1959-1961 | | |
Explanatory Variable	Logit-coefficient	SE	Odds-Ratios[a]	Logit-coefficient	SE	Odds-Ratios
Qualification required in first job:[b]						
Technical college (skilled worker)[b]	-1.174	(.644)	.309	-3.078*[c]	(1.021)	.046
None	1.652*	(.266)	5.216	1.639*	(.300)	5.149
Cohort						
1929-1931 (1939-1941)	-.913*	(.249)	.401			
1951-1953 (1959-1961)				.455	(.281)	1.576
Strategies used for combining family and work, number of children, and child care arrangement:						
No child or one child in institutional care	.880*[d]	(.275)	2.410	.0002	(.448)	1.000
One child in noninstitutional care	.028	(.359)	1.028	-1.566	(1.132)	.209
Two or more children in institutional care (two or more children in noninstitutional care)	.315	(.278)	1.370	.091	(.418)	.913
Type of labor force participation						
Continuously employed or employed with disruptions of 7 months or less (employed with longer disruptions)	.766*[e]	(.219)	2.152	-.265	(.331)	.768
Temporal arrangement of work						
Always full-time (not always full-time)	-.079	(.238)	.924	.708*[f]	(.342)	2.030

Party membership						
Until age 35 member of the SED or a linked party (not a party member)	.949*	(.282)	2.584	.928*	(.319)	2.529
Constant	−2.201	(.304)	.111	−2.742	(.486)	.064
Proportion of women with upward mobility compared to N	151/570 = .265			73/526 = .139		
Log-likelihood	−283.1			−174.2		
Chi-square	92.8			75.2		
Degrees of freedom	9			9		

SOURCE: Author's calculations; East German Life History Study (Huinink & Mayer, 1995).

NOTE: Cohort 1959-1961 is included in 1989, instead of at age 35.

a. Equal or close to 1 indicates that there is no difference from the respective reference category. An odds ratio greater than 1 indicates an increased chance of experiencing an upward move, whereas an odds ratio of less than 1 indicates a decreased chance of experiencing an upward move.

b. Items in parentheses in the left hand column are reference categories.

c. Difference between both cohort groups $p = .11$.

d. Difference between both cohort groups $p = .20$.

e. Difference between both cohort groups $p = .01$.

f. Difference between both cohort groups $p = .07$.

* $p \leq .05$.

women's child care arrangements in the different cohorts? Whereas 43% of all children borne by women of the oldest cohort did not attend any child care facilities, the proportions were reversed for children born to women of the two younger cohorts. Children with or without little institutional care became an exception (10% to 11% of children born to women of the younger cohorts). Across educational groups, there was no indication that younger families were reluctant to place small children in institutional care as it might have been motivated by a resistance to state educational goals. About 54% of all children borne by women of the two younger cohorts spent at least 5 years in public child care, compared to 10% of children of the oldest cohort. This suggests that women of the two earlier cohorts themselves were temporally more involved in child care than younger women. Grandparents were most important for the care of children borne by women in the cohort 1939-1941, which reflects the curious middle position of these women with respect to provision of child care. Because the generation of grandparents was increasingly still employed, their importance for child care decreased in the younger cohorts (results not shown).

These phenomena show up in the employment patterns (see Table 1.2). Almost 65% of all employment disruptions were family-related ones, with a duration of at least 8 months. About 8% were disruptions with a minimum length of 8 months because of nonfamily-related reasons, and 27% of all interruptions were shorter ones (Trappe, 1995, p. 131). In contrast to the United States (see Wenk & Rosenfeld, 1992), the majority of women's employment interruptions in the GDR were for family-related reasons, such as pregnancy, childbirth, child care, and marriage.

The most striking development across the cohorts was the decrease in the median duration of family-related employment disruptions from 4.7 years (cohort 1929-1931) to 1.1 years (cohort 1959-1961) while the variation of this duration was growing smaller. Even in the two earlier cohorts, where this variation was still larger, there were almost no differences in the duration of family-related employment interruptions according to women's education. Single mothers tended to reenter the labor force faster, significantly so in the two earlier cohorts (results not shown). The trend away from extended employment disruptions was supported by improved access to public child care, but it also reflects the lower fertility and the slightly increasing number of single mothers within the younger cohorts. Whereas women of the two earlier cohorts (especially cohort 1929-1931) tended to have at least one longer period when they were out of the labor force and during which they often had more than one child, women of the two younger cohorts interrupted their employment more often and for shorter time periods. Thus their employment became more unstable. The repeated change between work and family was supported by the implementation of paid maternity leave, which started in the mid-1970s.[8]

Table 1.2 shows also that not all women had any employment disruptions or any disruptions that exceeded 7 months. The slight increase of continuously employed women in the youngest cohort should not be interpreted because these women have not been in the labor force as long as the other cohorts. Among those with employment disruptions of less than 8 months, the proportion was especially high in the two earlier cohorts. Although in the 1950s and 1960s there were not many supporting measures to facilitate the combination of family responsibilities and employment, some women managed to combine both at the same time.

Table 1.3 gives an overview of different temporal work arrangements until age 35. It is important to take into account that the meaning of part-time work changed during the history of the GDR. In the 1960s, it was considered to be a possibility for integrating women into the labor force. Because this goal was reached to a large extent in the beginning of the 1970s, state institutions tried to avoid a further expansion of part-time work. Young women, especially, who worked part-time were expected to change to full-time work. Part-time work was officially considered as a temporary necessity for women with exceptional family demands (Trappe, 1995). This would support the assumption that a reduction of working hours was more common among women of the earlier cohorts as a strategy to combine family responsibilities and employment. Table 1.3 does not show a clear tendency. Part-time work seemed to be most important for women of the cohort 1951-1953 (see also Table 1.1). Also, in a more detailed analysis regarding part-time work around the birth of the first and the second child, there was no clear trend (results not shown). The only interesting result was that across all cohorts, part-time work occurred more often for women who experienced longer labor force disruptions than for those who worked continuously. This pattern seems to reflect different work commitments among women in a society where the economic and political conditions made it difficult for women with stronger family identity to leave the labor force. It is also important to keep in mind that there were at all times families with ill or disabled children who needed special attention.

In accordance with the hypotheses stated in the beginning, women used different strategies to combine family and work. Whereas women who formed their families before supporting measures became widely available tended to sequence their work and family roles, younger women combined employment and child rearing at the same time. Most of those younger women used strategies favored by the state, such as full-time work with short employment disruptions and a far-reaching institutional child care system. This does not mean that other reasons—for example, rising consumption tastes, a higher education and work commitment among younger women, and changing norms about the care of young children—were unimportant for women's strategies, but these developments were often fostered politically.

UPWARD MOBILITY OF WOMEN AND THEIR CHANGING LIFE COURSES

In the last step, I asked how women's adjustments to family responsibilities influenced their occupational careers with respect to their chances to be upwardly mobile (see Table 1.4). I estimated logit regression models of moves to different levels of qualification required in a job between their first job and the job held at age 35. Recognizing the different qualification levels women started to work in, it is not surprising that women of the two earlier cohorts were upwardly mobile to a greater extent than younger ones. For women of the oldest cohort (1929-1931), this process included first moves to jobs on the skilled level. For the three younger cohorts, these moves led mainly to jobs that required a technical college degree. The underlying process for getting access to jobs that required more qualifications was participation in a further qualification leading to a corresponding degree; the process was linked to different educational investments. For jobs on the level of technical college, this included an additional training of at least 2 years. I would assume that the underlying mechanisms for upward mobility were different for women of the two earlier and the two younger cohorts because of their different adjustments to family responsibilities. Therefore, I estimated separate logit regressions for these two groups, as well as a pooled model to test the significance of differences.

In the GDR, educational qualification of adults took place mainly during regular working hours by delegation of the enterprises where people were working. This suggests that child care and continuous employment were important prerequisites for participation. Because getting more qualifications always implied additional individual efforts, it should have been less likely that women in part-time work could do so, especially in this period when part-time work was politically unwelcome. Party membership is presumed to have favored upward mobility of women, independent of their adjustment strategies. There existed a certain expectation that party members should constantly qualify (Penrose, 1993).

In all cohorts, women who started to work in unqualified jobs had the best chance of upward mobility. Not only were these women on the lower end of the occupational hierarchy, they were also in the center of the state qualification offensive in the 1960s and 1970s. After controlling for the required qualification in the first job, women of the cohort 1939-1941 were more likely to realize an upward move than women of the oldest cohort. In accordance with the hypothesis, child care arrangements played an important role for women's occupational careers in the two earlier cohorts. Women without children or with only one child in institutional care, compared to women with two or more children in noninstitutional care, were more than twice as likely to experience an upward move. Obviously, the type of child care arrangement was more important than the number of children. In the two earlier cohorts, women with continuous employment or short disruptions had a higher chance of upward mobility than women who worked discontinuously. Summarizing these results, women who adjusted their employment to their family demands in a "more modern way," with continuous employment facilitated by institutional child care, had the best chances of improving their qualifications.

In contrast to this, the number of children, the child care arrangements, and the type of labor force participation had no significant impact on the chance of upward mobility for women of the two younger cohorts.[9] It was also insignificant whether these women already had a child when they first entered the labor force, whether they were single mothers for a longer period of time, or how often they interrupted their employment (results not shown). These results suggest that state social policies contributed to a convergence in women's adjustments to child rearing. Differences among women resulting from different strategies became smaller and therefore less powerful for the prediction of upward mobility. This has been true, in particular, for child care arrangements and the continuity of women's employment. However, part-time work sharply reduced the chance of being upwardly mobile. This can be interpreted as a coincidence of state and individual exclusion from further qualification. Since the beginning of the 1970s, part-time work among young women was politically unwelcome and thus not connected with occupational advancement. On the other hand, one important reason to change to part-time work was to save time for the family and to avoid additional occupational efforts.

For women of all cohorts, party membership favored their chances of improving their qualifications considerably. Including this variable in the models changed all other coefficients only marginally, thus assuming an independent impact of party membership on women's careers is justified. Hence party membership opened specific opportunities for improving one's qualifications, for example, special promotion plans for women that were not accessible to nonmembers in a similar manner.

CONCLUSIONS

Analyzing the influences of structural conditions on women's lives in the former GDR proved to be productive in several ways. There is empirical evidence that many changes in women's lives were induced politically. The high labor force participation, even for women of the oldest cohort, shows this clearly. Almost all women who interrupted their employment for longer time periods while they had small children started working again and did not remain housewives. This was a principal difference between them and women of the same generation in West Germany. Because these women shared important experiences, for example, entry into the labor force immediately after World War II, it is obvious that the diverse shape of their labor force participation in later life resulted from different social circumstances.

The most important change regarding women's employment patterns in the GDR was the transition from disrupted and less qualified work histories to steady and qualified ones. This process was supported by a considerable improvement of women's qualifications and an extension of public child care. The changing societal conditions shaped women's opportunities to combine family responsibilities and employment differently. Whereas women who formed their families before supporting measures became widely available tended to sequence employment and child rearing, younger women synchronized both roles. An important implication of social policies was a homogenization of women's adjustments to family demands with the consequence that the strategies they used, except part-time work, were no longer a cause for different career opportunities. On the other hand, the decreasing variation in women's strategies toward a pattern with repeated changes between employment and family-related interruptions contributed to the emergence of a pervasive statistical discrimination against women. Employers tended to disadvantage young women compared to men because they perceived them as less stable and reliable labor regardless of their actual behavior (Sørensen & Trappe, 1995). In this sense, social policies had ambiguous consequences on women's lives, providing protection and restriction at the same time.

The main differentiation regarding labor force participation, quality of work, and adjustments to family responsibilities could be found between women who formed their families in the 1950s and 1960s and younger women who experienced the full force of social policies, with the latter more similar than the first. Despite clear connections between state policies and the ways in which women reconciled employment and family, the analysis also indicates that the state did not fully determine such choices. In every period, there were women who chose unpopular and unrewarded ways of working.

The complexity of the relationship between social welfare policies and women's lives should have implications for East German women in the unified Germany. In the same way as the increase in women's labor force participation did not simply follow the provision of child care, the severe decline in the availability of affordable child care is not expected to lead automatically to younger women's exclusion from the labor market. Other "solutions," as indicated by the vast decrease in fertility (Witte & Wagner, 1995) or a renewed importance of child care provided by other family members, are possible as well. Although East German women have been particularly hard hit by unemployment and are less likely than men to reenter the labor market, so far there is no evidence that younger women withdraw from employment voluntarily (European Commission, 1995). Furthermore, at the attitudinal level, East German women continue to favor strategies that balance family and employment simultaneously with considerably shorter interruptions than those desired by West German women (Störtzbach, 1995). The lack of facilitating structures for combining employment and child rearing will most likely contribute to an increasing diversity of women's strategies, with a higher proportion of privately organized arrangements. At the same time, it is possible that younger women's pragmatic use of social benefits and the routinized ability to change between family and work will pay off in the future.

NOTES

1. The special promotion of women was initiated by the enterprises where women were working. The enterprises guaranteed them a workplace corresponding to their qualifications. Women were allowed to use a certain number of regular workdays to study (e.g., 100 days a year for a technical college or university degree since the beginning of the 1980s). This promotion addressed working women who had to care for children or elderly people.

2. Labor force participation over the life course is carried forward to 1989 for women of the earlier cohorts to make the overall shapes more visible. It is the only measure where age 35 has been purposely exceeded for those women.

3. This definition is rather restrictive and different from the more conventional 35 hours cutoff (Rosenfeld, 1993). For the GDR, the 40 hours cutoff is the most appropriate one, because all people who worked fewer than 40 hours were considered to be working part-time and did not receive the full benefits connected with full-time work.

4. To become a skilled worker usually required 2 years of vocational training. Three years of vocational education were necessary to get a degree at a technical college. These programs provided students with very specific skills and qualifications needed in narrowly defined occupations, which to a large degree were located in the service sector. Because this degree included medical and pedagogical occupations, such as nurse or nursery school teacher, it became more and more typical for women.

5. By U.S. standards, these figures might not indicate an early age but compared to West Germany, they do. For women of the cohorts 1949-1951 and 1959-1961, the median age at first marriage was 21.6 and 25.7 years. For the same cohorts, the median age at the birth of the first child was 25.0 and 28.7 years, respectively (Huinink, 1995).

6. For women of the 1951-1953 and 1959-1961 cohorts, 13% and 16% of first children were born before these women entered the labor force. Preemployment childbearing was closely related to the increasing time women spent in acquiring an education. The government reacted to this development with special measures for mothers still pursuing an education to make it possible for them to get their degrees. These women received even more benefits, for example, preferential treatment in the allotment of child care, than employed women. The birth of children during the mother's vocational education became part of a strategy itself and was in the 1970s and 1980s encouraged by the state (Trappe, 1995).

7. As a result of these policies, since 1979, all children ages 3 to 6 could attend day care facilities if the parents so desired. The GDR offered inexpensive public child care to an extent that has not been matched by any other state socialist society. This was especially true for children ages 0 to 3 years. In 1989, the GDR covered the day care needs for 80% of these children (compared to 16% in Czechoslovakia, 13% in Bulgaria, 9% in Hungary, 6% in Romania, and 5% in Poland) (Makkai, 1994). West Germany provided less child care than most European capitalist countries. Therefore, the two German states embodied extremes on the scale of European institutional child care (Deutsches Institut für Jugendforschung, 1993).

8. It could be possible that the expansion of discontinuous employment among women represents a more general trend. Hakim (1993) argues for Great Britain that the simple, three-phase, broken work profile has declined in importance, replaced by an expanding workforce of women with increasingly numerous breaks in employment.

9. I would hesitate to interpret the effects of child care arrangements for the younger cohorts any further because there were very few children in noninstitutional care.

REFERENCES

Behrend, H. (1990). Die Hypertrophie des Vergangenen. Aufbruch und Elend der DDR-Frauen [The hypertrophy of the past. Departure and misery of GDR women]. *Das Argument, 32,* 859-864.

Braun, M., Scott, J., & Alwin, D. F. (1994). Economic necessity or self-actualization? Attitudes toward women's labor-force participation in East and West Germany. *European Sociological Review, 10,* 29-47.

Bütow, B., & Stecker, H. (Eds.). (1994). *Eigenartige Ostfrauen. Frauemanzipation in der DDR und den neuen Bundesländern* [Strange women from the East. Women's emancipation in the GDR and the New States]. Bielefeld: Kleine Verlag.

Deutsches Institut für Jugendforschung (DIJ). (Ed.). 1993. *Tageseinrichtungen für kinder. Informationen-erfahrungen-analysen* [Day care for children. Information-experiences-analyses]. München: Author.

Einhorn, B. (1993). *Cinderella goes to market. Citizenship, gender, and women's movements in east central Europe.* London: Verso.

Elder, G. H., Jr. (1993). Foreword. In K. D. Hulbert & D. T. Schuster (Eds.), *Women's lives through time: Educated American women of the twentieth century* (pp. xii-xvii). San Francisco: Jossey-Bass.

European Commission. (1995). *Employment observatory East Germany 16/17.*

Friedan, B. (1963). *The feminine mystique.* New York: Norton.

Gornick, J. (1992). *The economic position of working-age women, relative to men: A cross-national comparative study.* Paper presented at the Conference on Comparative Studies of Welfare State Development, Bremen, Germany.

Hakim, C. (1993). The myth of rising female employment. *Work, Employment, and Society, 7,* 97-120.

Heinen, J. (1990). The impact of social policy on the behavior of women workers in Poland and East Germany. *Critical Social Policy, 10,* 79-91.

Huinink, J. (1995). *Warum noch Familie? Zur Attraktivität von Partnerschaft und Elternschaft in unserer Gesellschaft* [Why still family? To the attraction of partnership and parenthood in our society]. Frankfurt/New York: Campus Verlag.

Huinink, J., & Mayer, K. U. (1995). Einleitung [Introduction]. In J. Huinink, K. U. Mayer et al. (Eds.), *Kollektiv und Eigensinn: Lebensverläufe in der DDR und danach* (pp. 7-23). Berlin: Akademie Verlag.

Huinink, J., & Solga, H. (1994). Occupational opportunities in the GDR: A privilege of the older generations? *Zeitschrift für Soziologie, 23,* 237-253.

Kolinsky, E. (1991). Women in the New Germany. *Politics and Society in Germany, Austria, and Switzerland, 3,* 1-22.

Lesthaeghe, R. (1995). The second demographic transition in Western countries: An interpretation. In K. O. Mason & A.-M. Jensen (Eds.), *Gender and family change in industrialized countries* (pp. 17-62). Oxford: Clarendon.

Lewis, J. (Ed.). (1993). *Women and social policies in Europe: Work, family, and the state.* Brookfield, VT: Edward Elgar.

Makkai, T. (1994). Social policy and gender in eastern Europe. In D. Sainsbury (Ed.), *Gendering welfare states* (pp. 188-205). Thousand Oaks, CA: Sage.

Mayer, K. U., & Solga, H. (1994). Mobilität und Legitimität. Zum Vergleich der Chancenstrukturen in der alten DDR und der alten BRD oder: Haben Mobilitätschancen zu Stabilität und Zusammenbruch der DDR beigetragen? [Mobility and legitimacy. To the comparison of opportunity structures in the former GDR and the former FRG or: Did mobility chances contribute to stability and breakdown of the GDR?]. *Kölner Zeitschrift für Soziologie und Sozialpsychologie, 46,* 193-208.

Meyer, D. (1991). Einheitsverliererinnen. Zur Situation ostdeutscher Frauen [Unification losers. To the situation of East German women]. *Blätter für deutsche und internationale Politik, 36,* 1326-1333.

Myrdal, A. R. (1941). *Nation and family. The Swedish experiment in democratic family and population policy.* New York: Harper.

Ostner, I. (1993). Slow motion: Women, work, and the family in Germany. In J. Lewis (Ed.), *Women and social policies in Europe: Work, family, and the state* (pp. 92-115). Brookfield, VT: Edward Elgar.

Penrose, V. (1990). Vierzig Jahre SED-Frauenpolitik: Ziele, Strategien und Ergebnisse [Forty years of the Socialist Party's women's policies: Goals, strategies, and results]. *Frauenforschung, 8,* 60-77.

Penrose, V. (1993). *Orientierungsmuster des Karriereverhaltens deutscher Politikerinnen. Ein Ost-West-Vergleich* [Orientation patterns of career behavior for female German politicians. An East-West comparison]. Bielefeld: Kleine Verlag.

Pischner, R., & Giele, J. Z. (1993). Erwerbsverläufe der Deutschen in Ost und West in den Jahren 1949 bis 1989 [Employment histories of the Germans in the East and in the West in the years 1949 to 1989]. *DIW Wochenbericht, 60,* 207-211.

Rosenfeld, R. A. (1993, August 11). *Women's part-time employment: The influence of country context.* Paper presented at the meeting of Research Committee No. 28 of the International Sociological Association, Durham, NC.

Sainsbury, D. (Ed.). (1994). *Gendering welfare states.* Thousand Oaks, CA: Sage.

Solga, H. (1995). *Auf dem Weg in eine klassenlose Gesellschaft? Klassenlagen und Mobilität zwischen Generationen in der DDR* [On the way to a classless society? Class positions and mobility between generations in the GDR]. Berlin: Akademie Verlag.

Sørensen, A., & Trappe, H. (1995). Frauen und Männer: Gleichberechtigung-Gleichstellung-Gleichheit? [Women and men: Equal rights-equal opportunity-equality?). In J. Huinink, K. U. Mayer, et al. (Eds.), *Kollektiv und Eigensinn: Lebensverläufe in der DDR und danach* (pp. 189-222). Berlin: Akademie Verlag.

Statistisches Amt der DDR. (Ed.). (1990). *Statistisches Jahrbuch der DDR '90* [Statistical yearbook of the GDR '90]. Berlin: Rudolf Haufe Verlag.

Störtzbach, B. (1995). Germany: Unification in attitudes? In H. Moors & R. Palomba (Eds.), *Population, family, and welfare: A comparative survey of European attitudes* (Vol. 1, pp. 122-138). Oxford: Clarendon.

Trappe, H. (1995). *Emanzipation oder Zwang? Frauen in der DDR zwischen Beruf, Familie und Sozialpolitik* [Emancipation or coercion? Women in the GDR between work, family, and social policy]. Berlin: Akademie Verlag.

Trappe, H., & Rosenfeld, R. (1996, May 10). *Family and gender inequality in the labor market: A comparison of young adults in the former East Germany and the former West Germany.* Paper presented at the annual meeting of the Population Association of America, New Orleans, LA.

Ulrich, R. (1990). *Die Übersiedlerbewegung in die Bundesrepublik und das Ende der DDR* [The migration movement to the Federal Republic of Germany and the end of the GDR]. Wissenschaftszentrum Berlin Working Paper P90-302.

Wendt, H. (1992). Kein Platz für Nostalgie—Kritische Anmerkungen zur Wirklichkeit des Frauenalltags in der ehemaligen DDR [No room for nostalgia—critical remarks about the reality of women's everyday life in the former GDR]. *Frauenforschung, 10,* 89-95.

Wenk, D., & Rosenfeld, R. (1992). Women's employment exit and reentry: Job-leaving reasons and their consequences. In R. P. Althauser & M. Wallace, *Research in social stratification and mobility* (Vol. 11, pp. 127-150). Greenwich, CT: JAI.

Witte, J. C., & Wagner, G. G. (1995). Declining fertility in East Germany after unification: A demographic response to socioeconomic change. *Population and Development Review, 21,* 387-397.

CHAPTER 2

Public Opinion and Congressional Action on Work, Family, and Gender, 1945-1990

PAUL BURSTEIN

SUSAN WIERZBICKI

I t is widely believed throughout the social sciences that both women's labor market outcomes and the division of labor in the household are affected by public policy and by how people think about work, family, and gender. The historian Cynthia Harrison (1988, ch. 10), for example, writes that the march toward gender equality was long stymied by a virtually universal inability, even among feminists, to imagine how full-time careers for women could be reconciled with women's primary responsibility for child care. Only a "theoretical leap of great consequence" (p. 200)—the argument by the National Organization for Women that fathers as well as mothers had the responsibility to care for children—made it possible for women "finally to make a claim

AUTHORS' NOTE: We would like to thank participants in the University of Washington Center for Studies in Demography and Ecology seminar for their helpful advice and comments. An earlier version of the paper appeared as Seattle Population Research Center Working Paper no. 97-9. Support for this research was provided in part by the National Science Foundation (grant SES-9008217) and the Royalty Research Fund of the University of Washington; Susan Wierzbicki was supported in part by NICHD Grant 5 T32 HD07394.

for complete equality both in and outside the home" (p. 192). The sociologist
Kathleen Gerson (1985, ch. 6; 1993, ch. 9) argues that deep changes in ideology and beliefs about gender roles necessarily play a key part in the struggle
over gender equality, and goes on to say that change among individuals must
be matched by change in public policy, which is "a critical ingredient in determining whether social change reduces or exacerbates the problems women
experience" (1985, p. 224). The economist Claudia Goldin (1990) concludes
that "gender equality may be fostered by economic progress but must be as-
sisted by legislation and social change" (p. 217). Many others point to the importance of ideology and public policy as well: For example, Mayer and
Schoepflin (1989) on the relationship between state action and family and
gender roles; Reskin and Padavic (1994, p. 71) on the impact of federal laws
on women's access to nontraditional jobs; Strober and Dornbusch (1988) and
Bergmann (1986) on policy proposals for furthering the revolution in men's
and women's roles in the labor market and at home.

Not only do ideas and public policy affect labor market outcomes and the
division of labor in the household—in democratic societies, they almost
surely affect each other. The views of the public and legislators shape public
policy (though to what extent is a matter of dispute); public policy, in turn, affects their views (Page & Shapiro, 1983; Skocpol, 1992; Wlezien, 1995).
Thus, a full explanation of women's labor market outcomes and the division
of labor in the household must incorporate an examination of the relationship
between the views of legislators and the public on the one hand, and public
policy on the other.

Unfortunately, no one has systematically analyzed this relationship, at
least in the United States. There have been many studies of public opinion on
issues related to work, family, and gender, but none relate public opinion to
policy change (see, e.g., Cherlin & Walters, 1981; Erskine, 1971; Ferree,
1974; Mason, Czajka, & Arber, 1976; Mason & Lu, 1988; Schreiber, 1978;
Spitze & Huber, 1980; Thornton & Freedman, 1979; Wilcox, 1992; Wilkie,
1993). And studies of policy making on work, family, and gender do not analyze how it was affected by public opinion (e.g., Harrison, 1988).

This chapter begins to fill this gap in our knowledge, by analyzing how
changes in policies linking work, family, and gender have been related to the
views of legislators and the public. Our focus is congressional action since
1945 on policies relating to work, family, and gender. This was a period of
dramatic change. As World War II ended and returning soldiers and sailors
rejoined the labor force, the public and policymakers often called for a return
to "separate spheres," with men as breadwinners and women as homemakers
and mothers. Women had few career options. The continued existence of the

women's units of the armed forces was in doubt. Neither law nor opprobrium stopped employers from paying women less than men for the same work or from firing women who married or became pregnant. By the early 1990s, federal legislation prohibited employers from discriminating against women, not only in pay for doing the same work, but in hiring, promotion, firing, and other terms and conditions of employment as well. Other legislation had integrated the women's units of the armed forces into the regular services and allowed women's military roles to expand greatly. Federal law had abrogated state protective labor legislation and prohibited discrimination based on pregnancy. Furthermore, the federal government required many employers to offer at least a limited, unpaid leave to employees—female and male equally—to care for newborns, other dependents, and parents.

Our approach to this transformation in policy is based on Kingdon's work (1984) and on recent work on public opinion and public policy. In Kingdon's view, the federal policy-making process is essentially "organized anarchy" (p. 92). Those who make policy confront a complex environment; they are bombarded by far more demands and information than they can process satisfactorily; they are urged to address problems that have no obvious solution. In such an environment, Kingdon argues, policy making proceeds in three "streams": (a) the stream of problem definition, in which particular conditions come to be seen as problems potentially amenable to solution by government; (b) the stream of policy creation, in which alternative policy proposals are developed and refined; and (c) the stream of politics, in which public opinion, election campaigns, interest groups, and other forces push the government to act.

Although one could imagine the three streams neatly related to each other—for example, the public could see a problem and demand congressional action, and Congress could act after carefully examining alternative policy proposals—the streams often move independently. Groups struggle to get the public and policymakers to define some condition as a problem; those who have developed policies seek to expand their scope (as, e.g., those who favor "deregulation" try to find more policy domains to deregulate); and pressures on government rise and fall, sometimes predictably, as in the electoral cycle, and sometimes unexpectedly, as in an international crisis or a plane crash. Significant policy change comes about most often when the three streams are joined—for example, when a crisis attracts public attention, some groups manage to get the public to see the problem a particular way, the public demands government action, and Congress turns to the most readily available solution. The process is orderly (it is *organized* anarchy): Some groups have more of the resources helpful in winning public attention, some policy proposals can be expected to seem widely acceptable while others seem outrageous, changes in the party balance will often affect policy outcomes, and so on. There is a great deal of randomness as well (it is organized *anarchy*); unpredictable events may have major consequences.

Public opinion plays an equivocal role in Kingdon's approach. No serious discussion of democratic politics can ignore public opinion, because democratic political institutions were designed to give the public substantial influence over public policy. Yet the complexities of mass politics makes such influence problematic. Unlike some social scientists and much of the public, Kingdon (1984) sees politicians as very sensitive to public opinion (pp. 68-71, 217). Public opinion can force the government to take up certain issues and sometimes causes government to adopt particular policies. More often, however, public opinion only prevents government action; it does not cause it. Because the public is not concerned about most issues, policymakers have considerable freedom of action, but they also know that there are many policies the public would not accept; they "sense some boundaries that are set on their actions by the mood of the mass public . . . and believe they must operate within them" (p. 217).

Other social scientists have higher expectations. While acknowledging the complexities of mass politics highlighted by Kingdon, they argue that public opinion often does cause policy change. Stimson, MacKuen, and Erikson (1995) argue that American politics is characterized by what they call "dynamic representation," "that public opinion moves meaningfully over time, that government officials sense this movement, and that . . . those officials alter their behavior in response to the sensed movement" (p. 543). Their view is echoed by many others (e.g., Arnold, 1990; Erikson, Wright, & McIver, 1993; Jones, 1994; Page & Shapiro, 1983).

Thus, we will describe (a) how Congress defined the "problem" of work, family, and gender from 1945 on, (b) the policy alternatives members of Congress proposed as solutions to the problem, (c) public opinion on work, family, and gender, and (d) how these three "streams" came together to transform public policy.

WHAT CONGRESS WAS DOING: CONCEPTS AND DATA

We are interested in public policies regulating relationships among work, family, and gender in the United States. We cannot study all such policies; the task of analyzing the potentially relevant areas of the law (including labor and family law) at the state and federal levels is too immense. Instead, we focus strategically on how members of Congress proposed, between 1945 and 1990, to regulate how employers (both private and public) address gender issues and family roles. We focus on Congress because of its central role in American politics; on regulation of the labor market (rather than family law) because it has been a major focus on federal policy making; on the period since 1945 because it has been a time of great change that is better-documented than earlier periods; and on congressional proposals, and not just laws, because it seems important to analyze how changes in public opinion were related to congressional support for new policies—that is, we are concerned about the process of policy making, and not only its results.

What's the Problem?

Members of the 1945 Congress introduced only one bill proposing that men and women receive equal pay for equal work, and none to prohibit gender discrimination in the labor market more generally or to require employers to provide family and medical leave, as we understand those terms today, for a simple reason: The problems such bills would address—gender discrimination and men and women juggling obligations to job and family—did not exist.

This is not to say that employers treated men and women the same way, or that it was easy to balance the demands of job and family. Obviously, neither was the case. Rather, the problems did not exist in the sense that the difficulties people faced were not viewed as public problems—as conditions the government could, and should, do something about. In current terminology, a "difficult condition" becomes a *problem* only when people think something can be done about it, and a *public* problem when they argue that the *government* should do something (see Kingdon, 1984, p. 115). Public problems are socially constructed—and many of the problems whose existence we take for granted hadn't been constructed yet.

If we want to understand the transformation of federal policy on work, family, and gender, we have to learn how Congress defined the "problem" of work, family, and gender. If most members of Congress do not see any public problem associated with work, family, and gender, Congress will not act. If they do see a problem, the action they take will be influenced by how the problem is defined. Although the connection between problem and solution is often rather loose, Congress is likely to respond quite differently if its members see the problem as women neglecting their families when they work outside the home, as opposed to seeing the problem as women being denied job opportunities because of discrimination by employers.

Of course, there is no reason to expect that all members of Congress will define the problem the same way. In fact, competition among problem definitions often plays a critical role in policy change. As Weiss (1989) has written, competition "lays the fundamental groundwork for the ensuing struggle over the construction of useful policy alternatives [and] authoritative adoption of a policy choice." The victory of a particular definition "shapes the ensuing action [and] . . . legitimates some solutions rather than others." So important is the competition that "much policymaking, in fact, is preoccupied with whose definitions shall prevail" (pp. 97-98).

In Congress, the key locus of problem definition is the congressional committee. The committees decide which of the thousands of bills introduced during each Congress will win a hearing, decide who will have the opportunity to present their views formally, and gather and organize the evidence for and against competing proposals. Although committees draw heavily on ideas provided by others (most immediately, by sponsors of bills), it is they who define the problems Congress is to address, propose particular solutions, and channel the debate.

To describe how congressional committees defined the problem of work, family, and gender, Burstein and Bricher (1997) content-analyzed all reports on work, family, and gender issued by House and Senate committees between 1945 and 1990—69 reports in all.[1] That study focused on two key aspects of how the committees defined the problem: the *harm* they identified and its *cause* (Stone, 1989, and Weiss, 1989, provide much of the basis for this discussion).

On the basis of prior work and a preliminary reading of the reports, the study identified five types of harm that committee members might plausibly have associated with work, family, and gender (more than one of which could have been identified in any given report): harms stemming from (a) women not fulfilling their "traditional" roles; (b) inequality in sex-segregated contexts (such as the military, where sex segregation was long taken for granted, but concerns could be raised about how women were treated anyway); (c) minors being insufficiently protected from the working of labor markets (as addressed in child labor laws); (d) unequal treatment by gender, broadly construed; and (e) difficulties balancing obligations to home and work. Burstein and Bricher read every committee report—meaning the report supported by a majority of the committee—to determine how the particular committee, at the particular time, had seen the harm associated with work, family, and gender. They also read the 51 minority reports that accompanied the committee reports (some committee reports were accompanied by more than one minority report).

The harms could have been attributed to seven different causes (possibly more than one cause in any given report): (a) innate differences between men and women (most likely, biological); (b) decisions by individual women (in what might be an individualistic, free-market view of the harm); (c) decisions by individual men; (d) economic organizations (businesses, unions); (e) the federal government; (f) other organizations; and (g) macrolevel social change. Thus, the range of *possible* problem definitions was considerable. Committee members could have seen women causing harm by neglecting their traditional roles, as the result of their own decisions; women suffering from employment discrimination by employers; families being damaged by the difficulties parents were having trying to balance work and family responsibilities, with the difficulties stemming from broad patterns of social change; and so on. How did the committees *actually* define the problems? This question we address below.

What's the Solution?

How did members of Congress propose to deal with the problems defined by the congressional committees? What alternative policies did they consider?

For members of Congress, policy alternatives are embodied in bills. To analyze what Congress proposed to do about work, family, and gender, therefore, Burstein, Bricher, and Einwohner (1995) analyzed all bills and joint resolutions introduced between 1945 and 1990 in which members of Congress proposed to regulate how organizations in one sphere—the paid workplace—are to treat individuals as they are defined in the other sphere, in terms of family status and gender—as men, women, minor children, parents or potential parents (pregnant women and those seeking to adopt), and spouses.

Virtually all such bills were one of three types. *Separate spheres* bills proposed to limit the opportunities available to women and children, or maintain the physical separation of home and workplace. Essentially, their goal was to keep women and children out of the paid labor force or restrict them to subordinate positions. They would do this by barring access to certain jobs, permitting differential rates of pay or time at work, singling workers out by sex for special treatment, discouraging family ties in the workplace (e.g., through antinepotism rules), or limiting paid work in the home. Examples of separate spheres bills included "protective" labor bills limiting women's hours or access to jobs; bills providing leave for mothers to care for newborns, but not for fathers; and bills keeping children out of the labor force. Some separate spheres bills, especially those limiting child labor, were customarily seen as progressive, but they often had the effect of limiting mothers' opportunities to work outside the home.

Equal opportunity bills challenged limitations on women's opportunities in the public sphere by requiring employers to employ and evaluate women in the labor force on the same terms as men, or at least to move in that direction. They reduced the separation between home and work by making it easier and more rewarding for women to enter the paid labor force, but did not directly address men's or women's family responsibilities. Specifically, the bills required equal opportunity for jobs, equal pay, and equal time in the workplace regardless of family status or sex. Examples included bills mandating equal pay for men and women doing the same jobs, equal access for men and women to certain positions in the military, and general equal employment opportunity bills.

Work-family accommodation bills narrowed the separation between home and paid work by requiring employers to take employees' family responsibilities into account without making any distinctions on the basis of gender. Thus, they went beyond equal opportunity bills by requiring equal treatment not only with regard to job performance, but with regard to family obligations as well. Often this meant enabling men and women workers to meet family obligations during hours they would normally devote to paid work; many such bills went beyond requiring equal treatment in the labor force to encouraging, or at least facilitating, a more equal division of labor in the home. Such bills might permit differential time at work for parents or both men and women (treating both sexes identically), give employees of both sexes control over time at work so they can care for children, permit family in the workplace or paid work at home, or require employers to take employees' family circumstances into account in other ways. Examples of work-family accommodation bills included bills requiring employers to provide leave to employees to care for newborn babies or sick family members; bills subsidizing employer-provided child care; and bills prohibiting employers, when determining benefits, from penalizing employees who take time off when children are born.

The study gauged support for each type of bill two ways: number of sponsors and enactment. Number of sponsors indicated support for proposals that had not reached the floor for a vote. Enactment indicated the greatest support, of course; it requires, in addition to majorities in both houses, either presidential approval or enough support—two thirds of each House—to override a veto.

We might expect to find any one of a number of patterns of congressional support for competing policy alternatives. For example, the conventional wisdom about the postwar period might lead one to expect substantial support for separate spheres bills during the 1940s and 1950s; similarly, there could have been a resurgence of support for separate spheres in recent years, as talk of "family values" has become prominent in congressional debate. There could have been long periods of struggle between proponents of different visions of work, family, and gender, with one view winning over the other only gradually; or dramatic events might have changed the balance of support overnight. We describe the actual patterns of support below.

PUBLIC OPINION: THEORY AND DATA

As noted above, Kingdon (1984) has rather low expectations for the impact of public opinion on policy—he thinks public opinion often prevents congressional action but seldom causes it—while other social scientists believe that public opinion exerts a substantial impact on policy. The disagreement is more empirical than theoretical, however. Both sides see Congress as sensitive to public opinion; both also agree that Congress often has considerable latitude in what it does because the public cares little about most issues and does not demand that Congress do anything in particular. The disagreements are about just how sensitive Congress is, how often the public may be brought to care about an issue, and how clear and consistent the public's opinions are likely to be. Congressional responsiveness is not simply a matter of translating majority opinion into public policy. Congress is most likely to respond when the public makes *unambiguous* and *intense* demands that the government *act*.

It is important that public opinion be unambiguous because members of Congress fear that votes out of line with public opinion make them vulnerable to attack; their preference is to avoid acting until the majority favoring one side is large and growing larger.

Demands must be intense because Congress normally delegates much of its work to its committees, which in turn often consult the groups most interested in particular issues and best organized to make their wishes known. This decentralization usually works well; it enables Congress to deal with many issues at once and respond to the desires of those who care most about issues. Members of Congress try not to antagonize the public unnecessarily, but also know that most people don't care much about most issues. For Congress as a whole to pay acute attention to the public as a whole on a particular issue, many of its members must become convinced that the public cares so intensely about the issue that the issue will play a significant role in the next election.

Finally, it is important that the public not only have opinions on an issue—possibly strong opinions—but that its opinions demand that the government act. Much of the public distinguishes between wanting something done and wanting the government to do it. For example, during the 1950s a majority of Americans opposed racial discrimination in employment and public accommodation, but also believed that the issues should be dealt with privately and not by the federal government; similarly, millions of the Americans who believe abortion to be morally wrong also believe that it is a matter to be decided by women and their physicians rather than by government (Blendon, Benson, & Donelan, 1993).

Thus, to determine congressional responsiveness to public opinion, one should have data on what the public wants, preferably over decades; how badly it wants it; and whether it wants the government to act. Unfortunately, such data are not available on most issues. There are very few issues on which good public opinion data are available going back to at least 1945, and even fewer on which the public is regularly asked whether it wants government action. Data on the intensity of public concern may be said to be available by inference. The Gallup organization has been asking people for more than 50 years what they see as the most important problems facing the country; few issues are mentioned often enough to be reported, so the many others may be assumed relatively unimportant (or at least not "most important") to the vast majority of Americans. The lack of data means that virtually any analysis of public opinion and public policy must rest on far less evidence than would be desirable. Yet public opinion is so central to theories of democratic politics that it must be taken into account as much as possible in any serious analysis of policy change.

Data for this analysis come from Gallup polls from 1945 through the 1970s, the General Social Survey, the National Election Studies surveys, Harris/Virginia Slim polls from the early 1970s, and individual surveys from the 1980s and early 1990s conducted on behalf of ABC News, CBS News, the *Washington Post,* and the *New York Times.* Sources for specific questions are presented in the appendix. These time-series data will show how trends in public opinion relate to the legislation on work, gender, and family.

WHAT CONGRESS WAS DOING: FINDINGS

What's the Problem?

How did congressional committees define the "problem" of work, family, and gender? Here we describe what harm they saw themselves addressing and what they saw as its cause.

The conventional view of the immediate postwar period might lead us to expect that the committees would have been very concerned about harm caused by women's participation in the paid labor force and their neglect of traditional roles as wives and mothers. But that was not the case. In fact, not a single committee report—majority or minority, then or later—proposed congressional action to deal with harm resulting from women not fulfilling their traditional roles (Table 2.1).

Instead, even in the immediate postwar period, the committees focused on harm imposed on women as the result of their being treated worse than men. During the 1940s and 1950s, two views of gender inequality were on the congressional agenda. In the narrower view, committee members saw harm in women being rewarded less than men of equal rank and experience, but saw no harm in segregating jobs by sex, and, indeed, explicitly favored it (this view was expressed by the armed services committees). In the broader view, committee members simply saw harm in unequal treatment of any kind. At first, reports reflecting the narrower view outnumbered those with the broader view. Then, quite abruptly, the narrow view disappeared. Of the 27 reports focusing on unequal treatment issued after 1960 (26 focusing on unequal treatment alone, and 1 on unequal treatment together with competing obligations), not a single one took the narrower view. This is not to say that committee members have always viewed sex discrimination the way we do today; probably no member of Congress in the 1940s, 1950s, or 1960s could even have imagined how ideas about sex discrimination would change in subsequent decades. But their focus on unequal treatment by gender and their proposals to do something about it marked a clear conceptual break with the doctrine of separate spheres, and redefined the "problem" of work, family, and gender in a way that led to today's views.

From the early 1960s to the mid-1980s, the harm of greatest concern to the committees was that associated with unequal treatment by gender. Then a new concern won committee attention: Committees first recognized harm caused by the difficulties meeting competing obligations to family and paid work in 1985, and addressed it in reports issued in that Congress and every subsequent one. The "new" problem did not displace the old; there is no

TABLE 2.1 What Harm Is Identified by Committee Majorities and Minorities?[a]

Congresses	Women Not Traditional	Inequality in Sex-Segregated Context	Unequal Treatment	Competing Obligations	Treatment and Competing Obligations	Minors Not Protected	Other[b]	No Problem[c]	Total
1945-1960	0	12	8	0	0	3	1	1	25
1961-1984	0	0	22	0	0	3	7	3	35
1985-1990	0	0	4	5	1	0	0	4	14
Total	0	12	34	5	1	6	8	8	74

SOURCE: Burstein & Bricher, 1997.
NOTES: a. Cells represent the number of committee majority and minority reports referring to the various harm categories. Tables 2.1-2.2 report on majority and minority reports together.
b. Includes other harms to children and spouses.
c. This means that no problem is identified, not that there is an explicit denial that a problem exists.

necessary contradiction between concerns about equal opportunity and about work-family contradiction, and both have been the ongoing focus of committee activity.

What did the committees identify as the causes of the harms they identified? As noted above, the committees could have attributed harm to a variety of causes, including innate biological differences between men and women, and the freely made choices of men and women themselves. It is easy to imagine such attributions being made by committee members during the 1940s and 1950s, and perhaps even by conservatives today.

In fact, however, only one report ever argued that harm was caused by innate differences between men and women, and none suggested that men's or women's choices were responsible (Table 2.2; there are more "causes" in this table than "harms" in Table 2.1 because committees could attribute harms to more than one cause). Instead, the committees see harm as caused mainly by economic organizations, unanticipated consequences of federal laws, and social change not associated with any particular organizations.

Thus, we may say that since 1945 congressional committees never defined the problem of work, family, and gender as one in which harm was being done by women abandoning their traditional roles or as caused by men's or women's innate characteristics or individual decisions. Through the 1950s, two problem definitions competed for dominance on the congressional agenda: a narrower one seeing harm in some types of unequal treatment but not in sex segregation in the labor market, and a broader one simply seeing harm in unequal treatment; from 1960 until the mid-1980s the concern was unequal treatment, broadly defined; and since the mid-1980s, the focus has been on the twin problems of unequal treatment and competing obligations to family and paid work.

What's the Solution?

What did members of Congress propose to do about work, family, and gender? To some extent, we would expect the bills they introduce to propose solutions to the problems defined in the committee reports. Yet, as Kingdon (1984) points out, the link between "problems" and "solutions" may not be as tight as we might expect intuitively. Individual members of Congress may introduce virtually any bill they like; they need not define the problem the way the committees do, and indeed may be trying to influence the committees' view of the problem.

In a general way, the pattern of support for separate spheres, equal opportunity, and work-family accommodation bills, as gauged by sponsorships, is

TABLE 2.2 What Causes the Harm?[a]

Congresses	Federal Government	Macrolevel Change	Economic Organizations	Macro & Federal Gov't.	Econ. Orgs. & Gov't.	Macro & Econ. Orgs.	Macro, Econ. Orgs., & Gov't.	None Mentioned	Total
1945-1960	18	1	3	2	0	0	0	8	32
1961-1984	11	5	6	3	2	0	1	6	34
1985-1990	2	9	1	0	2	2	2	1	19
Total	31	15	10	5	4	2	3	15	85

SOURCE: Burstein & Bricher, 1997.

NOTE: a. Cells represent the number of committee majority and minority reports referring to the various causes. "Macrolevel change" refers to macrolevel economic, political, or social change not attributed to specific groups. "Economic organizations" are businesses and unions. In addition to the categories in the table, one report (issued in 1963) argued that the harm was caused by innate differences between men and women, and one (issued in 1975) argued that political parties caused the harm.

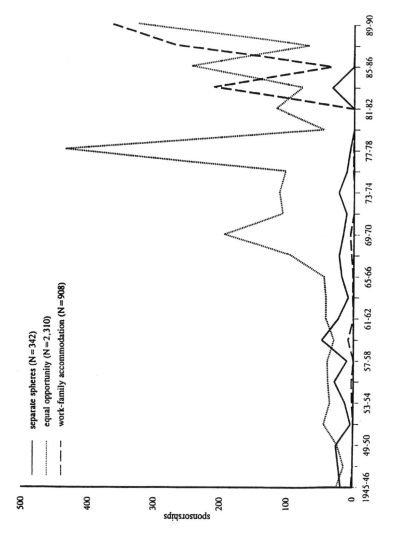

Figure 2.1. Number of Sponsorships, Three Packages

NOTE: Total = 3,560.

separate spheres (N=342)
equal opportunity (N=2,310)
work-family accommodation (N=908)

45

quite consistent with the pattern of problem definition by committees (Figure 2.1; the nature of the data did not permit us to distinguish between bills addressing inequality in a sex-segregated context from those directed at unequal treatment more broadly; both are treated as equal opportunity bills). Equal opportunity bills got far more support than the other types (2,310 sponsorships out of 3,560); work-family accommodation bills suddenly got a great deal of support beginning in the mid-1980s, just before the committees began to define competing obligations to family and paid work as a problem (the timing suggests that sponsorships led to committee action rather than the reverse); and work-family accommodation and equal opportunity bills are on the agenda simultaneously beginning in the mid-1980s.

There is one significant way in which support for bills diverges from the pattern of problem definition by committees. Although no committee defined threats to traditional gender roles as a problem, a fair number of separate spheres bills were introduced by individual members of Congress. Indeed, until the end of the Eisenhower administration, separate spheres and equal opportunity bills competed for support, with the former winning a majority of sponsors in some congresses and the latter in others. There has been some support for separate spheres bills in most congresses since then, with a small upsurge in 1983-1984 associated with child-labor legislation. This support for separate spheres is perhaps more in line with the conventional wisdom about the immediate postwar period than the committee problem definitions were; we can't help thinking there must have been some support for separate spheres, and the data on sponsorships show that there was. Nevertheless, support for separate spheres was never very strong, and over the entire period less than 10% of sponsorships were of separate spheres bills.

It is also worth noting that the number of sponsorships can be quite volatile, far more volatile than either committee reports or changes in public opinion (see below) would suggest. Most often, rapid changes in the number of sponsors is associated with specific events in what Kingdon would call the stream of politics. The dramatic peak in support for equal opportunity bills in 1977-1978, for example, was the congressional response to a 1976 Supreme Court decision declaring that differential treatment on the basis of pregnancy did not constitute sex discrimination. Enactment of laws reflects both committee concerns and sponsorships. Only one separate spheres bill was enacted between 1945 and 1990 (H.R. [House of Representatives bill number] 5856, in 1949), and it tightened the child labor law—a way of maintaining separate spheres, but not a major assault on equal opportunity. In fact, no separate spheres bill has made it out of committee since 1956; again, the ones that did dealt with child labor, not explicit support for traditional roles.

By way of contrast, 31 equal opportunity bills were enacted, at least 1 during every presidential term between 1945 (Roosevelt and Truman) and 1984 (the first Reagan term). Up through 1960, all the laws were directed at giving women more and better opportunities in the military. The breakthrough to greater gender equality in the civilian labor force came with adoption of the Equal Pay Act in 1963. This rather narrow bill, mandating only equal pay for men and women doing the same jobs, was followed just a year later by enactment of the law ushering in what we may think of as the modern era in the legal treatment of gender in the labor market: Title VII of the Civil Rights Act of 1964, which prohibited sex discrimination in hiring, promotion, discharge, and many other aspects of employment as well as pay.

Title VII immediately became the focus of efforts to expand opportunities for women in the civilian labor force. (Congress also continued to address the issue of gender equality in the military.) At first, the fight was to strengthen Title VII in ways affecting women and minorities the same way. The prohibition of sex discrimination had been adopted unexpectedly and with little debate—it was added during floor debate to a bill originally directed at discrimination on the basis of race, religion, and national origin—and for a decade almost no attention was devoted to considering what differences there might be between sex discrimination and discrimination against minorities.

This changed in a crucial way in the mid-1970s, as the issue of pregnancy entered the ongoing debate about equal employment opportunity. Traditionally, one of the key tenets of the ideology of separate spheres was that bearing children made women marginal members of the labor force; although women might be in the labor force when young and childless, the arrival of children required them to leave the labor force and devote themselves full time to their families. Employers could give practical force to this view—and many did—by firing pregnant employees, refusing to hire women who were pregnant or the mothers of young children, or treating pregnant women less well than other employees.

Did Title VII prohibit employers from treating pregnant women less well than other employees? Title VII prohibited sex discrimination, but did not mention pregnancy, so the legal question was one of definition: Was differential treatment on the basis of pregnancy a form of sex discrimination? When the Supreme Court was asked to answer this question, its answer, in 1976, was no: Such treatment did not distinguish between men and women but rather between pregnant and nonpregnant persons.

The Court's reasoning might have seemed plausible to most people when Title VII was adopted, but by 1976 it seemed absurd to those favoring equal opportunity for women. So strong was the reaction that Congress overruled the Court by amending Title VII (in the Pregnancy Discrimination Act [PDA] of 1978) to *define* differential treatment on the basis of pregnancy as sex discrimination.

Although the PDA was ostensibly only a small amendment to a major law, it may be seen in retrospect as a breakthrough of tremendous importance, because it brought a key element of women's role in the family—as prospective mothers—into discussions of equal employment opportunity. It was the PDA that first linked work, family, and equal employment opportunity in American law. Even if employers believed in traditional gender roles, it said, even if they wanted to maintain separate spheres by pushing women out of the labor force when they were about to become mothers, they could not legally act on their beliefs; women about to become mothers had the same right to employment as any other adult.[2]

The PDA ratified and possibly accelerated a decades-long trend: Women were returning to the labor force more quickly after having a child; for example, in 1948, 10.8% of married women with spouse present and children under 6 were in the civilian labor force, while in 1987, 56.8% were (Edwards, 1997). This increasingly common pattern of departure-and-reentry led to further legal and personal problems that became, in turn, political issues for Congress.

The legal problem was this: During the 1970s, Congress began to regulate not only how employers dealt with pregnancy, but how they dealt with pensions as well, in the Employee Retirement Income Security Act—ERISA (29 USC 1001 et seq., 1974). Soon the departure-and-reentry pattern of so many women raised a question for those implementing ERISA: how to deal with "breaks in service" associated with having and caring for children when calculating eligibility for, and the amount of, pensions. The response—in a context becoming more favorable to women's working for pay even when they had children (more on this below)—was a law (the Retirement Equity Act of 1984, Public Law 98-397) requiring employers to preserve pension rights for employees who take some time off for childbirth and child rearing and to provide partial credit toward pensions for time taken off for that purpose.

Again there was a situation in which a seemingly modest change in current law—supported by many conservatives interested mainly in resolving unanticipated inconsistencies between laws—actually represented an important shift in public policy. With passage of the Retirement Equity Act, employers were required not only to provide equal opportunity regardless of pregnancy, but to take some employees' family situations into account on an ongoing basis as well. The next, and much better known, movement in this direction, began in 1985 with the introduction of the first family and medical leave bills.

Family and medical leave bills address one of the most fundamental problems stemming from women being in the labor force even when they have young children: With mothers as well as fathers in the labor force, there is no one at home to care for children. This is a serious problem under ordinary circumstances because good child care is expensive and often hard to find; but it is far more serious when a child is newborn, ill, or injured, and is seen as requiring parental care. Traditionally, mothers would have been expected to quit their jobs to care for their children under such circumstances, and might have been pressured to do so by employers who became aware of the problem. Such expectations and pressures become less tenable as the idea of gender equality becomes more deeply embedded in law and economic institutions and women win access to better jobs—but the needs of the children remain. Family and medical leave bills proposed to address this problem by requiring employers to provide time off to care for newborns and sick or injured children—and, in a true break with tradition, to provide such time to men and women equally.

The issue of caring for family members was most obvious, and most clearly linked to prior changes in the law, with regard to newborns; but others sometimes need care as well. By the time the Family and Medical Leave Act was signed into law, in 1993, it required employers to provide employees time off to care for adopted as well as biological children, dependent parents, and spouses.

Although the major impetus for work-family accommodation has been change in ideas about women's labor force participation—particularly the belief that having children required them to leave the labor force—it has had another source as well: the economic consequences of divorce. Along with the dramatic increase in divorce in recent years has come an increase in the number of noncustodial parents (most of them fathers) failing to provide for their children financially. Concerned that some such failures were forcing women onto welfare and thereby increasing government expenditures, Congress in the 1970s adopted a law mandating that states seek out the noncustodial parents of children on welfare and, if they were behind on court-ordered child-support payments, require employers to withhold part of their wages for that purpose. In 1983, members of Congress proposed for the first time that states and employers do this for all custodial parents—not just those on AFDC—requesting help in getting child-support payments. The proposal won immediate support, and was enacted into law (Public Law 98-378) without opposition (the vote was 413-0 in the House and 99-0 in the Senate) in 1984. Employers were thus required, under some circumstances, to take account of family circumstances (as noncustodial parents behind in support payments) in their treatment of employees.

It can easily be argued that at this point much of what Congress was doing was stimulated by the consequences of its own prior actions and the actions of other governmental institutions (including the Supreme Court). The prohibition of sex discrimination was bound to lead eventually to questions about pregnancy. Once the PDA was adopted and women were, in essence, granted the right to remain in their jobs through pregnancy, Congress was, arguably, bound to find itself dealing with the implications of women remaining in the labor force continuously, with only relatively short breaks for childbirth and caring for infants and toddlers (Edwards, 1997).

This does not mean that there was any inevitability to the questions Congress wound up asking, or to the answers it reached. What the questions were at any given time was a function of previous decisions; and what the decisions were depended on how problems were defined, which solutions seemed plausible, and what circumstances were in what Kingdon calls the "political stream," that set of forces that determines whether Congress will act. Among the potentially important forces was public opinion, and it is that to which we now turn.

PUBLIC OPINION AND CONGRESSIONAL ACTION

Separate Spheres

Congressional support for separate spheres was greater in the immediate postwar period than it has ever been since, yet, in contrast to what we might have expected, it was not very strong even then (Table 2.3 summarizes some key congressional actions). Why so little congressional support for separate spheres? Could congressional inaction have been consistent with public opinion? What was public opinion on work, family, and gender right after World War II, when congressional support for separate spheres was at its peak? And what were the trends thereafter?

It would probably be fair to say that in the years just after the War, the public favored men and women occupying separate spheres; they certainly did not see men and women participating in the labor market on equal terms. Most people—76% in 1945—did think that women doing the same work as men should be paid the same amount, in principle (see Table 2.4). But support

TABLE 2.3 Highlights and Turning Points in Congressional Action

1945-1960: Support for separate spheres, and narrow and broad views of gender inequality

1955, last separate spheres bill reported out
1960, last committee report focusing on inequality in a sex-segregated context
1959-1960, last time sponsors of separate spheres bills outnumber sponsors of equal opportunity bills

1961-1982: Equal opportunity dominates congressional agenda

1961-1982, 90% of sponsorships support equal opportunity bills
1963, enactment of Equal Pay Act (first proposed, 1945)
1964, enactment of Civil Rights Act; Title VII prohibits sex discrimination in employment
1972, enactment of amendments to Title VII, expanding coverage and strengthening enforcement
1978, enactment of Pregnancy Discrimination Act

1983- : Congress adds work-family accommodation to the agenda

1983-1984, first Congress in which work-family accommodation bills win many sponsors
1984, first work-family accommodation bill enacted
1985, family and medical leave bills first introduced
1986, first committee report on family and medical leave bill
1989, family and medical leave bill passes both Houses, vetoed by President Bush
1990, bill to strengthen Title VII passes both Houses, vetoed by President Bush
1991, bill to strengthen Title VII enacted
1993, Family and Medical Leave Act enacted

SOURCES: Burstein & Bricher, 1997; Burstein, Bricher, & Einwohner, 1995.

fell to 66% when the question asked was whether a young, single woman should be paid the same as a married man with children, and in 1946 more than two thirds thought that if women were being paid less than men for doing the same job, there was often a good reason for it. Moreover, the proportion thinking that women would, or should, be doing the same work was probably small. Women's very participation in the labor force was seen as a function of their marital status and their husband's ability to earn a living. Although 79% of the public felt (in 1949) that it was all right for women to work during the first few years of married life if that were necessary to make the marriage feasible, less than half (39% in 1946) approved of a woman "earning money in business or industry" if she had a husband capable of supporting her. Those women in the labor force could expect difficulties if they aspired to supervisory positions: Three quarters of men and more than half of women preferred that a boss in a new job be a man (in 1953).

TABLE 2.4 Public Opinion on Work, Family, and Gender, Mid-1940s to Early
1950s

Women in the Civilian Labor Force:	
Women should be paid same as men for same work, 1945	76%
Young, single women should be paid the same as married man for same work, 1945	66%
Often a good reason for paying women less than men, same job, 1946	
men	65%
women	72%
OK for women to work when first married, 1949	79%
OK for woman to earn money if she has husband who can support her, 1946	39%
Prefer that boss in a new job be a man, 1953	
men	75%
women	57%
Makes no difference whether boss is a man or a woman, 1953	
men	21%
women	29%
Women in the Military:	
Approve of drafting nurses, 1945	73%
Favor drafting young single women to fill typing and clerical jobs in armed forces, 1951	48%
After the war, require one year's military training of:	
men	70%
women, in women's branches of armed forces, 1945	22%
Should be units of armed forces in which women could enlist, in peacetime, 1947	53%
Women and Public Office:	
Would vote for woman for president	
1945	33%
1949	48%
... for governor, 1945	56%
Approve of woman in president's cabinet, 1945	38%
... on Supreme Court, 1945	47%

SOURCES: Erskine, 1971; Gallup, 1972.

The public also saw women's role in the military as limited and stereotyped. Most could imagine drafting women to fill critical, stereotypically female positions during wartime—three quarters approved of drafting nurses
when Congress was thinking of doing so early in 1945—and almost half

favored drafting women to fill typing and clerical jobs in wartime (48% in 1951). But when asked about "military training" rather than specific jobs, only a fifth of the public favored drafting women, a third as many as favored drafting men, even when the question specified that women would serve in women's branches of the armed forces. Barely half the public favored providing women with the opportunity to enlist in the military—in women's (i.e., sex-segregated) units.

Willingness to vote for a woman for president has often been seen as an indicator of a more general openness to women in untraditional roles. In the years just after the War, a growing minority of the public expressed a willingness to do so, and substantial minorities—with regard to voting for a woman for governor, a small majority—were willing to accept women in other important public roles.

Unfortunately, there are no data on trends in public opinion on separate spheres for the entire period between 1945 and 1990. Trend data are available since the early 1970s, however, on two questions that ask relatively directly whether people believe women should play an important role in the public sphere or should confine their activities mainly to the home: One asks whether women should take care of running their homes and leave running the country to men, and the second asks whether women's place is in the home, as opposed to having a role equal to men's in business, industry, and government (Table 2.5).

Both trends show the public increasingly willing to see women occupying important roles in the public sphere. If we were to extrapolate the trends back to the 1940s—a plausible procedure but not one on which to place great reliance—it would probably be fair to guess that a majority of the public then saw women's place as primarily in the home. The actual data, though, may provide some idea why separate spheres proposals have not gotten very far in Congress since the early 1970s; at that time, approximately half the public opposed limiting women to the domestic sphere, and the proportion has been increasing fairly steadily ever since (data are provided through 1994, when available, to add credibility to the trend line).

Probably none of this mattered a great deal to most people. The "most important problem" question does set a high threshold—"*most* important." Had many people considered work, family, and gender issues important, however, it seems likely that enough would consider them "most important" to show up in the Gallup's published reports—but they never did. No doubt many people were concerned about men's and women's roles, but other issues had higher priority.

TABLE 2.5 Should Women Have a Public Role, or Stay Home?

Year	Don't Agree That Men Should Run Country[a] (%)	Women Should Have Equal Role[b] (%)
1971	50	
1972		46
1974	64	50
1975	64	
1976		50
1977	62	
1978	68	57
1980		58
1982	72	58
1983	77	
1984		54
1985	74	
1986	76	
1988	79	65
1989	80	
1990	82	
1991	81	
1993	85	
1994	86	

SOURCES: Gallup, 1982; National Election Studies; Harris, 1971.
NOTES: a. "Do you agree or disagree with this statement? Women should take care of running their homes and leave running the country to men." [disagree]
b. "Recently there has been a lot of talk about women's rights. Some people feel that women should have an equal role with men in running business, industry, and government. Others feel that women's place is in the home. Where would you place yourself on this scale, or haven't you thought much about this?" [categories 1-3, "equal role," on 7-point scale]

So was Congress responding to public opinion when it did little to preserve separate spheres? Perhaps it is fair to say that had Congress done more, the public would not have objected; support for equal opportunity was weak. But there is not much evidence to show that the public wanted more congressional action, either.

There is much less data on public opinion than we might like. Yet it is important to keep in mind that the lack of data meant that Congress, too, was operating in an environment of uncertainty. Had the public been demanding more action, polling organizations would probably have sensed that the preservation of separate spheres was a major issue and therefore have asked more questions. Our inability to find much evidence of public demand for the preservation of separate spheres suggests that Congress did not see itself confronting demands for action; and, in the absence of a clear message from the public, Congress is not likely to do much to respond to it. Perhaps the most plausible conclusion is a weak one: Congress was not being unresponsive to the public when it failed to do much to preserve separate spheres.

Equal Opportunity

As we know, congressional action on work, family, and gender focused on equal opportunity almost exclusively between the early 1960s and the mid-1980s. Was this what the public wanted? Unfortunately, as with separate spheres, the data needed to address this question directly and comprehensively do not exist. But there are enough data to provide a fairly clear picture of the broad trend in the public's attitudes.

The focus of equal opportunity bills is equal opportunity *in the labor force*. What we want, therefore, are public opinion data that ask only about the labor force, and not about home and family. It is important to keep this in mind, because questions often thought of as tapping attitudes about women in the labor force actually make their labor force participation contingent upon their family status—for example, the question, "Do you approve or disapprove of a married woman earning money in business or industry *if she has a husband capable of supporting her?*" (emphasis added).

Since the 1940s, the public has moved consistently toward greater acceptance of women taking on a wider variety of roles in both the civilian labor market and the military, and toward greater willingness to see women as just as competent as men (stretching the definition of "labor market" a bit to include the presidency; see Tables 2.6 and 2.7). The public has become more willing to vote for a woman for president, have a woman as a boss, and agree that women can run most businesses as well as men. Rates of change vary over time and for different questions, but there are no reversals, no movement away from egalitarian attitudes.

These findings are not trivial. Although claims that there was a major "backlash" against women in the 1970s or 1980s cannot be substantiated on the basis of these data, there is no reason to think that attitudes about gender in the labor market inevitably move only one way. While there need not be a perfect correlation between the attitudes of the general public and the attitudes of employers setting women's wages, it is plausible that there is some connection between the two; and there is considerable evidence that sex discrimination in wages increased substantially between roughly 1900 and 1940 (Goldin, 1990). If attitudes about women in the labor market *can* move in

TABLE 2.6 Trends in Public Opinion on Women in the Civilian Labor Market (Percentages)

Year	Vote for Woman[a]	Boss's Gender Makes No Difference[b]		Women Run as Well[c]	Equal Pay for Same Work[d]
		Women (%)	Men (%)		
1945	33				
1949	48				
1953		29	21		
1954					87
1955	52				
1958	52				
1962					90
1963	55				
1969	54				
1970				51	
1971	66				
1972	73				
1973					95
1974	80				
1975	80				
1976		27	32		
1977	79				94
1978	82				
1982	86	30	46	72	
1983	86				
1985	82				
1986	86				
1987		39	57		
1988	88				
1989	86				
1990	90				
1991	91				
1993	91				
1994	92				

SOURCES: "Woman for president": Gallup, 1972, 1982, General Social Surveys; "boss's gender makes no difference," "women run as well," "equal pay for same work": Gallup, 1972, 1982; General Social Surveys; Simon & Landis, 1989.

NOTES: a. "If your party nominated a woman for president, would you vote for her if she were qualified for the job?"

b. "If you were taking a new job and had your choice of a boss, would you prefer to work for a man or for a woman?"

c. "Do you think women could run most businesses as well as men, or not?"

d. Variously worded questions asking whether women should be paid the same as men if they are doing the same work.

TABLE 2.7 Public Opinion on Women in the Military, 1945-1992

1945:		
February		
Approve of drafting nurses?	73%	
After the war, require one year's military training of:		
men (May):	70%	
women, in women's branches of armed forces (February):	22%	
1947:		
Should be units of armed forces in which women could enlist, in peacetime	53%	
1951:		
Favor drafting young single women to fill typing and clerical jobs in armed forces	48%	
1954:		
Favor drafting women for non-combat duties if there's a third world war	55%	
1979-1980:	*1979*	*1980*
If draft becomes necessary, against drafting women	50%	47%
For drafting women, but not in combat roles	22%	25%
For drafting women, including for combat roles	19%	22%
1982:		
How has increasing number of women in armed forces affected effectiveness?		
Raised effectiveness	20%	
Made no difference	60%	
Reduced effectiveness	8%	
Don't know	12%	
1984:		
9% of armed forces are women.		
Is this too many?	8%	
About the right number?	58%	
There should be more	34%	
1982:		
Woman in armed forces should be assigned to this job, assuming she is trained to do it:		
typist at the Pentagon	96%	
nurse in a combat zone	92%	
truck mechanic	82%	
jet transport pilot	71%	
jet fighter pilot	61%	
air defense missile gunner in the U.S.	57%	
commander of a large military base	57%	
crew member on a combat ship	55%	
soldier in hand-to-hand combat	34%	

SOURCES: Questions from 1945 through 1980, Gallup, 1972, 1982; from 1982-1992, General Social Surveys.

both directions, it means something that, since World War II, they have moved in only one.

Trends in attitudes about women in the military are harder to gauge than attitudes about women in the civilian labor market, because there do not seem to be any questions asked of the public repeatedly over substantial periods of time, and no questions at all between the mid-1950s and late 1970s. Nevertheless, the trend does seem to be toward acceptance of women playing a larger part in the military, in a wider range of roles.

At the end of World War II, the public saw women's role in the military as limited and stereotyped. As already noted, most Americans could imagine drafting women to fill critical, stereotypically female positions during wartime, but most opposed drafting women for "military training" more generally, and barely half favored women enlisting even in sex-segregated units.

There are some real uncertainties involved in trying to compare attitudes about women in the military in the 1940s and 1950s to the attitudes expressed when again asked about the issue, beginning in the late 1970s. Although the Cold War was still on in the late 1970s, questions about drafting women may not have had the same meaning for people then as they had earlier, because the draft no longer existed and war did not seem as likely. Nevertheless, it would be difficult to argue that the data do not suggest a substantial change in attitudes. In 1945, about a fifth of respondents favored drafting women once the War was over; in 1979-1980, about two fifths did, and one fifth favored drafting them for combat roles—something that was not even suggested in earlier questions. In the early- to mid-1980s, a third of Americans wanted to see more women in the military and a fifth thought increasing their number would raise the military's effectiveness. It is easy to imagine almost everyone approving of women typists in the Pentagon in the late 1940s, as they did in 1992; but it is very difficult to imagine that Americans in the late 1940s would have had the same distribution of preferences as in 1982 on other military roles for women: 71% approving of women as transport pilots, 61% of women as fighter pilots, 57% of women commanding large military bases.

Our data on public opinion tell a consistent story, albeit one without much detail. At the end of World War II, most Americans probably felt that women's major commitment should be to the home and men's to the paid workforce—they supported separate spheres of activity for men and women. There was some support for gender equality, but with limits so much taken for granted that they were not even discussed—people favored equal pay for the same work, but not equal treatment in hiring or promotion.

Yet the distribution of views was not static. Every time series we have, and every inference we can make, suggests that the public's attitudes about women in the labor force were becoming more egalitarian.

Congressional action was consistent with this trend. Although it might be argued that there was some competition right after the War between the proponents of separate spheres and the proponents of equal opportunity—both kinds of bills got roughly comparable numbers of sponsors, both were the subject of hearings, and both led to the passage of laws—the contest was over by the second Eisenhower administration. As the public became more egalitarian, members of Congress defined unequal treatment as a problem, sponsored more equal opportunity bills, and enacted some into law. It would be difficult to argue that congressional action was being propelled by intense public demands for action; but it does seem to be true that, in a general way, Congress and the public were moving in the same direction.

Work-Family Accommodation

Family and medical leave bills differ from equal opportunity bills in two fundamental ways: They require employers to take cognizance of employees' family responsibilities, and forbid them from acting on the presumption that women alone bear the responsibility for taking care of family members—that is, the employers have to make leave available to women and men equally. One can readily hypothesize that such bills would receive little support unless people were willing to imagine women and men being equal at the workplace and in the home, committed to independent careers and sharing responsibilities for the care of family members.

Trends in attitudes on careers and family responsibilities are similar to trends on equality in the workplace, and consistent with increasing support for work-family accommodation. Increasing proportions of Americans approve of wives taking on roles traditionally assigned to husbands, and of husbands taking on roles traditionally assigned to wives: They increasingly approve of a married woman earning money (even) if she has a husband to support her, devoting herself to her own career rather than her husband's, achieving outside the home as well as caring for her family, and sharing household responsibilities (Table 2.8). They have also collectively changed their minds about one of the strongest normative impediments to a woman remaining in the workforce once she has a child—the belief that by returning to the workforce a mother harms the child; increasing proportions believe that "a working mother" can have a warm relationship with her child, and that the child need not suffer if his or her mother works (Table 2.9). It is easy to imagine Americans wanting to guarantee that women who have to care for family members should be able to do so without losing their jobs, and even wanting to provide men the same right—though it would be far better if we had data on whether they wanted federal legislation on these issues.

TABLE 2.8 Trends in Public Opinion on Women, Work, and Husbands

Year	Approve Women Earning[a] (%)	Husband's Career Not Primary[b] (%)	Not Better if Man the Achiever[c] (%)	Spouses Share Responsibilities[d] (%)
1938	21			
1945	18			
1969	55			
1970	60			
1971				
1972	64			
1974	68			45
1975	69			
1976				
1977	65	43	34	47
1978	72			
1979				51
1980				
1982	74			
1983	75			
1984				
1985	84	62	52	54
1986	77	64	52	
1988	79	69	58	
1989	78	72	59	
1990	81	71	60	

SOURCES: "Approve women earning": Erskine, 1971, Gallup, 1972, General Social Surveys; "Husband's career," "Not better if man the achiever," "Spouses share responsibilities": General Social Surveys.
NOTES: a. "Do you approve or disapprove of a married woman earning money in business or industry if she has a husband capable of supporting her?" (approve)
b. "It is more important for a wife to help her husband's career than to have one herself" (disagree)
c. "It is much better for everyone involved if the man is the achiever outside the home and the woman takes care of the home and family." (disagree)
d. "In today's society there are many different lifestyles, and some that are acceptable today that weren't in the past. Regardless of what you may have done or plan to do with your life, and thinking just of what would give you personally the most satisfying and interesting life, which one of these different ways of life do you think would be the best as a way of life? [card shown respondent]
. . .
    b. a marriage where the husband and wife share responsibilities more—both work, both share homemaking and childcare responsibilities."

The trends in congressional action are thus consistent with the trends in public opinion. One thing the changes in opinion do not tell us, however, is why Congress shifted its attention to work-family accommodation when it did and in the way it did—quite abruptly in the mid-1980s. Answering this

TABLE 2.9 Public Opinion on "Working Women" and Their Children

Year	*Can Relationship Be Warm?*[a] *agree*[c] *(%)*	*Will Preschool Child Suffer?*[b] *disagree (%)*
1977	49	33
1985	61	46
1986	62	49
1988	63	52
1989	64	52
1990	63	51
1991	65	52
1993	67	57
1994	70	58

SOURCES: General Social Surveys for years included.
NOTES: a. "A working mother can establish just as warm and secure a relationship with her children as a mother who does not work."
b. "A preschool child is likely to suffer if his mother works."
c. "Agree" includes both "agree" and "strongly agree"; "disagree" includes both "disagree" and "strongly disagree."

question brings us to our conclusions about how the three streams of problem definition, alternative policy solutions, and public opinion interacted to prompt particular actions by Congress.

CONCLUSIONS: PROBLEMS, SOLUTIONS, PUBLIC OPINION, AND PUBLIC POLICY

Was Congress responding to public opinion when it transformed federal policy on work, family, and gender in the decades after World War II? In general, it seemed to be, but indirectly. The public was not clamoring for federal legislation specifically on work, family, and gender, although the outcry after the Supreme Court's decision on pregnancy discrimination shows that the public was not indifferent either. Still, even when the public called for a policy change, it tended to have no opinion—it could not be expected to have any opinion—on most aspects of most bills. Instead, as the public moved toward more egalitarian views of men's and women's roles in the labor market and at home, Congress enacted laws to mandate equal treatment and require employers to make some accommodation to the needs of working parents. To return to Stimson et al.'s (1995) view that American politics is characterized by "dynamic representation," we can say that with regard to work, family, and gender, it appears that "public opinion move[d] meaningfully over time . . . government officials sense[d] this movement, and . . . those officials alter[ed] their behavior in response to the sensed movement" (p. 543).

The specific form of the response, however, was strongly influenced by what had been occurring in the "streams" of problem definition and policy alternatives as well as by public opinion. When something happened that seemed to require Congress to act, what it did was very much a function of how the issue was viewed, what policy proposals seemed most plausible, and what public opinion seemed to demand, or at least permit.

To take a key example: The public was not demanding in 1964 that Congress prohibit sex discrimination in employment. It was, however, demanding that Congress act against discrimination against minorities, and public discourse (outside the South) was filled with powerful arguments about the evils of discrimination and the moral necessity of federal action to ensure equal treatment (Burstein, 1998). Then, as Congress debated bills that would ban discrimination on the basis of race, religion, and national origin, a representative moved that sex discrimination in employment be prohibited as well. At this point, the three streams came together. Had members of Congress not seen sex discrimination as a problem, the amendment surely would have failed. But congressional committees had been defining sex discrimination as a problem for a long time, and had been providing evidence of its seriousness in their reports; they had not been thinking of sex discrimination defined as broadly as in the bill being debated, but nevertheless their orientation was toward seeing unequal treatment as a problem. Had there been no obvious legislative solution to the problem, no law would have been adopted; but the bill potentially being amended was seemingly such a solution. Had the public opposed the amendment, it might very well have been defeated; but the public was moving toward becoming more egalitarian. Thus, problem, solution, and public opinion joined—and Congress prohibited sex discrimination in employment.

Once it did so, the policy process in this area developed its own logic. A plausible scenario: The passage of Title VII raised the expectations of women who had been working for equality (in the fight for passage of the Equal Pay Act, for example); their disappointment at the failure of the newly created Equal Employment Opportunity Commission to take sex discrimination seriously led to the formation of the National Organization for Women and other groups; intellectual developments prompted by the resurgence of the women's movement led to the development of new policy proposals and new arguments about sex discrimination and gender roles (on these points, see Harrison, 1988); these new arguments won enough acceptance so that when another potentially key moment arrived (such as the 1976 Supreme Court decision on pregnancy), Congress found relevant problem definitions and policy proposals readily available; women's continuing entry into the labor market and their increasingly continuous participation in it led to pressure for new definitions of the problem of work, family, and gender, and for new policy proposals; and in a climate of public opinion (possibly itself influenced by past policy changes) becoming increasingly egalitarian, policy proposals favoring equality in the labor market and at home became the seemingly obvious ones to support. By the mid-1980s, 20 years after the adoption of Title VII and just a few after adoption of the Pregnancy Discrimination Act, the time was ripe for work-family accommodation—and when work-family accommodation proposals were made, they rapidly won support.

What are the implications of our analysis for future changes in policy? One thing that should be clear is that major changes in policy are unpredictable, in the sense that they require the conjunction of three processes (or "streams") that are only loosely connected: problem definition, the development of new proposed solutions, and pressure on Congress for action. For those who want to influence the direction of change, however, long-term involvement in the political process, preparing for that unpredictable conjunction, is essential. Although interest organizations cannot predict when (or if) their efforts to arouse public opinion will succeed, if they cease their efforts it is unlikely that public pressure will rise to the level seemingly requisite for major policy change. And they have to remain active in the legislative and bureaucratic arenas as well. When Congress decides to act, the chances are good that it will enact policy proposals that have been "on the shelf"—familiar and available—for some time; without ongoing involvement by interest organizations, their favored proposals are likely to fade from view (Kingdon, 1984; Polsby, 1984).

Although it is virtually impossible to predict when major changes in policy will occur or what the changes will be, one can predict with considerable confidence that small changes in policy will be a regular occurrence in Congress, the administrative agencies, and the courts, as loopholes, inconsistencies, and unforeseen consequences of the law come to the attention of those concerned about policy implementation and impact. Sometime a series of seemingly small changes, each responding to issues raised by previous changes, will add up to major change in unanticipated ways, as when the ban on discrimination on the basis of pregnancy ultimately had ramifications for laws regulating pensions and helped bring work-family accommodation onto the political agenda. Here, too, it is clear that ongoing activity by interest organizations can make a difference; such organizations can help draw attention to issues before administrative agencies or the courts and can influence how the issues are defined and remedied (Burstein, 1990, 1991).

What are the prospects for dramatic change in policies affecting work, family, and gender in the immediate future? Probably not very great. Pressure to expand the coverage and improve the benefits mandated by the Family and Medical Leave Act will continue, but whatever changes may occur will be incremental. Dramatic changes in social policy seem to require the development of new ideas, their careful cultivation over a substantial period of time, and events that lead the public to demand change. It is not at all obvious at the moment that new ideas about work, family, and gender are working their way on to the congressional agenda. Yet at the same time we can expect incremental change to continue; Congress and the American people have hardly worked through the implications of the movement toward gender equality in the labor market and at home. We cannot really predict what the small changes will add up to; but we do know that continuing involvement by those concerned about policies affecting work, family, and gender can influence the direction they take.

NOTES

1. The committee reports are based on hearings held to consider bills on work, family, and gender. The bills themselves are described in the next section. Because the introduction of bills precedes the hearings, it might seem reasonable to describe bills first and committee reports second. We proceed in the reverse order because logically it makes sense to describe problems before proposed solutions. The bills obviously influence committee action, but it is really the committee reports, defining the problem and trying to show how it will be mitigated by a particular bill, that prompt serious consideration by the House and Senate. Congressional activity is reported by "congress," not by year, because congressional activities are organized around the 2-year period between elections.

2. This is not to claim that there was no resistance to the PDA, that employers did not fight to keep its scope as narrow as possible, or that its consequences were foreordained; with regard to work and family, the PDA was a beginning, not a culmination. See Edwards (1996) for a broad discussion of pregnancy discrimination litigation.

REFERENCES

Arnold, R. Douglas. (1990). *The logic of congressional action*. New Haven, CT: Yale University Press.

Bergmann, B. R. (1986). *The economic emergence of women.* New York: Basic Books.

Blendon, R. J., Benson, J. M., & Donelan, K. (1993). The public and the controversy over abortion. *JAMA* [Journal of the American Medical Association] *270,* 2871-2875.

Burstein, P. (1990). Intergroup conflict, law, and the concept of labor market discrimination. *Sociological Forum, 5,* 459-476.

Burstein, P. (1991). Legal mobilization as a social movement tactic. *American Journal of Sociology, 96,* 1201-1225.

Burstein, P. (1998). *Discrimination, jobs, and politics.* Chicago: University of Chicago Press.

Burstein, P., & Bricher, R. M. (1997). Problem definition and public policy: Congressional committees confront work, family, and gender, 1945-90. *Social Forces, 76,* 135-168.

Burstein, P., Bricher, R. M., & Einwohner, R. (1995). Policy alternatives and political change. *American Sociological Review, 60,* 67-83.

Cherlin, A., & Walters, P. (1981). Trends in United States men's and women's sex-role attitudes, 1972 to 1978. *American Sociological Review, 46,* 453-460.

Edwards, M. E. (1996). Pregnancy discrimination litigation. *Social Forces, 75,* 247-269.

Edwards, M. E. (1997). *Toward explaining accelerated rates of employment among American mothers of preschoolers.* Unpublished doctoral dissertation, Department of Sociology, University of Washington.

Erikson, R. S., Wright, G. C., & McIver, J. P. (1993). *Statehouse democracy.* New York: Cambridge University Press.

Erskine, H. (1971). The polls: women's role. *Public Opinion Quarterly, 35,* 275-290.

Ferree, M. M. (1974). A woman for president? Changing responses, 1958-1972. *Public Opinion Quarterly, 38,* 390-399.

Gallup, G. (1972). *Gallup poll: Public opinion, 1935-1972* (3 vols.). New York: Random House.

Gallup, G. (1982). *The Gallup poll.* Wilmington, DE: Scholarly Resources.

Gerson, K. (1985). *Hard choices: How women decide about work, career, and motherhood.* Berkeley: University of California Press.

Gerson, K. (1993). *No man's land: Men's changing commitments to family and work.* New York: Basic Books.

Goldin, C. (1990). *Understanding the gender gap.* New York: Oxford University Press.

Harris, L., and Associates. (1971). *Harris Survey yearbook of public opinion.* New York: Louis Harris and Associates.

Harrison, C. (1988). *On account of sex: The politics of women's issues, 1945-1968.* Berkeley: University of California Press.

Jones, B. (1994). *Reconceiving decision-making in democratic politics.* Chicago: University of Chicago Press.

Kingdon, J. (1984). *Agendas, alternatives, and public policies.* Boston: Little, Brown.

Mason, K. O., Czajka, J., & Arber, S. (1976). Change in U.S. women's sex role attitudes, 1964-74. *American Sociological Review, 41,* 573-596.

Mason, K. O., & Lu, Y.-H. (1988). Attitudes toward women's familial roles: Changes in the United States, 1977-1985. *Gender and Society, 2,* 39-57.

Mayer, K. U., & Schoepflin, U. (1989). The state and the life course. *Annual Review of Sociology, 15,* 187-209.

Page, B. I., & Shapiro, R. Y. (1983). Effects of public opinion on policy. *American Political Science Review, 77,* 175-190.

Polsby, N. (1984). *Political innovation in America.* New Haven, CT: Yale University Press.

Reskin, B., & Padavic, I. (1994). *Women and men at work.* Thousand Oaks, CA: Pine Forge Press.

Schreiber, E. M. (1978). Education and change in American opinions on a woman for president. *Public Opinion Quarterly, 42,* 171-182.

Simon, R. J., & Landis, J. M. (1989). Women's and men's attitudes about a woman's place and role. *Public Opinion Quarterly, 53,* 265-276.

Skocpol, T. (1992). *Protecting soldiers and mothers.* Cambridge, MA: Belknap Press of Harvard University Press.

Spitze, G., & Huber, J. (1980). Changing attitudes toward women's nonfamily roles: 1938-1978. *Sociology of Work and Occupations, 7,* 317-335.

Stimson, J. A., MacKuen, M. B., & Erikson, R. S. (1995). Dynamic representation. *American Political Science Review, 89,* 543-565.

Stone, D. (1989). Causal stories and the formation of policy agendas. *Political Science Quarterly, 104,* 281-300.

Strober, M. H., & Dornbusch, S. M. (1988). Public policy alternatives. In S. M. Dornbusch & M. H. Strober (Eds.), *Feminism, children, and the new families* (pp. 327-55). New York: Guilford.

Thornton, A., & Freedman, D. S. (1979). Changes in the sex role attitudes of women, 1962-1977. *American Sociological Review, 44,* 832-842.

Weiss, J. A. (1989). The powers of problem definition. *Policy Sciences, 22,* 97-122.

Wilcox, C. (1992). Race, gender, and support for women in the military. *Social Science Quarterly, 73,* 310-323.

Wilkie, J. R. (1993). Changes in US men's attitudes toward the family provider role, 1972-89. *Gender and Society, 7,* 261-279.

Wlezien, C. (1995). The public as thermostat: Dynamics of preferences for spending. *American Journal of Political Science, 39,* 981-1000.

PART II

The Juggling Act

This set of chapters gets to the heart of "the juggling act" that parents who work experience on a daily basis. Jerry Jacobs and Kathleen Gerson investigate the distribution of workers' work hours to provide new evidence concerning whether Americans are overworked, underemployed, or whether each model is true, but for different sets of workers. They take as point of departure Juliet Schor's (1991) *The Overworked American*, which argues that work hours have increased over time in the United States. Jacobs and Gerson argue that her evidence is more consistent with relatively constant work weeks over time in terms of length, with possibly less vacation time annually than had been true earlier. Still, the image that Americans are overworked is a compelling one. But, if true, how does that image reconcile with what we know regarding the phenomenon of underemployment, a condition where workers are employed fewer hours than they desire? Jacobs and Gerson use data from the National Study of the Changing Workforce, a national probability sample of 3,381 men and women employed in 1993. They demonstrate that both models of overwork and underemployment exist simultaneously, but apply to different segments of the workforce. The most educated workers are likely to work higher numbers of hours per week, at least partly because for salaried workers, employers do not pay for overtime and can spread costly benefits across more hours of worker productivity. The least educated workers are most likely to work at part-time jobs. In analyses of worker preferences, the most educated workers prefer to work less, while the least educated workers would like to work more. Associated with educational differences, professional, managerial, and technical workers tend to report feeling overworked. Their study of gender differences suggests substantial similarity in men's and women's preferences for work hours, thus indicating that both genders seek a reasonable balance between work and home. Additional findings regarding age, marital status, and life cycle stage reinforce the conclusion that men and women both seek work arrangements that provide sufficient material support along with time to manage family responsibilities. Their findings also help us view Arlie Hochschild's findings through a critical lens. While some of her arguments suggest that workers prefer to spend more time at work than at home, Jacobs and Gerson's data suggest that many workers would prefer to spend less time at work.

Amy Cox and Harriet Presser are also concerned with the juggling act and provide an important piece of the puzzle concerning how families manage both responsibilities at work and at home. In a series of papers, Presser (1988, 1989, 1995) has argued that an important strategy for a nontrivial proportion of households with two employed parents is having each parent work a different shift; that is, at least one parent will work a nonstandard work schedule. In the current work, these authors are concerned with why nonstandard work schedules are a frequently chosen option among mothers who are not married. They hypothesize that job constraints encourage nonstandard schedules among never married mothers, followed by formerly and currently married mothers, and that child care preferences influence choice of nonstandard schedules for currently married mothers, followed by never and formerly married mothers. Their data come from the May 1991 Current Population Survey, specifically a subsample of 7,199 currently married, 1,499 formerly married, and 609 never married mothers who completed employment schedules as part of the interview. They find that nearly a third of never married mothers work nonstandard hours, while only 20% of currently and formerly married mothers work these hours. Occupational differences influence choice of nonstandard work schedules, with those in service occupations being especially likely to work nonstandard schedules. Currently married mothers are more likely to cite child or family care as the primary reason for adopting nonstandard work hours than are formerly or never married mothers. Job-related factors are more frequently cited among never and formerly married mothers than among currently married mothers as primary reasons for working nonstandard hours. Their findings sensitize us to how family structure may be influencing the strategies that mothers adopt to manage the responsibilities to care for children as well as pursue paid employment.

The transition to motherhood is one that has major implications for women who are already working, and issues surrounding this transition are central to the next three chapters. Sandra Hofferth uses data from two sources: the 1990 National Child Care Survey, a survey of 4,400 families with children under age 13, and A Profile of Child Care Settings, a nationally representative study of child care facilities that was produced at the same time in the same communities as the family survey. Studying 613 mothers who had a child in the year before the survey, Hofferth finds that employer policies have an impact on how quickly mothers return to work after childbirth. Mothers adopt part-time work more quickly when employers provide access to part-time work and child care is available at the work site. Mothers with access to liberal unpaid leave and a flexible spending account return to full-time work at a faster rate than mothers who lack these benefits. Hofferth also documents the importance that family income plays in these decisions. She finds that mothers in low-income families return to full-time work quickly after childbirth, whereas, net of other family income, mothers with higher earning power return to part-time work promptly, presumably as a way to balance work and family responsibilities. The policy theme in her work focuses primarily on employer policies, particularly the effects of part-time work, liberal leave policies, and flexible spending accounts as incentives for mothers to return to work rapidly after childbirth. Hofferth raises the issue of inequality among mothers in access to family-friendly benefits. Clearly, higher-income women have more options regarding time allocation to work and family roles than do low-income women.

Joanne Sandberg and Daniel Cornfield are interested in the circumstances under which men and women will terminate a family or medical leave. Since the implementation of the Family and Medical Leave Act in 1993, eligible employees may take up to 12 weeks of leave per year, with continued health coverage and a guaranteed return to the same or comparable job upon return. They use a national survey of United States adults who worked for pay between January 1994 and the survey date 18 months later and studied 937 leave-takers. They found that women were more likely than men to terminate their leaves in response to work pressures, while men were more likely to return to work voluntarily. They argue that women, normatively expected to bear greater responsibility for care of family members, return to work because of financial need or pressure from supervisors or co-workers, while men, consonant with their own expectations and others', return to work because they "want to." That both work and family factors influence women's decisions to return to work while men's reasons are less patterned also reinforces the idea that it is not possible to separate gender from discussion of work and family conflict and accommodation.

REFERENCES

Presser, H. B. (1988). Shift work and child care among young dual-earner American parents. *Journal of Marriage and the Family, 50,* 133-148.
Presser, H. B. (1989). Can we make time for children? The economy, work schedules, and child care. *Demography, 26,* 523-543.
Presser, H. B. (1995). Job, family, and gender: Determinants of nonstandard work schedules among employed Americans in 1991. *Demography, 32,* 577-598.
Schor, J. B. (1991). *The overworked American: The unexpected decline of leisure.* New York: Basic Books.

CHAPTER 3

Do Americans Feel Overworked?

Comparing Ideal and Actual Working Time

JERRY A. JACOBS

KATHLEEN GERSON

The late 20th century has witnessed dramatic changes in the ways Americans organize their work and family lives. As men's earnings have stagnated and women have become increasingly committed to long-term, full-time employment, the breadwinner-homemaker household that predominated at mid-century has given way to a diverse range of work-family arrangements. Today, dual-earner and single-parent families outnumber so-called traditional households, leaving most workers striving to juggle the competing demands of work and family.

These far-reaching social changes have created new options and dilemmas for American workers. They have also posed new questions and spawned vig-

AUTHORS' NOTE: The authors wish to thank Kathleen Christensen for her encouragement and support for this research, and the editors of this volume for their detailed comments on an earlier draft. This research was funded by a grant from the Alfred P. Sloan Foundation.

orous debates about the current state and future prospects of work and family life in America. Amid the growing controversy, two debates stand out. The first, triggered by the publication of Juliet Schor's *The Overworked American,* centers on the question of whether or not contemporary Americans are overworked. Schor (1991) contends that an increase in working hours has produced an "unexpected decline of leisure" in American society, with American workers logging more time at the workplace than did their parents or grandparents. Although much evidence indicates that the average number of hours worked per week for the labor force as a whole has changed little in recent decades, there is no question that changes in family structure, and especially the rise of working mothers, have raised new questions about how Americans balance their ties to paid work and family work (Jacobs & Gerson, 1997).

Questions about the links between work and family point to a second emerging controversy, which has gained renewed attention with the publication of Arlie Hochschild's *The Time Bind.* Hochschild (1997) argues that a cultural and social transformation has produced a society in which "home has become work and work has become home" and in which workers have shifted their allegiance from the home to the workplace. Like Schor's analysis, Hochschild's study draws attention to the new dilemmas faced by workers trying to balance multiple and conflicting obligations. From the perspective of the American labor force as a whole, however, it raises more questions than it answers about the changing nature of the link between family and work. Do most workers actually prefer time spent at the workplace over time spent at home, or do they face new economic and social constraints? And, more generally, does the balance people strike between work, family, and leisure actually reflect their preferences, or does it emerge from the social, cultural, and economic options they face?

Given the fundamental restructuring of family life in America and the increasing social and political concern over the fate of our children, these questions are not merely academic. Their answers hold important implications not only for how we address policy issues regarding employment, child rearing, and the workplace, but also for how we approach issues of gender equity at work and in the home. Our analysis focuses on the questions of how contemporary workers feel about the time they spend at work and how they would prefer to allocate their work time with other life pursuits. Since the concept of overwork depends as much on perception as on actual working time, we examine the differences between workers' real and ideal working hours. In light of their working hours, do workers feel overworked, and, if given more choice, what kind of balance would they prefer to strike between work, family, and leisure time?

We argue that the debate about whether or not Americans are overworked should focus not only on historical trends but also on what workers want. We draw on a data set collected in 1993 by the Families and Work Institute that solicits information regarding both workers' actual hours worked and information on their preferred allocation of work time. We conclude that, contrary to the argument that workers are using work to avoid family time, those who are putting in long hours at work would prefer a more private and family-centered balance in their lives. Only those working relatively short hours would actually prefer to work more.

This chapter begins with a brief discussion of historical trends in working hours. We then turn to an examination of the factors that may be producing a mismatch between employers' demands and workers' preferences regarding working time. To understand this process, we investigate the economics of the work week as well as broad historical changes in the factors influencing workers' preferences. Next, we consider the issue of how much time Americans want to spend at work. We then develop a set of expectations regarding how desired working time should vary by education, age, gender, and marital status. After presenting our data, methods, and results, we discuss some theoretical and policy implications of these findings.

HISTORICAL TRENDS IN WORKING HOURS

In *The Overworked American,* Juliet Schor (1991) contends that Americans are working more in recent years than at any time since the Second World War. Much subsequent research has challenged the argument that there has been a general increase in working hours among employed Americans. However, a careful review reveals that Schor never actually claimed that the average *work week* had lengthened substantially since the 1970s. Indeed, her own figures make it clear that there has been little change for either employed men or women. Schor thus reports that the average number of hours worked for men declined slightly between 1969 and 1989 (42.8 to 42.3) while the average for women increased by less than 1 hour per week (35.2 to 36.1; Leete & Schor, 1994). Instead, Schor argues that the increase in time spent working stems from a change in *annual,* not weekly, hours worked. Many difficulties complicate a calculation of annual working hours, including the fact that the

Census and Current Population Survey data do not distinguish between work and paid vacations.[1] Thus, Schor's empirical claims center more on vacation deprivation than on the growth of the typical work week.

When we focus on weekly working hours, our analysis of the time-series evidence shows, as have many others, that the past 25 years have seen few changes in the average number of hours worked for the labor force as a whole. Contemporary men work about 42 hours on average per week, and contemporary women average about 36 hours.[2] Yet we also find that focusing on the average worker tells only one part of the story. When we examine variation around the average, we find evidence of an emerging bifurcation in working hours among workers: There has been an increase in the proportion of workers who work long hours (50 hours or more per week) as well as an increase in the proportion who work fewer than 40 hours a week. Moreover, the length of the work week is linked to education and occupational position. The longest working hours are more likely to occur at the high end of the labor market, in professional and managerial jobs requiring college degrees. Part-time work is concentrated in lower echelon positions, particularly in retail sales and personal service occupations (these and related findings are presented in more detail in Jacobs & Gerson, 1997).

A second important phenomenon has been the growth of women's labor force participation. Life in two-earner households with children at home has always felt rushed, and now there are many more such families. Less than 15% of American households now consist of a married couple with a male earner only. With the exception of retired people, the remaining households are divided among dual-earner couples, single (predominately female) parents, and self-supporting individuals (Gerson, 1993).

These considerations suggest that, while the general argument contained in the "overworked American" thesis is not sustained by the evidence, there are several kernels of truth to draw from it. First, there is an emerging group of Americans who work long hours, but they represent one segment of the labor force rather than American workers en masse. Second, the changing demographic makeup of the labor force, which now contains many dual-earning couples and single parents, has produced a growing sense of overwork even while average working hours have not substantially changed.

THE EMERGENCE OF LONG AND SHORT WORK WEEKS

Why has the work week expanded for one group of workers while shrinking for another? Hidden beneath the static average, we argue, are special forces at work that encourage employers to offer *both* long and short work weeks. While some workers are facing pressures to put in longer hours at the workplace, others may find it harder to secure jobs that offer them as much work as they would like.

What factors are promoting long work weeks? First, employers have a stake in encouraging long work weeks from salaried employees. These workers do not receive extra wages for every extra hour worked, and from the employer's point of view, there is little or no marginal cost to persuading (and expecting) them to work extra hours (Landers, Rebitzer, & Taylor, 1996). The increasing cost of benefits provides a second reason that employers may push for longer work weeks. The costs of many of the most expensive fringe benefits, such as health care, are fixed for a full-time worker no matter how many hours he or she works. Consequently, the hourly cost of such benefits declines as the worker devotes more hours to the job. As the cost of benefits rises as a fraction of total compensation, employers may be inclined to seek longer hours from their employees. And, finally, the pressures of corporate downsizing may increase the incentive for employers to get more work per employee, increasing the hours and intensity of work. There is good reason to expect, therefore, that salaried employees such as managers and professional workers are likely to face increasing pressure to put in more than the once obligatory 40-hour work week.

For hourly employees and other workers who must be paid for each hour worked, however, the situation is likely to be quite different. When employees can expect a sharp increase in pay per hour (such as time-and-a-half payments) for working more than a 40-hour week, employers may be more restrained in their requests. Indeed, they may take active steps to limit the amount of work available and to convert full-time into part-time work. The rising costs of benefits contribute to this trend. Since employers need not and typically do not offer benefits to part-time workers, they can substantially reduce their compensation costs by encouraging part-time employment.

A set of economic and social factors is thus encouraging employers to offer or even demand both long *and* short work weeks. Moreover, these opportunities are not likely to be distributed equally across the labor force. While well-educated and highly trained employees who are paid on a salaried basis, such as managers and professionals, may face increased pressure to put in long hours at the office, those with less secure jobs, such as hourly workers, part-time employees, and contingent workers, may have a difficult time getting the work they need and desire. In this context, the supply of jobs available may not reflect or mesh well with workers' preferences. Rather, we are likely to see a widening gap between those who would prefer to work less and those who wish to work more.

THE CLASH BETWEEN WORKER PREFERENCES AND EMPLOYER EXPECTATIONS

While employers have good reasons to offer a supply of jobs with both long and short work weeks, workers face a different set of contingencies. Changes in family life over the past several decades, which have been nothing less than revolutionary, have altered Americans' perceptions of how much they would like to work as well as how they would like to schedule their working hours. As men have faced stagnant wages and women have become increasingly committed to work outside the home, the breadwinner-homemaker family that predominated in the 1950s has given way to a diverse range of family types. Among married couples, the dual-earner couple has replaced the male breadwinner model as the predominant arrangement. In 1970, in more than half (55.8%) of married couples only the husband worked, while husband and wife were both employed in less than one third of couples (31.2%). By 1990, this pattern had reversed, with working couples representing a new majority of couples (51.0%), and breadwinner husbands representing a minority (32.8%; Jacobs & Gerson, 1998). These changes are generating changes in worker preferences that may not fit with the supply of jobs.

Changes in family structure and the family economy have transformed worker needs and preferences in several ways. Most households now rely on women's earnings, and these economic responsibilities have fueled women's desire for secure, well-paying jobs. At the same time, members of dual-earner and single-parent households, who cannot count on an unpaid worker at home, face new needs for flexibility in their working hours and schedules. While women are especially likely to prefer good jobs with reasonable hours, fathers who share breadwinning with an employed wife also need flexible hours and some measure of control at work.

There is good reason to conclude that worker needs and preferences are increasingly at odds with employer expectations and demands. Just as the economic pressures facing employers are fueling longer work schedules for the best jobs and less security for jobs with shorter hours, working parents face new pressures to secure good jobs that also give them more time and flexibility to be with their families.

A DIVIDED LABOR FORCE

In light of this analysis, the debates about overwork and work-family conflict need to be reframed in several ways. First, rather than focusing on whether or not Americans are overworked, we need to assess the ways in which Americans increasingly face a divided labor market in which some experience overwork while others are not able to work as much as they would like. As Barry Bluestone and Stephen Rose (1997) point out, we need to "unravel the economic enigma" of both overwork and underemployment.[3] Each of these situations is problematic, since overworked Americans must sacrifice family and leisure time, and underworked Americans experience economic hardship and thwarted opportunities. To generalize from only one of these situations is to ignore the experience of an important segment of the labor force and to misunderstand the dynamics of social change. (According to Robert Lerman, 1997, for example, the increase in earnings inequality results not from changes in the wage rate but rather from changes in the dispersion of hours worked.)

Second, we need to clarify how this economic and social transformation has created a gap between employer demands and worker needs and preferences. Employers may benefit from dividing jobs into categories that distinguish strongly and weakly committed workers, but workers, including both employed women and men, increasingly need employment that offers a balance somewhere in the middle. They need jobs with long enough hours to support their families but short enough hours to meet their families' needs for time and attention.[4]

On the surface, the rise of long work hours for some and contingent, part-time jobs for others may appear to provide an innovative solution to the dilemmas faced by working parents and nontraditional families. However, in the context of rising economic insecurities, such workplace innovations are likely to intensify these dilemmas rather than resolve them. Neither families nor the economy are likely to fare well over the long run if workers are forced to choose between well-rewarded jobs with expanding opportunities and jobs that allow them to take their family commitments seriously. Moreover, the problem can only be exacerbated if this division of jobs serves further to divide men and women workers. Our analysis is thus guided by the conviction that American workers of both sexes need employment that offers both opportunity and family time. The social and economic fabric of American society can only benefit when working parents are able to balance paid employment and family life without endangering their economic security or long-term work prospects.

DO WORKERS FEEL OVERWORKED? RECONSIDERING WORKERS' COMMITMENTS TO FAMILY AND WORK

As families diversify and workers face new challenges in meeting their multiple commitments, there is a rising sense of being torn between public and private worlds. Whether individual workers are working more or less, new conflicts between work and family are creating pressures and dilemmas that most of them must address. Given the changes in American households, it is understandable that the notion of a "time bind" would capture the popular imagination in much the same way as the image of overworked Americans. Yet we need to know if this bind reflects new constraints on workers and a growing gap between what they prefer and what they feel they must do, or if, alternatively, this bind reflects a growing desire to spend more time at work at the expense of private pursuits. To answer this question, we turn to an examination of the link between workers' actual and ideal working hours.

Hochschild's (1997) study captures the emergence of "time binds" in illuminating detail. Yet her analysis of how and why workers cope with these binds is problematic in several ways. While a study based on one company at one point in time can provide some rich and suggestive ideas, when the company is clearly atypical, it cannot support broad conclusions about general cultural, structural, or individual change.[5] To capture the complex links between workplace arrangements and the variety of strategies workers create to cope with their situations, we need to make comparisons among workers in a range of companies, with varied workplace structures and cultures.

Even more fundamentally, a focus on broad cultural and social change as the primary cause of workers' choices ignores the ways in which workers experience a conflict between what they prefer and what they feel compelled to do. Individual values, whatever their content, rarely provide a complete explanation of behavior because few have the opportunity to enact their fondest desires—especially at the workplace, where so much is influenced by organizational rules and those wielding power from above. Only by overlooking the real constraints that workers face can one argue that workers get just what they want.

Hochschild, for example, argues that economic forces are not at the root of decisions about working time because those with the highest levels of education and the highest wages are working as much as other employees. Yet affluent workers, no less than other workers, face economic and other workplace constraints.[6] Indeed, we find that highly educated workers in the professional and managerial sectors of the labor force are the very workers who face the greatest demands to put in long hours at work. Rather than insulating one from overwork, well-paid jobs that offer advancement may actually increase the pressures to work more as well as the penalties for working less.[7]

A focus, then, on a shift among workers in the relative valuing of work and home overlooks other possible explanations for the balance people strike between family and work, including social-structural, economic, and demographic forces.[8] Without denying the importance of cultural influences outside the workplace, we argue that they are not the only or even the primary factors shaping workers' choices.[9] To understand how workers balance their work and family commitments, we need to pay attention to such factors as the demands that jobs impose, the structure and culture of the workplace in which those jobs are embedded, and a range of demographic factors that influence where workers are placed in the economy, the labor market, and the family life course. For example, do those workers who put in very long hours at work do so because they prefer work over family or leisure? Or do their actions reflect perceived and real pressures and constraints? To answer these questions, we examine the link between actual working hours and the expressed ideals and preferences of workers. We are especially interested in ascertaining if those who work 50 or more hours per week prefer such a lifestyle or, alternatively, if they would prefer to have a different balance in their lives.

WORKER PREFERENCES, WORK-FAMILY CONFLICTS, AND IDEAL VERSUS ACTUAL WORKING HOURS

While average work hours have not increased substantially, there is still reason to believe that more workers are *feeling* overworked. Even though most families can no longer rely on the support of a woman at home, the structure of work has not changed sufficiently to accommodate the changes in workers' private lives. Working parents may thus feel squeezed in ways that are altogether new. Yet the debate has focused on historical trends in actual time spent at paid work rather than on whether workers feel overworked, squeezed, or overburdened. Since most national surveys do not include information on workers' desired work schedules, it has been difficult to address the subjective aspect of change.

In this vacuum, some have argued that since most workers are currently working a few minutes less than were their counterparts in 1950, they do not feel overworked (e.g., Kneisner, 1993). Such a conclusion not only ignores the widespread and fundamental changes that have taken place in family structure over this period, but also overlooks the question of what kinds of work schedules contemporary workers desire. Regardless of the historical trajectory in working hours, we need to understand how Americans feel about their current work commitments in light of their commitments and responsibilities outside the workplace.

We argued above that changes in the demographic makeup of the labor force may be clashing with economic forces shaping the structure of jobs. As a result, we expect that a significant proportion of workers will experience a discrepancy between their actual and preferred, or ideal, working time. We expect that some individuals will report a preference for fewer hours than they are actually working, while others will indicate they wish to work longer hours. We also anticipate that the group desiring shorter hours will be the larger of the two because of the large number of working couples and working parents in the labor force.

In addition, we expect the relative size of the groups wishing to work more or fewer hours will vary with the number of hours worked. Specifically, among those working very long hours, a sizable proportion are likely to report a desire to work fewer hours. Conversely, among those working short work weeks, a sizable fraction are likely to report a preference for working longer hours. Since those working the longest hours are highly educated workers and workers employed in managerial, professional, and technical positions, the greatest gap between ideal and actual hours is likely to be found among the best educated members of the labor force as well as among professional and managerial workers.

The age patterns of preferred hours should reflect, to some extent, the demographic forces shaping workers' preferences. We thus expect that the greatest gap between actual and ideal hours for working women will occur when they have children at home. The gap between ideal and actual hours worked should grow as women reach their thirties and forties, the prime childbearing and -rearing years, and only wane as they grow older and their children leave the household. Because men do not contribute equally to domestic work, we expect this pattern will be less marked, if evident at all, for men.

Similarly, since family commitments increase the demands of domestic work as well as the expectations to spend time at home, marital status should also influence the gap between ideal and actual hours. We expect this gap to be larger among married couples than it is among singles. And, again, since wives continue to bear a greater share of the burden of domestic work, the gap should be more pronounced for wives than for husbands.

Like age and marital status, parental status should influence the perceived gap between ideal and actual working hours. Employed mothers with children under 6 should prefer to work less than those who have not borne children or whose children are older. Indeed, if they cannot realize this preference in their choice of jobs, then the gap between ideal and actual working hours is likely to be largest among this group. For men, however, the influence of parental status is likely to be quite different. Fathers may want to be with their families, but they also face an increased pressure to earn enough to support their families. These conflicting forces may dampen the influence of parental status for men, leaving the fathers of young children with preferences for working hours that are similar to other men.

DATA AND METHODS

To examine the contours and causes of workers' actual and ideal working time, we analyze information from the National Study of the Changing Workforce, a national probability sample of 3,381 employed men and women aged 18 through 64 based on hour-long telephone interviews. The response rate was 50.5%, and the data were weighted in order to reflect the characteristics of the U.S. labor force as estimated by the March 1992 Current Population Survey (Galinsky, Bond, & Friedman, 1993). Conducted by the Families and Work Institute in 1993, this survey is distinctive in terms of the range of questions asked regarding workers' values and preferences and in its focus on the links, tensions, and conflicts between work and family. Since respondents were asked about their ideal as well as their actual working hours, we can examine whether the overall level of work activity reflects the desires of workers. We can also ascertain whether variation in preferences across groups of workers corresponds to variations in actual work levels.

The Changing Workforce survey collected a wide array of information about actual working time, ideal working hours, and how people would prefer to balance their commitments to work, family, and personal pursuits. Several questions regarding working time asked people how many hours per week they usually worked on their principal job and also on any additional jobs they held. Here we examine hours worked on all jobs together (we examine the issue of dual job holders elsewhere; see Jacobs & Gerson, 1997). In order to ascertain ideal work hours, respondents were also asked: "Ideally, how many hours, in total, would you like to work each week?" Using this information on total and ideal hours, we were able to construct a measure indicating the difference between a person's usual hours worked on all jobs and his or her ideal hours.

RESULTS

In Table 3.1, which compares ideal hours to total hours worked for employed women and men, it becomes clear that most American workers experience a significant gap between how much they work and how much they would like to work. While one third of respondents reported that their actual and ideal hours corresponded precisely, nearly half indicated that their usual work week was longer than their ideal hours, and an additional one in six reported that they would prefer to work more than they currently do. (The unemployed should also be added to this group of "underworked" Americans, but the Changing Workforce survey includes information only on currently employed individuals.)

The vast majority of those who expressed a preference for shorter working hours indicated that they wished to work at least 5 hours less per week than they currently do. Nine in 20 of the total sample (90% of those wanting to work less) preferred to work at least 5 hours per week less. Nearly one third of the total sample (32% of both men and women) expressed the desire to work 10 hours less per week, and about one in seven of the total sample wanted to work at least 20 hours less per week.[10]

While women on average work about 6 fewer hours per week than men, the difference between the actual and ideal hours is quite similar for men and women. By approximately the same amount, both sexes indicated a desire to work less. Men reported a preference for working 5.51 fewer hours, compared to 5.14 fewer hours for women, a difference that is not statistically significant. If both groups were able to realize their preferences, the gender gap in hours worked (which is about 6 hours per week) would probably not change significantly.

These findings suggest that, whether or not they are actually working more than earlier generations, the majority of contemporary Americans feel overworked—at least compared to their ideals. Most workers do not appear to prefer long work hours over family and personal pursuits. Nevertheless, a notable group of workers would like to work more. As we shall see, however, these workers are not currently putting in long work weeks but rather are likely to wish to extend relatively short work hours.[11]

In Table 3.2 we gain a clearer picture of how the gap between ideal and total working hours is linked to the number of hours a person works. The results

TABLE 3.1 Comparison of Total Hours Worked Per Week and Ideal Hours, by Sex

	Men (n = 1,300)	Women (n = 1,539)
Total Hours Usually Worked (all jobs)	45.77*	39.71
Ideal hours	40.26*	34.82
Difference (Ideal–Actual)	–5.51	–4.89
Percentage wanting to work less	50.06	45.58
Percentage ideal equals actual	33.78	37.61
Percentage wanting to work more	17.16	16.84
Percentage wanting to work at least 5 hours less	45.36	41.25
Percentage wanting to work at least 10 hours less	32.39	32.40
Percentage wanting to work at least 20 hours less	15.30	13.19

SOURCE: National Study of the Changing Workforce, 1992
NOTE: * The difference between men and women is statistically significant, $p < .01$. None of the other sex differences in Table 3.1 are statistically significant at the conventional $p < .05$ level.

indicate that those who work few hours prefer on average to work more, while those who work very long weeks prefer on average to work less. The great majority of both men and women who work more than 50 hours per week would prefer shorter schedules. Indeed, more than 80% of those who worked over 50 hours per week indicated a preference for fewer hours. The excess work was substantial: Those working between 50 and 60 hours per week preferred working 12 hours less, while those working more than 60 hours indicated a preference to work a full 20 hours less. While the preferences of individuals vary, we found that only 6.4% of women and 15.8% of men expressed a desire to work more than 50 hours per week. Yet roughly one in four men and 1 in 10 women actually put in that much time at work.

This evidence provides further support that an increasingly bifurcated labor market is a major aspect of social change. It has implications not only for how much time workers spend at work but also for how workers feel about their work arrangements. Those at the top appear to feel overworked, while many of those in less attractive positions express a desire to work more. These data also raise questions about whether employers are heeding the needs and preferences of their employees when it comes to structuring employment options. A "taste" for "overwork" does not appear to explain why those putting in long work hours are doing so.

We now turn to education and occupational differences in working patterns (see Table 3.3). Since actual hours worked increase with educational

TABLE 3.2 Comparison of Total Hours Per Week Worked and Ideal Hours, by Hours Worked and Sex

A. Women	Number of Cases	Total Hours	Ideal Hours	Difference	Percentage Wanting to Work Less
Total	1,539	40.13	34.99	-5.14	45.58
Total Hours Usually Worked					
Less than 30	188	19.83	25.34	5.51	10.91
30-39	328	34.41	33.70	-0.72	27.73
40-49	742	41.38	35.91	-5.46	48.48
50-59	183	51.80	38.71	-13.09	86.24 ns
60+	98	66.52	43.75	-22.77	88.43

B. Men	Number of Cases	Total Hours	Ideal Hours	Difference	Percentage Wanting to Work Less
Total	1,300	45.77	40.26	-5.51	50.06
Total Hours Usually Worked					
Less than 30	59	20.45	29.67	9.21	8.77 ns
30-39	110	34.19	37.39	3.20	9.59
40-49	694	42.19	40.41	-1.78	38.40
50-59	257	51.91	39.65	-12.26	84.01 ns
60+	180	66.55	45.93	-20.62	84.98

SOURCE: National Study of the Changing Workforce.

NOTE: We conducted tests of statistical significance for every pair of adjacent groups, by sex. For example, women who worked less than 30 hours were compared to those working 30-39 hours. Women working 30-39 hours were compared again with those working 40-49 hours. All paired differences are statistically significant, $p < .05$, except the three entries marked "ns."

TABLE 3.3 Total Hours Per Week Worked and Ideal Hours, by Education, Occupation, and Sex

A. Women	Number of Cases	Total Hours	Ideal Hours	Difference	Percentage Wanting to Work Less
Education					
Less than high school	102	38.59 ns	39.57*	−0.98*	31.57*
High school graduate	457	38.56 ns	35.33*	−3.23 ns	35.62 ns
Some college	544	38.75 ns	33.75*	−5.00*	44.90*
College graduate	236	42.22 ns	33.62 ns	−8.60 ns	63.04 ns
Some graduate education+	200	43.14	35.30	−7.83	60.71
Managerial, professional, and technical occupations	671	42.12*	34.20 ns	−7.92*	58.28*
Other occupations	868	37.96	35.27	−2.70	36.39

B. Men	Number of Cases	Total Hours	Ideal Hours	Difference	Percentage Wanting to Work Less
Education					
Less than high school	130	44.11 ns	43.74*	−0.36*	32.11*
High school graduate	388	44.95 ns	40.87*	−4.08 ns	43.66 ns
Some college	379	44.24*	39.35 ns	−4.89 ns	49.09 ns
College graduate	226	48.37 ns	38.48 ns	−9.89 ns	64.61 ns
Some graduate education+	177	49.22	40.50	−8.72	63.00
Managerial, Professional, and technical occupations	562	48.59*	39.66 ns	−8.93*	66.80*
Other occupations	738	43.66	40.71	−2.95	37.50

SOURCE: National Study of the Changing Workforce.
NOTE: * p < .05. We conducted tests of statistical significance for every pair of adjacent groups, by sex. For example, women with less than high school education were compared to those with a high school degree. Women with a high school degree were compared again with those who had attended some college. Paired differences that are statistically significant, p < .05, are indicated with a star, and those that are not are marked "ns."

85

level while desired hours decline, the gap between ideal and actual hours is highest among the most educated workers of both sexes. Interestingly, desired hours are highest among male high school dropouts, who must work relatively long hours at low rates of pay to earn an adequate income. In contrast, actual hours worked are highest for college graduates and those with graduate training. The gap between actual and ideal hours is highest for these two groups. More than 60% of both men and women with at least a college education reported wanting to work fewer hours.

Occupational differences show a similar pattern. Professional, managerial, and technical workers are most likely to report feeling overworked. Women in these high-status positions would prefer to work 8 hours less than they do, while men in these professions indicate wanting to work just under 9 hours less. For workers in other occupational categories, the average respondent indicated wanting to work between 2 and 3 hours less. We find it especially interesting that, while professionals and managers work much longer hours than other workers, their *ideal* working hours do not differ from those of other workers. For both men and women, the differences in ideal working hours between professional and managerial versus other workers is not statistically significant. These differences thus appear to reflect the structure of work demands, driven by powerful economic forces, rather than the desires of workers.

These findings add support to our view that occupational position is critical in shaping the needs and desires of both men and women. Despite the persistent view that female professionals are less committed to work than their male counterparts, we find that workers of both sexes are looking for a reasonable balance between home and work. Those who put in long hours, regardless of gender, would like to cut back, while those who face shortened work weeks would like to work more. Ironically, it is the most highly educated and well-remunerated professional and managerial workers who, in the face of heightened pressure to work long hours, would prefer less time at the workplace.

Does age, and the related aspects of life stage, make a difference in shaping the gap between actual and ideal hours? If work-family conflict is the principal force driving the desire for fewer hours, then the biggest gap between actual and ideal hours should be concentrated among those in their late twenties, thirties, and early forties, the years during which workers are most likely to marry, become parents, and face the heavy demands of caring for young children.

Table 3.4, which displays actual and ideal hours by age for men and women, largely confirms our expectations, although differences across age

TABLE 3.4 Age Profile of Total Hours Per Week Worked and Ideal Hours, by Sex

A. Women	Number of Cases	Total Hours	Ideal Hours	Difference	Percentage Wanting to Work Less
Age Group					
16-25	144	36.65*	36.32 ns	−0.33*	35.50*
26-35	505	39.56 ns	34.44 ns	−5.12 ns	47.19 ns
36-45	476	40.48 ns	34.34 ns	−6.14 ns	48.82 ns
46-55	265	41.21*	35.23 ns	−5.98*	49.68*
56-65	149	38.32	35.18	−3.14	33.33

B. Men	Number of Cases	Total Hours	Ideal Hours	Difference	Percentage Wanting to Work Less
Age Group					
16-25	126	38.64*	38.52*	−0.13*	26.69*
26-35	490	46.50 ns	41.50 ns	−5.00*	48.74*
36-45	353	47.24 ns	40.77 ns	−6.47 ns	54.85 ns
46-55	222	46.97*	38.89 ns	−8.08*	61.34*
56-65	109	44.02	38.68	−5.33	43.46

SOURCE: National Study of the Changing Workforce.
NOTE: * $p < .05$. We conducted tests of statistical significance for every pair of adjacent groups, by sex. As in previous Table 3.3, paired differences that are statistically significant, $p < .05$, are indicated with a star, and those that are not are marked "ns."

groups in ideal working hours are remarkably small and often statistically insignificant. We can see that for men, actual working hours increase until ages 46 through 55 and then begin to fall somewhat. Ideal hours increase slightly until age 35 and then remain roughly constant. Thus, the gap between actual and ideal hours grows for men until age 55. Among the 46 to 55 age group, the gap is 8 hours. More than three fifths of this group of men indicated a preference for shorter hours. Notably, it does not appear to be fathers of young children but rather men in their fifties (whose children are likely to be older) who are most likely to express a strong interest in working fewer hours.

For women, ideal hours are remarkably consistent across the age groups. None of the paired comparisons are statistically significant. The gap between ideal and actual work hours peaks at 6 hours among the 36- to 45-year-old age group. However, the gap remains virtually unchanged at 6 hours for women between the ages of 46 and 55, and it drops to 3 hours only for women over 55.

From age 26 through 55, between 45% and 50% of women expressed a preference for working fewer hours.

For both men and women, the desire to work fewer hours is not restricted to the years in which young children are living at home. Nor is there evidence of a clear generational shift: There is as much or more interest in working less among the middle-aged as there is among the youngest group of workers.[12] When gender differences emerge, it appears that men in their fifties may be seeking more leisure, while women in their thirties may be seeking more time for family responsibilities. However, gender differences in the effects of life stage are small, indicating a growing convergence between men and women in their strategies for building work careers over the life course.

The gap between ideal and actual working hours appears to be driven more by the shifting demands of work over the life course than it does by age gradations in workers' preferences. During the thirties and forties, both men and women are trying to build their careers, and their time in paid jobs increases. Their desire for increased working time does not show a corresponding increase, and consequently a gap between ideal and actual work time emerges.

Despite the similarities we have found among women and men, it is reasonable to expect that the unmet desire for fewer hours might be concentrated among those employed women who have small children. If so, then allowing everyone to work their ideal hours might result in women disproportionately taking advantage of shorter schedules, thus reinforcing the gender gap both in hours worked and earnings. We have seen, however, that the unmet demand for fewer hours is roughly equal for men and women. In Table 3.5 we examine the relationship among gender, family situation, and ideal working hours in more detail.

These results confirm a difference between married and single workers of both sexes. Married women work almost 1.5 hours less per week than women who are not currently married, but they would like to work 4.5 hours less. The gap between actual and ideal working time is thus 3 hours greater for married than for single women. In other words, married women would ideally prefer to work 6 hours less per week, while single women would prefer to work 3 hours less per week.

In contrast, married men work more than do single men, by about 5 hours per week. However, married and single men wish to work about the same amount of time. The difference between single and married men in terms of ideal working hours is not statistically significant. As a result, married men report a larger gap between actual and ideal hours (6.5 hours per week) than do single men (2.7 hours per week). Thus, for both men and women, married life is characterized by a significant time deficit. The reasons for this deficit,

TABLE 3.5 Comparison of Total Hours Per Week Worked and Ideal Hours, by Marital and Family Status, by Sex

A. Women	Number of Cases	Total Hours	Ideal Hours	Difference	Percentage Wanting to Work Less
1. Married (or living with partner)	872	39.14*	33.21*	-5.94*	48.29*
2. Not currently married	667	40.71	37.69	-3.03	40.78
3. Married, working spouse	703	38.97	32.79*	6.18	49.22
4. Married, non-working spouse	169	39.94	35.10	-4.83	43.98
5. With children under 6	283	37.48*	31.40*	-6.08	51.17
6. Without children under 6	1,256	40.18	35.54	-4.64	44.40

B. Men	Number of Cases	Total Hours	Ideal Hours	Difference	Percentage Wanting to Work Less
1. Married (or living with partner)	879	47.00*	40.53	-6.47*	52.93
2. Not currently married	421	42.18	39.48	-2.71	41.65
3. Married with working spouse	341	46.55	40.73	-5.81	52.31
4. Married, non-working spouse	538	47.28	40.40	-6.88	53.32
5. With children under 6	263	48.27*	41.71*	-6.56*	55.57
6. Without children under 6	1,037	45.15	39.90	-5.25	48.69

SOURCE: National Study of the Changing Workforce

NOTE: * $p < .05$. Tests of statistical significance are reported for paired comparisons within sex. Thus, married women are compared with not currently married women (row 1 vs. row 2). Similarly, tests compare rows 3 and 4, and rows 5 and 6, for women and men, respectively.

however, differ by gender. For men, it emerges from spending more time on the job; for women, it stems from a desire to cut back on working time.

Within marriage, differences are evident among women living in different family situations, but these differences are not as large as might be expected. Women with working husbands work about one hour per week less than those few whose husbands do not work, but this small difference is not statistically significant. Women in dual-earner marriages report wanting to work 33 hours per week instead of the 39 hours they report working, for a 6 hour per week gap. For those with husbands who are not employed, the gap is 5 hours (and the difference between the two is not statistically significant).

A similar pattern is evident for women with preschool children. These women work 37.5 hours per week on average, but would prefer to work 31.5 hours per week, for a gap of 6 hours per week. For women without children under 6, there is a 4.5 hour per week differential, which is statistically indistinguishable from the 6-hour gap for those with preschool children. Thus, for women, having preschool children and employed husbands affects both desired and actual working time, but does not create a dramatic change in the gap between actual and desired working time.

Marital and parental status also influence men's actual and ideal working time, but, as in the case of women, these effects are modest. Men in this sample with employed spouses do not differ from those with stay-at-home spouses on actual or ideal working time. Having preschool children in the household does increase the total hours worked per week for men, but it also increases desired working time. The fathers of young children are thus likely to perceive that their family's financial needs require them to put in more time at work. And since actual work time increases by more than does desired work time, a higher proportion of this group want to work less.

These results stem, in part, from the fact that women have already made strategic adjustments to avoid work-family conflict. After all, their average working hours are lower than men's at the outset. Nevertheless, the larger pattern suggests that family status is as important as gender and that both mothers and fathers with young children want more time away from work than do other groups. Marriage clearly provides an incentive that pulls both women and men toward personal commitments outside of work. Yet we find little support for the oft-stated argument that married women with young children are the primary group wishing to work less. Rather, about half of married men and women across a range of family situations express this desire.

We have examined how actual and ideal hours are shaped by a range of individual and social factors, including age, educational level, occupation, family situation, and gender. This analysis has found no trend suggesting, as

Hochschild does, that those putting in long hours at work are doing so out of a preference for long hours and a desire to avoid family commitments. To the contrary, we have consistently found that workers in high-demand jobs would prefer to work less. The wish for more work prevails at the opposite end of the occupational spectrum, where less-educated workers in less-prestigious jobs face underemployment and economic squeezes.

Our findings also suggest that the labor market is not producing employment options that reflect the preferences of workers. In the Changing Workforce survey, a majority of workers reported a preference for a different work schedule than they had. In particular, those working the longest were most likely to report a desire to work less. We thus conclude that the growth in long hours among some groups of workers is not being driven by a broad cultural shift in the commitment to work. Rather, it represents a change initiated by employers that employees are responding to and attempting to accommodate.

We have found that both women and men are facing this apparent bifurcation of work into overdemanding and underdemanding jobs. As women and men cope with converging situations, they are responding in similar ways. The problems caused by the changing nature of the labor force thus affect both sexes and cannot be solved by re-creating a distinct, separate, or unequal set of options for women and men. If "family-friendly" policies are designed to treat mothers (or women who may be "potential mothers") as a separate and problematic group, they risk not only re-creating gender inequality at work but also failing to address the needs of both female and male workers.

CONCLUSION: REORIENTING THE ANALYSIS OF WORK AND FAMILY

Much of the debate concerning work and family change in America remains shrouded in ideological controversy. Disagreement about whether such changes are beneficial or detrimental has often overshadowed careful analyses of the contours, causes, and consequences of change. We have addressed these controversies by offering a revised view of the nature of change and an alternate explanation for how these changes are being experienced by American workers. Our analysis also holds implications for the causes of the current difficulties and what kinds of social policies need to be crafted to address them. In this concluding section, we would like to consider the significance and policy implications of our analysis.

In considering the prospects for work and family life in America, it behooves us to keep in mind that most Americans share a common desire for strong families and good jobs. In addition, with the exception of those "cultural conservatives" who believe that a return to the 1950s model of the breadwinner-homemaker family is both possible and desirable, most women and men agree that gender equity should be an important aspect of social efforts to forge a just and viable balance between family and work. We share these values and goals with other analysts, including Schor and Hochschild.

Indeed, Schor and Hochschild deserve much credit for focusing public attention on the issue of work-family conflict. Schor's research has helped undermine the ill-founded idea that American workers are not working as hard as their international peers in the global economy. It has also drawn attention to how changes in the family economy, which now typically depends on the earnings of women, have created a sense of overwork in many American households. Hochschild, too, has helped to deflate some distorted stereotypes. Her work rightly suggests that, whatever the economic incentives, American women are also working because they find personal gratification in public pursuits. Women have become strongly committed to work outside the home and cannot be expected to return to domesticity. Her descriptions of the links between family and work also help us move beyond idealized and misleading visions of family life as a haven from the problems of the marketplace.

Alongside these contributions, however, are some noteworthy analytic and political limitations. In Schor's case, the danger lies in overestimating the extent of the problem of overwork, while ignoring a growing segment of the labor force that faces underemployment and economic insecurity. In Hochschild's analysis, the danger lies in holding workers primarily responsible for their (and their children's) problems by ignoring the constraints at work and attributing workers' choices to their own preference for work over family time. While some workers may indeed prefer work over family life, such an outlook cannot explain the behavior or desires of the majority of workers.

We argue that it is essential to recognize the wide variation in circumstances faced by American workers. Both family situations and workplace arrangements are now remarkably diverse. It is distorting to characterize trends in the economy as simply a general increase in the prevalence of the overworked American or to attribute the changes that have occurred to a broad-based decline in the value of family life and a corresponding rise in the value of work. Rather, a range of diverse trends and causes is pulling workers in different directions at once. Given the diversity of American workers and their families, it is essential to examine the variation in working experiences across a variety of employment settings and family situations.

We share the values and goals of those who stress the problems of over-work and time binds, but our analysis suggests a different approach to diagnosing the shape and causes of workers' dilemmas as well as different social strategies for resolving them. We argue that in order to resolve the work-family dilemmas that American workers increasingly face, we must pay attention not only to the economic constraints and family pressures on workers, but also to the social, cultural, and structural conditions of their jobs. Some workers, especially among the well-educated in the professional and managerial sectors, are facing enormous pressures to work more than they or their families would wish. They face severe constraints on working less and real penalties if they choose to do so. Other workers, and especially those with little education and limited white-collar skills, face the opposite problem—how to find enough work with sufficient pay to support their families and build a sense of security at home.

Although the problems workers face take different forms, most seem to desire the same outcome. Thus, when we look at what workers want, we find a notable convergence. Most workers desire gratifying workplace experiences, but they also value their families and their personal time. Put simply, in addition to job security and opportunity, they want balance between family and work and some measure of flexibility in how they choose to integrate the many obligations they shoulder. In a world where both mothers and fathers must work, they do not want to have to sacrifice job opportunities in order to make time for their families. In terms of their feelings about their current jobs and their desires for changes, women hold these goals and outlooks as strongly as men.

In the abstract, these goals seem simple and straightforward. Unfortunately, social-structural trends appear to be moving in a direction that makes them difficult to achieve. As employers encourage extremely long hours from some and part-time work from others, owners' incentives collide with the new realities of working mothers and fathers. If we are to craft a resolution to this predicament, we must first recognize the social-structural causes of change. Otherwise, we are left holding ordinary women and men responsible for conditions they did not create rather than offering them genuine opportunities to be both committed workers and involved parents.

NOTES

1. Rather than indicating a loss in vacation time, the trends detected by Schor's analysis are more likely due to changing patterns of labor force attachment, especially

among women. Most workers who report less than a full-year work schedule do so be-cause they joined or left the labor force at some point during the year. A decline in the frequency of these entries and exits probably accounts for the bulk of Schor's increase in annual working hours.

2. These results differ slightly depending on whether the question pertains to hours worked last week or hours typically worked last year.

3. While Bluestone and Rose are on the right track in exploring the increasingly polarized labor force, their analysis of working hours focuses on the mean, the aver-age worker. We take the need to explore polarization a step farther by using statistics more appropriate for a polarized labor force, namely measures of dispersion in hours worked.

4. Even Schor notes that an increasing number of workers would like to work more than they actually do. But, rather than incorporate this fact into an analysis of an increasingly bifurcated labor market, she stresses the general increase in working hours for the labor market as a whole.

5. For example, as reported by Hochschild, the average working hours at Amerco, the fictionally named research site, are longer than average working hours for the American labor force as a whole.

6. Indeed, the case histories presented in *The Time Bind* demonstrate that long hours were required at Amerco for those who were serious about career advancement.

7. The analysis in *The Time Bind* also downplays the role of workplace culture in shaping and constraining individual decisions. According to Hochschild, a lack of de-mand on the part of workers, and not constraints imposed by supervisors and the cul-ture of the workplace, led to the underutilization of flexible work arrangements. The focus on one company only, however, makes it impossible to examine whether compa-nies with a more deeply rooted family-friendly orientation, in which informal penal-ties are not attached to formally available policies, encourages and allows greater use of flexible scheduling options by employees. To that end, we examined the influence of supervisor and workplace support on the use of flexible schedules by employees. Our analysis (Jacobs & Gerson, 1997) shows that those workers who enjoy flexible scheduling options do, in fact, take advantage of these options at notably high rates.

8. For example, Hochschild concludes that the arrival of children increases the number of hours that both mothers and fathers spend at the workplace, even though much evidence suggests that women with small children reduce the time they spend at paid work, albeit to a smaller extent than in previous generations.

9. We need to specify and define what "culture" means in the context of growing work-family conflicts. Not only do cultural values in the wider society vary and con-flict, but the workplace also has a "culture" that influences the options and decisions of workers. Moreover, the culture of the workplace is likely to be shaped and con-strained by those at the top, leaving workers at the middle and lower rungs of the or-ganizational hierarchy coping to adjust as best they can.

10. Note that in Table 3.1, all percentages are of total male and female samples, re-spectively. Thus, 50.06% of men reported wanting to work less; 45.36% wanted to

work at least 5 hours less. This is not 45.36% of those who wanted to work less, but rather is 45.36% of the total. In other words, the great majority (45.36 over 50.06) of those men who reported wanting to work less reported at least a 5-hour gap between their actual and ideal working hours.

11. In a longer report, we examined the experience of dual job holders and compared them to the majority of workers who hold only one job. Dual job holders are indeed more likely to indicate a preference for fewer hours. Yet only 8% of the sample reported holding more than one job, and thus most of the sense of being overworked cannot be attributed to the experiences of people who work at two jobs. In other words, the total sample of workers feels only a bit more overworked than do single job holders.

12. Both age and cohort position undoubtedly influence these results. Younger workers in the current period may favor a more balanced work schedule than did previous generations at the same point in their life course, but we cannot establish this conclusion from this cross-sectional survey.

REFERENCES

Bluestone, B., & Rose, S. (1997). Overworked and underemployed: Unraveling an economic enigma. *The American Prospect, 31*(March-April), 58-69.

Galinsky, E., Bond, J. T., & Friedman, D. E. (1993). *The changing workforce: Highlights of the national study.* New York: Families and Work Institute.

Gerson, K. (1993). *No man's land: Men's changing commitments to family and work.* New York: Basic Books.

Hochschild, A. R. (1997). *The time bind: When work becomes home and home becomes work.* New York: Metropolitan Books.

Jacobs, J. A., & Gerson, K. (1997). *The endless day or the flexible office? Working time, work-family conflict, and gender equity in the modern workplace.* Report to the Alfred P. Sloan Foundation (June).

Jacobs, J. A., & Gerson, K. (1998). *Trends in hours of paid work.* Unpublished manuscript, Department of Sociology, University of Pennsylvania.

Kneisner, T. J. (1993). Review essay: The overworked American? *Journal of Human Resources, 28*(33), 681-688.

Landers, R. M., Rebitzer, J. B., & Taylor, L. J. (1996). Rat race redux: Adverse selection in the determination of work hours in law firms. *The American Economic Review, 86*(3), 329-348.

Leete, L., & Schor, J. B. (1994). Assessing the time-squeeze hypothesis: Hours worked in the United States, 1969-1989. *Industrial Relations, 33*(1), 25-43.

Lerman, R. I. (1997). Is earnings inequality really increasing? *Economic Restructuring and the Job Market, 1*(March): The Urban Institute.

Schor, J. (1991). *The overworked American.* New York: Basic Books.

CHAPTER 4

Nonstandard Employment Schedules Among American Mothers

The Relevance of Marital Status

AMY G. COX

HARRIET B. PRESSER

O ver the past three decades, the United States has witnessed striking rises both in the employment rates of mothers of young children and in the number of single mother families. These trends have led to the growing expectation that single mothers will be employed while retaining primary responsibility for child rearing. Yet the special problems that these mothers face with regard to balancing employment and child care have received minimal attention. For most mothers, regardless of marital status, there are both psychic and financial costs as they struggle to find adequate, affordable child care and limit their employment when they cannot do so.[1] Single mothers, and especially never married mothers, may find arranging child care particularly problematic, since they generally have less money for such care and less flexibility for limiting their employment than married mothers have. Although most married mothers are also employed and primarily responsible for children's care, their husbands generally help ease the financial burden, and to a lesser extent the child care burden, that comes with raising children.

Paid work and family considerations are further complicated by a growing diversity of work schedules, including employment during evenings, nights, weekends, and varying hours and days (Presser, 1989a; Smith, 1986). Employment during nonstandard times appears to have risen with the growth of the service sector, although research on trends does not exist (Hedges & Sekscenski, 1979; King, 1978; Presser, 1989a; Wetzel, 1995). Moreover, female-dominated service sector jobs continue to increase, and the demand for employment at nonstandard times appears to be growing, especially for women. Many of the jobs projected to have the largest growth over the next decade have disproportionately high rates of nonstandard schedules and are in female dominated occupations (Presser, 1995).

Among women, single mothers disproportionately work late hours, weekends, and/or rotating or variable schedules, a fact that parallels the difficulty they face in balancing paid work and family (Cox, 1994; Presser, 1989a). Nonstandard employment schedules conflict with the times when commercial child care is available, almost exclusively Monday through Friday during the day. For married couples, such schedules may serve to establish a cost-effective arrangement if spouses work at different times and share child care. Indeed, this is how one third of dual-earner married couples with preschool-age children manage child care (Presser, 1988). For single mothers, however, this split-shift arrangement with fathers is generally unavailable. While single mothers may coordinate child care with grandmothers by working different schedules (Presser, 1989b), research suggests that care by relatives generally is not preferable and that its availability is diminishing (Brayfield, Deich, & Hofferth, 1993; Leibowitz, Waite, & Witsberger, 1988).

A question thus arises about why single mothers are more likely to work nonstandard times than are married mothers. Employment schedules can either facilitate the balance between paid work and family, by allowing for a split shift or other informal, low-cost child care strategy, or inhibit it, by being an imposed requirement of certain jobs in the absence of desirable child care options. Because never married mothers in general have less money than formerly married mothers and both have less money and less time than currently married mothers, marital status may affect employment schedules in one of two ways. Never and formerly married mothers cannot share the time and financial expenses of child care with husbands, as currently married mothers can, and they are their families' primary breadwinners. Never and formerly married mothers thus may be more likely than married mothers to use nonstandard schedules as a low-cost child care strategy, or they may be willing to assume an imposed schedule more often than married mothers even when this means accepting undesirable child care arrangements.

In the remainder of this chapter, we explore this question as follows. First, we review the literature on women's employment schedules and child care use. Next we examine the prevalence of working nonstandard hours or days among mothers by marital status, distinguishing among never, formerly, and currently married women, and consider why mothers' rates of nonstandard schedules differ. Taking a labor market perspective, we distinguish the effect that differences in occupational distributions by marital status have on the rates of nonstandard schedules. With a multivariate analysis, we ask whether the effects of personal and family characteristics differ by marital status once we control for occupation. We then explain the pattern of determinants found by examining the reasons mothers give for working nonday or variable hours. Finally, we discuss the implications of our findings for research and policies that address child care needs and women's abilities to balance employment and family, given that both single motherhood and nonstandard work schedules are likely to remain highly prevalent in the near future.

PRIOR RESEARCH

Given the paucity of research on marital status in relation to nonstandard employment schedules, we draw on two related sets of literature for our hypotheses: research examining employment and child care by marital status, but without regard to time schedules, and employment schedule studies that do not center on marital status.

Employment and Child Care by Marital Status

As previously noted, the vast majority of single mothers, like married mothers, are employed, although single mothers tend to work more hours and have less advantaged positions in the labor market than do married mothers. Single mothers tend to work more hours the more children they have, while married mothers tend to work fewer hours the more children they have (Coverman & Kemp, 1987). Employed single mothers tend to have less education than employed married mothers; this is especially true for never married mothers, who tend to have less education and employment experience than formerly married mothers (Johnson & Waldman, 1983). Correspondingly, never married mothers, and to a much lesser extent formerly married mothers, are more likely to be in occupations characterized by low earnings and low status than are currently married mothers (Cox, 1994).

When mothers are at their paid job, their child care arrangement differs by marital status as well. Single mothers' children are most often cared for by commercial or family-based care, while married mothers' children are largely split between these arrangements and care by fathers and other relatives (Brayfield et al., 1993; Casper, 1993). Not including care by fathers, care by other relatives is a more common arrangement for single than for married mothers; 39% of employed single mothers used such care as their primary arrangement, compared to 19% of employed married mothers in 1991 (Casper, 1993).[2] While relative care is more often free or low cost and may have fewer time constraints for mothers working nondays and weekends, father care is generally unavailable to single mothers, and grandmother care often must be coordinated with grandmothers' employment, especially for single mothers. Twice as many of the grandmothers who provided child care in 1982 were employed when the mother was single as when she was married (Presser, 1986). This greater sacrifice of time by grandmothers—many of whom are themselves employed—again suggests the difficulty single mothers face in arranging child care with their paid jobs.

Employment Schedules

The literature on employment schedules reveals a growing diversity in the numbers of hours and days worked (Presser, 1989a, 1995; Smith, 1986). This growing diversity is an especially important development for women since they usually must coordinate their employment with the jobs of home and child care, and particularly for never and formerly married mothers who tend to be employed more hours than currently married mothers. Yet we know relatively little about how job demands and work-family preferences interrelate.

Differences between working a nonstandard schedule and working a fixed, daytime schedule, Monday through Friday, involve economic, health, and social considerations. The limited research that addresses these concerns looks at which hours people work—but not which *days,* although many of the findings that are based on hourly shifts can be generalized to which days of the week people are employed.

Economic considerations include a wage premium: Workers on evening, night, or rotating shifts have historically received a higher wage than those who worked a day shift at the same job (Finn, 1981; Hedges & Sekscenski, 1979). Although there is no up-to-date research on wage differences by schedule, the increased proportion of service sector jobs among nonday shift work suggests that this practice is far less prevalent today than in the past.[3] Moreover, nonstandard schedules tend to be associated with lower occupational status, which in turn is linked to lower earnings (Mellor, 1986).

Of special relevance to mothers who work nonstandard shifts are the consequences that these schedules have for family life, including both health and social considerations. Evening, night, and rotating shifts are associated with physiological disorders that probably do not apply to those who work nonstandard days, but for those with nonstandard hours, these disorders are associated with less safety and efficiency on the job[4] (Carpentier & Cazamian, 1977; Finn, 1981; U.S. Congress, 1991). We expect these detrimental health effects would also be associated with less energy and patience at home. Finally, mothers on these shifts have less time to spend with young children who go to bed early, and the time that they do have is likely affected by the fatigue resulting from less adequate sleep (Carpentier & Cazamian, 1977; Finn, 1981; U.S. Congress, 1991).

The few nationally representative studies that have examined the prevalence and determinants of women's employment schedules have included how they relate to job demands and family needs. More than one in six employed mothers with children under 14 work other than a fixed daytime shift, and about one in four work on weekends or variable days (Presser, 1989a). Single mothers are more likely to work nonstandard hours or days than married mothers, even when job, family, and individual characteristics are controlled (Presser, 1989a, 1995). These studies, however, do not distinguish among nonmarried mothers. Job characteristics associated with higher rates of nonstandard schedules include service occupations, the personal service industry, working part-time, and holding more than one job. In addition, having a preschool-age child (compared to having no children under 14), being young, having low levels of education, and being Black (compared to White) increase the odds that a woman works a nonstandard schedule. Having school-age children lowers the likelihood, as does being Hispanic.

These same studies have also addressed the reasons women report for working nonday, rotating, or irregular hours. A substantial minority of all mothers with children under 14 who worked nonstandard hours in 1991 reported that care for children or other family members was their main reason for working these shifts. Nearly half (45%) of mothers who had children under 5 and about a third (34%) of those with school-age children gave family or child care as their main reason. On the other hand, mothers were as likely to report job demands as their main reason for working nonstandard hours as they were to report child or family care. Among mothers whose youngest child was under 5, 35% reported as their main reason that their job required such a shift or that they could not get another job; among mothers with school-age children, the share was nearly half (44%; Presser, 1995). Moreover, differences by marital status in these reasons are striking. In 1985, married mothers with children under 6 who were in dual-earner couples were twice as likely as single mothers with children under 6 to report family or child care as their main reason for working nonstandard hours (53% vs. 27%, respectively; Presser, 1989a). Similarly, more than half (56%) of single mothers with a preschool child reported job demands as their primary reason for working a nonstandard shift, compared to 37% of their married counterparts in dual-earner couples (Presser, 1989a). This suggests that some nonday employment among single mothers occurs because of compatibility with others' shifts, but much less so than is the case for married mothers.

Finally, one study demonstrates more clearly the relevance of child care to shift work for mothers and shows important marital status differences. Presser (1986) analyzed the determinants of working evening or nighttime hours, the relationship between shift work and child care, and the constraining effects on employment of shift work and child care for mothers of young children in 1982. Marital status was a strong determinant of shift work among mothers employed full-time, though there was little difference by marital status among mothers employed part-time. Both shift work and marital status were related to the type of child care used. Married mothers who worked nondays were much more likely to have relatives, especially fathers, care for children than married mothers who worked daytime shifts. Indeed, among married mothers who worked nondays, father care was the most common child care arrangement. Among single mothers, however, care by a relative was about equally likely whether they worked days or nondays. Care by nonrelatives, followed by grandparent care, were the most common child care arrangements for single mothers who worked nondays. Thus, the type of child care appears related to which shift married mothers worked because of child care that fathers provided, but not to which shift single mothers worked. Finally, looking only at married mothers, shift work appeared to constrain the employment of those working part-time. Among those who worked part-time and who also had a nonday shift, more than one fourth said that they would work more hours if satisfactory child care were available, whereas only one sixth of those who worked daytime shifts reported such constraint. It is important to note that the 4% of employed mothers who work rotating shifts (Presser, 1989a) could not be delineated in this analysis, suggesting that employment constraints resulting from nonstandard schedules may be even greater.

Previous research, then, shows that single mothers tend to have lower labor market positions than married mothers. Earlier studies also demonstrate that women who work nonstandard schedules have lower labor market status than those who work fixed, weekday schedules. With regard to marital status, single mothers are more likely to work at nonstandard times than married mothers, and family care issues appear more related to married mothers' employment schedules than to single mothers' schedules. It remains to be seen, however, why single mothers are more likely than married mothers to work at nonstandard times and whether the circumstances under which they work these times differ. We also do not know whether never married mothers—with their lower labor market positions—differ from formerly married mothers in their rates and determinants of working nonstandard schedules.

CONCEPTUAL FRAMEWORK

Mothers are stratified by marital status in two ways that may affect why they work nonstandard schedules. The first difference is between single and married mothers: Single mothers are more disadvantaged than married ones because they lack most of the financial and child care resources that a present father contributes. Many single mothers do not receive child support, and even those who receive money do not pool income and expenses with fathers as married mothers do. Moreover, as previously noted, few if any single mothers are able to share child care with their children's fathers, compared to the more than one third of dual-earner couples with small children who share child care by working different schedules (Presser, 1988). Single mothers' economic disadvantage due to lower household income is thus often exacerbated by having higher child care costs, relative to income, than married mothers. In terms of employment schedules, the economic disparity between single and married mothers leaves single mothers more desperate for a paid job and more vulnerable to impositions of the job, including working at nonstandard times and accepting low-quality child care or unstable arrangements.

Second, among single mothers, never married mothers are generally at an economic disadvantage compared to formerly married mothers (Garfinkel & McLanahan, 1986). In 1992, the average annual income of never married mothers was only $8,609, compared to $17,503 for divorced mothers (who make up the majority of formerly married mothers; Saluter, 1993). Never married mothers are less likely than formerly married mothers to receive child support and to earn satisfactory wages (Lester, 1991; Saluter, 1993). Many of these women are or were teenage mothers and as such had little time to gain human capital resources when they began raising children. However, because of this background, never married mothers are also more likely than formerly married mothers to be living with extended family where their own mothers may be available and willing to share child care; between 32% and 41% of never married mothers, depending on race-ethnicity, lived with extended family in 1990, compared to 12% to 15% of separated and divorced mothers (McLanahan & Casper, 1995). In terms of employment schedules, this means that never married mothers may be more vulnerable to impositions of the job, yet better able to use nonstandard schedules as a low-cost child care strategy than formerly married mothers.

In short, the differences between single and married mothers and between never and formerly married mothers suggest two mechanisms through which mothers work nonstandard times. Nonstandard schedules can be either a burden resulting from job demands or a more voluntary decision made to share child care. We hypothesize that never married mothers are the most likely to work at nonstandard times because of financial hardship, followed first by formerly married and then by currently married mothers. The economic differences among mothers mirror their rates of nonstandard schedules, suggesting that economic burdens may drive the employment schedules of never married mothers the most and of currently married mothers the least. Correspondingly, we also hypothesize that nonstandard schedules are preferred by currently married mothers the most, followed by never married and then by formerly married mothers, since currently married mothers have the most potential child care partners. We use "preference" here strictly in comparison to economic hardship as a determinant of employment schedules. The need to balance work and family is hardly a choice (it is more of an obligation, especially for women compared to men), but working a nonstandard schedule because it eases this balance speaks of a more voluntary decision than working at such time because the available jobs require it. In this chapter, then, we test competing arguments about whether job demands or caregiving preferences drive mothers' employment schedules, hypothesizing that job constraints are most important for never married mothers, and that child and family care preferences are most important for currently married mothers.

DATA

Data for this study come from the May 1991 Current Population Survey (CPS). The CPS is a nationally representative, monthly survey of approximately 58,000 households in the United States. It is conducted by the Bureau of Labor Statistics primarily to estimate civilian unemployment. In May 1991, a supplement on work schedules was added. Our analysis draws on the subsample of women who were asked about their employment schedules; who had children of their own under age 14 living with them; and who were employed in civilian, nonagricultural occupations. The sample with all employment schedule data consists of 9,307 women,[5] 7,199 currently married, 1,499 formerly married, and 609 never married mothers. This sample represents 13.0 million currently married, 2.8 million formerly married, and 1.2 million never married mothers, respectively, in the United States. For the 5.7% of employed women with more than one paid job, our analysis focuses on the job in which they worked the most hours during the reference week.

ANALYSIS

Definitions

We consider both the hours and the days that women work. We define hourly schedules with seven categories, as follows:[6]

Fixed day: At least half of the hours worked during most days last week fell between 8 a.m. and 4 p.m.

Fixed evening: At least half of the hours worked during most days last week fell after 4 p.m. and through midnight.

Fixed night: At least half the hours worked during most days last week fell after midnight and before 8 a.m.

Irregular day: Usually having an irregular schedule determined by the employer, where at least half of the hours worked last week fell between 8 a.m. and 4 p.m.[7]

Irregular evening or night: Usually having an irregular schedule determined by the employer, where at least half of the hours worked last week fell after 4 p.m. and before 8 a.m.

Irregular, no hours given: Usually having an irregular schedule, but whether the hours fell mostly in the day, evening, or night cannot be determined.

Rotating: Schedules changing periodically from days to evenings or nights.[8]

We consider women as working "standard" hours when they work fixed daytime schedules and women as working nonstandard hours when they work any other type of shift, including irregular days.

We define daily schedules with three groups, as follows:

Weekdays: Usually working only during Monday through Friday, but not necessarily all of these days.

Some or all weekend: Usually working on Saturday and/or Sunday, only or in addition to weekdays.
Days vary: Usually having a variable schedule of days at work.[9]

We consider women working "standard" days when they work weekdays only and nonstandard days when they work either of the other schedules.

Descriptive Findings

Before addressing the determinants of nonstandard schedules, we ask first to what degree employment schedules vary by marital status. Table 4.1 presents the rates of nonstandard employment schedules for never, formerly, and currently married mothers with children under 14 at home.

Working a nonstandard hourly shift (i.e., other than fixed hours during the day) is much more common for never married than for either formerly or currently married mothers. Nearly a third of never married mothers work other than a fixed daytime shift, while roughly one fifth of both formerly and currently married mothers work these nonstandard hours. Never married mothers are especially likely to work fixed evening and rotating shifts compared to the other mothers. The differences between formerly and currently married mothers' shift rates are relatively small, showing that the greater prevalence of nonstandard hours among single mothers shown in earlier studies is driven largely by the high prevalence of such hours specifically among never married mothers.

In terms of days employed, never and formerly married mothers look similar to each other and have higher rates of working nonstandard schedules than currently married mothers have. The percentages working other than a fixed Monday to Friday schedule are 35.8%, 34.2%, and 29.9%, respectively. Never married mothers are especially likely to have workdays that vary, 21.5%, compared to about 16% of formerly and currently married mothers. Formerly married mothers are especially likely to work at least some days on the weekend; 18% of them work Saturdays and/or Sundays, compared to about 14% of never and currently married mothers.

Taken as a whole, then, never married mothers are the most likely to work nonstandard hours or days, followed first by formerly married and then by currently married mothers. Formerly married mothers look more like currently married mothers in terms of their hourly schedule, and more like never married mothers in terms of their daily schedule. Next we consider the extent to which marital status differences in employment schedules are determined by marital status differences in occupational composition.

TABLE 4.1 Prevalence of Working Nonstandard Schedules, Among Women With Children Under 14, Employed in Civilian, Nonagricultural Occupations, by Marital Status, Weighted—May 1991 Current Population Survey

	Never Married	*Formerly Married*	*Currently Married*
Which Hours Employed			
Fixed day shift	70.2	79.4	81.4
Irregular day shift	3.5	2.8	3.8
Fixed evening shift	13.8	8.2	8.1
Fixed night shift	3.9	3.8	2.8
Irregular nonday shift	2.7	1.7	1.4
Rotating shift	5.1	3.5	1.9
Irregular shift, no hours given	0.8	0.6	0.6
Total	100.0	100.0	100.0
Which days employed			
Monday to Friday only	64.2	65.8	70.1
Some or all days on the weekend	14.3	18.0	13.8
Days vary	21.5	16.2	16.1
Total	100.0	100.0	100.0
(N)	(609)	(1,499)	(7,199)

Standardizing on Occupation

If never married mothers are most subject to scheduling impositions of the job, followed by formerly married and then by currently married mothers, then occupational differences among the women should explain part of their differences in employment schedules. Differences in the occupational distributions of groups reflect the organization of the labor market, showing which occupations are most available to people with different socioeconomic characteristics.[10] Moreover, previous research has shown occupations to be highly related to employment schedules because occupations vary in the extent to which they represent the demand for services 24 hours a day, 7 days a week (Presser, 1995). Examining the occupational distributions of groups thus taps job requirements and captures some of the role that institutional factors (such as labor market demands and racial-ethnic and class segregation) may play in determining employment schedules. While recognizing that occupational preferences (supply factors) are also involved, the demand for labor is the principal determinant of occupational distributions (Cotter et al.,

1998). Of concern here is whether never married mothers are most likely to be in those occupations that demand nonstandard schedules, as we have hypothesized.

To answer this question, we examine never, formerly, and currently married mothers' rates of nonstandard employment schedules while controlling for differences in their occupational distributions. We do this by standardizing the occupational distributions of the three groups of mothers to the occupational distribution of all mothers. Standardization allows us to determine the degree to which the differences among never, formerly, and currently married mothers' rates of nonstandard schedules are due to differences in their occupational distributions. The smaller the differences among rates of nonstandard schedules when we constrain all groups to the same occupational distribution, the more relevant to employment schedules are the actual differences in occupational distributions among these groups.

The standardization process involved three steps. First, we grouped occupations into 16 categories, 10 detailed occupations and 6 broader occupational groups.[11] We then multiplied the proportion of all mothers in an occupation (without regard to marital status) by the nonstandard schedule rate of each marital status group of mothers in that occupation. This gives the percentage of each group of mothers that would have a specific occupation and would work a nonstandard schedule, if that group had the same occupational distribution as all mothers. Taking cashiers as an example, 6.6% of never married mothers are cashiers (before standardization), and 54.4% of them work nonstandard hours. If the same share of never married mothers were cashiers as of all mothers (after standardization)—3.3%—and 54.4% worked nonstandard hours, this would reduce the percentage of never married mothers who work nonstandard schedules. Accordingly, the total of all the occupation-specific rates provides an overall expected rate of nonstandard employment schedules, if the three groups had similar occupational distributions. These overall rates are presented in Table 4.2.

Table 4.2 shows that when we standardize occupational structure, never and formerly married mothers' rates of nonstandard schedules decline while currently married mothers' rates rise. If never married mothers had the same occupational distribution as all mothers, just under 26% would work nonstandard hours and 32.5% would work nonstandard days, compared to the roughly 30% and 36%, respectively, who actually work these times. The rates of nonstandard schedules among formerly married mothers fall from 20.68% to 19.20% for nonstandard hours and from 34.19% to 32.41% for nonstandard days, with the same occupational structure. Finally, currently married mothers' rates of nonstandard schedules rise a half of a percentage point with standardization, to 19.10% working nonstandard hours and 30.5% working nonstandard days.

Table 4.3 shows the strong impact that occupational distribution has on the differences in nonstandard schedule rates among the groups of mothers. Between never and formerly married mothers, the difference between their crude (or prestandardization) rates of nonstandard hours is 9.1 percentage points, while the difference in their standardized rates is 6.7 percentage points. This means that occupational differences between the two groups account for 26% of never married mothers' greater tendency to work nonstandard hours, compared to formerly married mothers. For never and currently married mothers, whose crude rates differ the most, the effect of occupation is even greater. The difference between their rates drops from 9 to just under 7 percentage points after standardization; 39% of never married mothers' greater likelihood of working nonstandard hours, relative to currently married mothers, is due to occupational differences. Finally, the difference between the rates of formerly and currently married mothers is nearly eliminated with standardization (95%), partly because their rates are more similar prior to standardization.

Occupation is particularly relevant in explaining why never married mothers are more likely than either of the other two groups to work *weekends or variable days*. Standardizing by occupation accounts for 92% of the difference between never and formerly married mothers' rates and 67% of the difference between the rates of never and currently married mothers. Between formerly and currently married mothers, occupational differences also explain more than half, 57%, of the difference in their rates of working nonstandard days.

These results lend credence to the strong link between occupation and employment schedules by showing that much of the difference among the nonstandard schedule rates is driven by differences among the mothers in occupational distribution. Given the impact of occupation, we turn next to the question of how influential children's characteristics are to the employment schedules of the three groups of mothers. To the extent that they are influential, child care preferences may be relevant.

Multivariate Analysis

Once we control for occupation, do child care preferences, as measured by children's characteristics, affect the employment schedules of currently married mothers the most, as we have hypothesized? We answer this question with a multivariate analysis that examines the determinants of nonstandard

TABLE 4.2 Percentages of Women Working Nonstandard Schedules Before and After Standardization on Occupation, by Marital Status. May 1991 Current Population Survey.

	Never Married	Formerly Married	Currently Married
Nonstandard Hours			
Actual percentage nonstandard	29.73	20.68	18.63
Standardized percentage	25.87	19.20	19.10
Nonstandard Days			
Actual percentage nonstandard	35.77	34.19	29,91
Standardized percentage	32.53	32.41	30.50
(N)	(609)	(1,499)	(7,199)

TABLE 4.3 Differences Among Mothers by Marital Status, in the Rates of Nonstandard Schedules, Before and After Standardization on Occupation. May 1991 Current Population Survey.

Comparison Groups	Never vs. Formerly Married	Formerly vs. Currently Married	Never and Currently Married
Nonstandard Hours			
Crude difference	9.05	11.10	2.05
Standardized difference	6.67	6.77	0.10
Percentage of crude difference explained	26%	39%	95%
Nonstandard Days			
Crude difference	1.58	5.86	4.28
Standardized difference	0.12	1.95	1.83
Percentage of crude difference explained	92%	67%	57%

schedules separately for each group of mothers. We use logistic regression to model the odds of working nonstandard hours and the odds of working nonstandard days.

As previously noted, differences among the groups of mothers center around income and child care. Since currently married mothers often have fathers available to pool income and share child care, their children's character-istics—acting as a proxy for child care need—will most likely affect their employment schedules. For formerly married mothers, who generally have neither of these resources, their children's characteristics are less likely to in-fluence work schedules. For never married mothers, the reasoning is uncer-tain. On the one hand, some never married mothers live with extended family members who may be willing to provide child care, indicating that children's characteristics would affect employment schedules, although likely less than for currently married mothers. On the other hand, the financial hardship faced by never married mothers may be extreme enough to dictate their em-ployment schedules over any other factors, including child care arrange-ments. In this multivariate analysis, then, we test the hypothesis raised at the outset: that caregiving needs, as measured by the characteristics of children, influence the schedules of currently married mothers the most, followed by those of never and formerly married mothers, and that job constraints influ-ence the employment schedules of never married mothers the most, followed by those of formerly and currently married mothers.

Definitions of all variables used in the multivariate analysis are in Appen-dix 4.A. We define nonstandard hours and days as we did previously. Non-standard hourly schedules are evening, night, irregular, or rotating shifts, and nonstandard daily schedules consist of weekend or variable days.

Children's characteristics, the proxy for child care need, relate to two fac-tors that most affect cost of care: the number of children and whether children are of preschool age. Where children's characteristics matter, we expect that having more children and having preschool-age children raise the odds of working a nonstandard schedule; they increase formal child care costs and thereby raise the benefit of adapting employment schedules around informal, low-cost child care arrangements.

With regard to the paid job, we include several characteristics that may di-rectly affect whether or not a respondent has a nonstandard schedule. These are whether a respondent is employed part-time, has more than one paid job, works in the government or the private sector, and the industry and occupa-tion of her job. We define part-time work as consisting of less than 35 hours per week at all paid jobs during the reference week and expect that mothers working part-time are more likely to work nonstandard schedules than those working full-time, since part-time jobs are associated with more nonstandard employment than full-time jobs. We define multiple job holders as those working at more than one paid job during the reference week.[12] We expect that they are more likely to work nonstandard schedules than those with only one paid job, as the arranging of two or more jobs is likely to involve schedules beyond Monday to Friday during the day more than is the scheduling of one job. We measure the private sector as any nongovernmental job, including self-employed jobs, and expect that mothers in the private sector have higher odds of working nonstandard schedules than those in the government; private sector jobs tend to have more nonstandard work than government sector jobs. We classified industry into five categories: distributive, extractive and transformative, producer services, social services, and personal services.[13] We expect that those in personal services are more likely than those in other industries to work nonstandard schedules, consistent with previous research (Presser, 1995). For occupation we specify the six most common detailed occupations of never married mothers and group the rest; we include occupation to control for the influence on employment schedules demonstrated in Tables 4.2 and 4.3.[14]

We also include several nonmarket characteristics that can affect labor market position. The differences in mothers' occupational distributions evident in Tables 4.2 and 4.3 are due to two factors beyond economic hardship that reflect never married and, to a lesser extent, formerly married mothers' vulnerability to impositions of the job. First is position in the life course; this is especially important for never married mothers, who are most likely to be young and to have had a child before gaining substantial human capital. We include education in completed years, age, and age squared to capture these differences, and expect that the odds of working nonstandard schedules are higher when women have less education and are younger. Second, we include race-ethnicity since racial-ethnic differences among the three groups of mothers correlate with racial-ethnic occupational segregation and leave never married mothers, who are more likely than the other mothers to be in a racial-ethnic minority, at an occupational disadvantage. In this sense, we expect that White mothers are less likely to work a nonstandard schedule than racial-ethnic minority mothers.

Multivariate Results

Tables 4.4 and 4.5 show the results of the multivariate regressions; each model shows the effects of family, job, and individual characteristics. Of particular focus in this analysis is the relationship between children's characteristics and employment schedules, and our findings support the hypothesis that this relationship is weakest for never married mothers and strongest for currently married mothers. Among never married mothers, neither the number nor the age of children significantly affects the likelihood of working nonstandard hours or days. Among formerly married mothers, the number of children raises their odds of working nonstandard hours by 26%, and neither measure significantly affects their odds of working nonstandard days. Among currently married mothers, both the number and age of children raise the likelihood of working nonstandard hours, by 12% and 59%, respectively, and the number of children also raises the odds of working nonstandard days, by 18%. For many currently married and at least some formerly married mothers, then, nonstandard schedules appear to be a way to balance job and family demands. This does not appear to be a prevalent strategy for never married mothers, who seem unable to take into account their family situations when they work at nonstandard times.

With regard to job characteristics, being employed part-time affects which hours worked, and being employed in the private sector affects which days worked among never and formerly married mothers. Among currently married mothers, both part-time and private-sector work affect hourly and daily schedules. All three groups are 2 to 2½ times as likely to work nonstandard hours when employed part-time, versus full-time, and currently married mothers are also twice as likely to work nonstandard days when employed part-time. All three groups are 2½ to 3 times as likely to work weekends or variable days when employed in the private sector, versus in the government, and currently married mothers are also 2.6 times as likely to work nonstandard hours when in the private sector.

The industry in which mothers are employed appears to affect the days more than the hours they work. Compared to those working in distributive industries, never married mothers' odds of working both nonstandard hours and days are higher among those employed in personal service industries. In addition, their odds of working nonstandard days are lower among those working in extractive or transformative and in producer service industries. Among formerly married mothers, those in extractive or transformative and in producer service industries have lower odds of working nonstandard hours and of working nonstandard days, and those in personal service industries have higher odds of working nonstandard days, compared to those working in distributive industries. Among currently married mothers, and again relative to those in distributive industries, the odds of working both nonstandard hours and nonstandard days are lower among those in producer service industries and higher among those in personal service industries. Currently married mothers' odds of working nonstandard days are also lower among those working in extractive or transformative and in social service industries. The overall effect of industry on employment schedules is also significant; the addition of industry improves the explanatory power of the models for all three groups of mothers (see Appendix 4.B).[15]

TABLE 4.4 Odds of Working Nonstandard Hours Among Women With Children Under 14, Employed in Civilian, Nonagricultural Occupations, by Marital Status, Weighted—May 1991 Current Population Survey

	Never Married	Formerly Married	Currently Married
Family			
Number of children under 14	1.07	1.26*	1.12**
Youngest child is under 5	1.18	1.25	1.59***
Paid Job			
Employed part time	1.93**	2.39***	2.64***
Has more than one job	0.95	0.88	1.48**
Job is in the private sector	1.27	1.59	2.62***
Industry			
(Distributive)	(1.00)	(1.00)	(1.00)
Extractive or transformative	0.90	0.54*	0.96
Producer services	0.99	0.46**	0.72*
Social services	0.91	0.98	1.20
Personal services	2.26*	1.05	1.40*
Occupation			
(Secretaries, stenographers, typists)	(1.00)	(1.00)	(1.00)
Managerial, professional specialty occ's	2.16	2.07	3.16***
Cashier	7.30**	10.49***	7.96***
Other technical and sales support occ's	1.92	4.30***	4.52***
Other administrative support occ's	1.30	1.47	2.11***
Waitresses	6.90*	7.33***	11.05***
Nursing aides, orderlies, attendants	11.20***	8.68***	9.65***
Cooks	5.19*	2.19	3.70***
Maids	1.12	0.66	1.22
Child care providers, except private	0.93	0.41	0.79
Other service occupations	4.16*	4.36***	3.32***
Precision production, craft, repair occ's	6.25*	3.52*	4.67***
Operators, fabricators, laborers	3.10	4.46***	4.25***
Individual			
Age	1.12	0.83**	0.92*
Age squared	1.00	1.00**	1.00*
Completed years of education	0.99	0.99	0.97
Race-ethnicity			
(White)	(1.00)	(1.00)	(1.00)
Black	0.71	1.48*	0.88
Hispanic	0.59	1.38	0.81
Other race-ethnicity	0.24	1.16	1.69**
Intercept (log odds)	−4.00	0.22	−2.63***
(N)	(573)	(1,425)	(6,838)

NOTE: * $p < 0.05$; ** $p < 0.01$; *** $p < 0.001$.

TABLE 4.5 Odds of Working Nonstandard Days Among Women With Children Under 14, Employed in Civilian, Nonagricultural Occupations, by Marital Status, Weighted—May 1991 Current Population Survey

	Never Married	*Formerly Married*	*Currently Married*
Family			
Number of children under 14	1.11	1.08	1.18**
Youngest child is under 5	1.16	1.34	0.93
Paid Job			
Employed part time	1.49	1.35	2.00***
Has more than one job	0.51	0.73	1.11
Job is in the private sector	3.16**	2.47***	2.43***
Industry			
(Distributive)	(1.00)	(1.00)	(1.00)
Extractive or transformative	0.10***	0.21***	0.37***
Producer services	0.31**	0.32***	0.50***
Social services	0.97	0.76	0.79*
Personal services	2.48*	1.83*	2.20***
Occupation			
(Secretaries, stenographers, typists)	(1.00)	(1.00)	(1.00)
Managerial, professional specialty occ's	3.12	2.40**	3.96***
Cashier	15.78***	7.04***	13.10***
Other technical and sales support occ's	18.02***	4.75***	8.91***
Other administrative support occ's	1.55	1.15	2.25***
Waitresses	7.61*	6.77***	10.81***
Nursing aides, orderlies, attendants	20.38***	15.19***	19.93***
Cooks	15.91**	2.71*	8.18***
Maids	4.57	5.69**	12.81***
Child care providers, except private	0.38	0.29	0.92
Other service occupations	4.89*	3.18***	4.38***
Precision production, craft, repair occ's	8.07*	2.36	3.66***
Operators, fabricators, laborers	4.63*	2.10*	2.66***
Individual			
Age	0.97	1.04	0.90*
Age squared	1.00	1.00	1.00*
Completed years of education	1.00	0.95	0.99
Race-ethnicity			
(White)	(1.00)	(1.00)	(1.00)
Black	0.62	1.06	0.97
Hispanic	0.60	1.27	0.68**
Other race-ethnicity	0.61	0.84	1.31
Intercept	−2.37	−2.29	−1.47*
(N)	(573)	(1,425)	(6,838)

NOTE: * $p < 0.05$; ** $p < 0.01$; *** $p < 0.001$.

The odds of working nonstandard schedules can vary dramatically across occupations as well. Relative to secretaries, the odds of working nonstandard hours are particularly high among cashiers; waitresses; and nursing aides, orderlies, and attendants in each group of mothers. The odds of working nonstandard days are especially high among cashiers; those in other technical and sales-support occupations; waitresses; and nursing aides, orderlies, and attendants as among secretaries. The odds of working nonstandard days are also quite high for cooks, among never and currently married mothers, and for maids, among former and currently married mothers. Finally, the explanatory power of all models is significantly greater with the addition of occupation, again demonstrating the strong impact of occupation on employment schedules (see Appendix 4.B).[16]

The remaining set of variables, women's individual characteristics, help predict the employment schedules of currently married mothers and, to a lesser extent, of formerly married mothers, but not of never married mothers. For never married mothers, individual characteristics do not significantly affect the odds of working nonstandard hours or days; their high rates of nonstandard schedules appear to exist regardless of their age, education, or race-ethnicity. Among formerly married mothers, younger women are less likely and African American (compared to White) women are more likely to work nonstandard hours; none of the characteristics affect their likelihood of working nonstandard days. Currently married mothers are more likely to work both nonstandard hours and nonstandard days when they are younger. Compared to married White mothers, married mothers in other racial-ethnic minorities are more likely to work nonstandard hours, and married Hispanic mothers are less likely to work nonstandard days. Education does not significantly affect employment schedules for any of the groups, possibly because the model also includes occupation.[17] These findings suggest that never married mothers, unlike currently and formerly married mothers, are willing to work these nonstandard times regardless of their individual characteristics, presumably because they are most dependent on income from employment and their job options may be most limited.

In general, the multivariate results support our hypothesis that children's characteristics affect the employment schedules most notably for currently married mothers. Children's characteristics also appear to influence the schedules of formerly married mothers but not of never married mothers. The determinants of employment schedules look quite different for never and currently married mothers, and the determinants of formerly married mothers fall somewhere between those of the other two groups. This suggests that caregiving demands precipitate nonstandard schedules among currently married and, to a lesser extent, among formerly married mothers and not among never married mothers. The influence of family characteristics is less consistent for formerly married than for currently married mothers; among formerly married mothers, the number of children affects the likelihood of working nonstandard hours but not days, while children's characteristics affect both types of schedules among currently married mothers. Since family characteristics are not significant determinants of never married mothers' schedules, we can assume that job demands are largely why these women work at nonstandard times. The multivariate analysis provides a rigorous assessment of the influence of family characteristics on employment schedules for all those employed—that is, the sample includes those who work standard as well as nonstandard times. Looking only at mothers with nonstandard schedules, it is also revealing to consider the reasons they give for working at these times.

Self-Reported Reasons

Mothers with nonstandard hourly schedules were asked their main reason for working these shifts, and their responses are tabulated in Table 4.6.[18] Looking at family demands, we see that, overall, 34.2% of all mothers report child or other family care as their main reason for working a nonday, rotating, or irregular shift.[19] By marital status, as Table 4.6 shows, substantially more currently married mothers report care of children or other family members as their main reason for working a nonstandard shift than do never or formerly married mothers. Among currently married mothers, 38.2% report these reasons, compared to 24.3% of formerly married and 18.7% of never married mothers. Of special note is the difference by marital status in reporting care of family members other than children. Currently married mothers are more than twice as likely as formerly or never married mothers to report care for other family members as their main reason, suggesting that currently married mothers are more likely to take on the responsibility of parents and parents-in-law as well as husbands, while single mothers may focus more on their own survival.

Similarly, the strong impact of job factors in predicting mothers' employment schedules corresponds with the fact that job considerations are the most commonly reported reasons for all groups of mothers. Moreover, as Table 4.6 shows, never and formerly married mothers are much more likely than currently married mothers to report job-related factors as their main reason for working nonstandard hours. Just over half of never and formerly married mothers report "requirement of the job" or "could not get any other job" as

TABLE 4.6 Main Reason Reported for Working Nonstandard Hours Among
Women With Children Under 14, Employed in Civilian,
Nonagricultural Occupations, by Marital Status, Weighted—May 1991
Current Population Survey

	Never Married	Formerly Married	Currently Married
Could not get any other job	6.3	7.0	3.2
Requirement of the job	47.8	45.1	37.0
Better pay	6.3	5.3	1.8
Care of children	13.5	17.8	24.6
Care of other family members	5.2	6.5	13.6
Allows time for school	7.5	4.1	2.5
Other	6.5	9.5	11.5
No response	6.9	4.7	5.8
Total	100.0	100.0	100.0
(N)	(187)	(325)	(1,505)

their main reason for working late or varying hours, compared to 39.2% of
currently married mothers. This finding suggests that nonstandard schedules
are often an imposition of the job for all mothers, but that this imposition is
more often experienced by never and formerly married mothers than by currently married mothers. The very low percentages reporting another job-
related reason, "better pay," as their main reason suggest that few women may
earn higher wages for working a nonstandard shift. However, single mothers
are more likely to regard a pay differential as a reason to work nonstandard
hours, despite the difficulties associated with these shifts. Among never married mothers, 6.3%, and among formerly married, 5.3%, report better pay as
their main reason for working nonstandard hours, compared to only 1.8% of
currently married mothers.

Finally, mothers differ in how often they report "allows time for school" as
their main reason for working nonstandard hours.[20] Never married mothers
are nearly twice as likely as formerly married mothers and are three times as
likely as currently married mothers to report school as their main reason for
working a nonstandard shift, although here, too, the percentages are relatively small for each group: 7.5%, 4.1%, and 2.5%, respectively. The higher
shares of never married mothers reporting this reason is consistent with their
younger ages and lower levels of schooling, compared to the other mothers.
In addition, the higher shares of both never and formerly married mothers re-

porting school suggests that working nonstandard schedules is more of a human capital strategy for these women—that is, a way of gaining education to increase their earning power. A chi square test of the association between the main reason for working nonstandard hours and marital status is significant at the 0.001 level (χ^2 = 117.79, 16 df).

DISCUSSION

Overall, the reasons that mothers report for working nonstandard hours are consistent with the multivariate findings that job factors determine the employment schedules of never married mothers the most and of currently married mothers the least, and children's characteristics predict the schedules of currently married mothers the most and never married mothers the least. The results of this study thus support our hypothesis that nonstandard schedules are the result of employment demand most for never married mothers, followed by formerly married and currently married mothers, and of caregiving preference most for currently married mothers. Marital status differences in the mothers' occupational distributions explain a substantial amount of the differences in their rates of nonstandard schedules. In addition, never married mothers report that they work nonstandard hours primarily because of job-related reasons most often, followed by formerly married and then by currently married mothers. Correspondingly, family characteristics determine currently married mothers' odds of working nonstandard schedules the most, followed by those of formerly married mothers, and they do not significantly affect never married mothers' likelihood of working at nonstandard times. Finally, currently married mothers report that they work nonstandard hours mainly because of caregiving most often, followed first by formerly married and then by never married mothers.

The determinants of working nonstandard hours or days are thus different for the three groups of mothers. For never married mothers, job factors, more than personal or family characteristics, determine employment schedules. For formerly married and currently married mothers, on the other hand, both job demands and children's characteristics determine schedules. The schedules of currently married mothers are more influenced by children's characteristics than are the schedules of formerly married mothers.

The differences in income and child care resources among the mothers help explain this pattern. With relatively low incomes, never married mothers are more vulnerable to labor market demands, including nonstandard schedules. Currently married mothers are both less vulnerable to job requirements and more able to share child care with others, because of contributions by their husbands. Between these two groups, formerly married mothers appear to have more resources for balancing employment and family demands than never married mothers but lack the resources from husbands that currently married mothers have. Comparing never and formerly married mothers, the latter tend to have more advantaged labor market positions and presumably share child care with grandmothers more often. Formerly married mothers may be more able to coordinate child care with grandmothers than never married mothers because of lesser economic burdens; the grandmothers in never married mother families may themselves be employed more often than those in formerly married mother families. In addition, formerly married mothers may be more able to pay grandmothers for care than never married mothers. However, rarely do never or formerly married mothers have the economic resources that husbands generally bring to married couple families.

Thus, the processes through which mothers come to work nonstandard schedules differ by marital status. For most never married mothers, the need for income is paramount, as the strong effects of occupation and the lack of influence of family characteristics suggest. As a result, many never married mothers likely arrange their child care around their need for employment and work nonstandard schedules when jobs so require, and if child care cannot be informally arranged at little or no cost, may be especially likely to resort to welfare. For formerly married mothers, economic burdens are also high; nearly as many of them reported job factors as their main reason for working nonstandard hours as did never married mothers. However, more formerly married mothers appear more able to prioritize their child care arrangements than never married mothers, given the influence of children on formerly married mothers' likelihood of working nonstandard shifts. Formerly married mothers likely adapt their employment around a child care arrangement when grandmothers are available but often work nonstandard schedules because of job requirements as well. Thus, nonstandard schedules often exacerbate the greater difficulty faced by formerly and, especially, never married mothers in balancing paid work and family, compared to currently married mothers. Not only are single mothers more likely than married mothers to work at nonstandard times, but single, and especially never married, mothers are more likely to do so involuntarily.

For many currently married mothers, on the other hand, the decision to work a nonstandard schedule appears to result from adapting employment around child care arrangements more often than is the case for never or formerly married mothers. Labor market demands are clearly relevant, as the reasons that mothers give for working nonstandard hours show. Unlike never married and, to a lesser extent, formerly married mothers, however, if these demands become too imposing, married mothers are more often able to work fewer hours or leave their paid job entirely and rely on husbands' income. Furthermore, the fact that personal and family characteristics help determine married mothers' schedules supports the findings of other research that shows that many married mothers adapt their employment needs around their child care arrangements by sharing care with their husbands (Presser, 1988). While this work-family balance is not likely to be easy, it is at least more flexible and likely involves lower psychic as well as financial costs than the situation that formerly married and, especially, never married mothers face.

CONCLUSIONS

For single mothers, then, and especially for never married mothers, we need to consider not only the number of hours that mothers are employed and require child care, but which hours and days that child care is needed as well. This issue shows no sign of diminishing in importance since single motherhood is unlikely to decline (Bianchi, 1995); more never and formerly married mothers are looking for permanent employment because of "welfare reform," or will be in the near future; and the demand for nonstandard employment, especially among women, appears to be increasing. The difficulty faced by formerly married and, especially, never married mothers in balancing employment and family demands is therefore likely to grow. Some of this difficulty can be alleviated by expanding both child care services with evening, night, and weekend availability and job opportunities with daytime and weekday schedules for these women.

The extent to which child care is available during nonstandard times is not known; there are no national estimates of prevalence or cost. Case studies suggest that commercial child care is a rare option for mothers working late hours and weekends (Women's Bureau, 1995). Some child care providers are unwilling to offer care at nonstandard times because they and their employees prefer to work during the day and during the week; others perceive a lack of demand for nonday and weekend care (Women's Bureau, 1995). Mothers who do find child care at nonstandard times may be expected to pay more than for weekday care, especially if child care providers receive a pay differential for working nonstandard schedules. Clearly, the availability of child care during nondays and weekends needs to be addressed by both researchers and policymakers.

The expansion of child care services into nondays and weekends is likely to be needed most by women in low status occupations that are characterized by low earnings and benefits, high rates of part-time work, and little unionization. Many of these occupations have some of the highest projected growth rates, as well as being among the most common occupations of never married mothers, such as cashiers; janitors and cleaners (including maids and housekeeping cleaners); waiters and waitresses; and nursing aides, orderlies, and attendants (Sylvestri, 1995) However, women in these occupations are unlikely to have either the money or the collective power to demand more prevalent or affordable care.

These high growth, highly nonstandard occupations are also among the most common occupations of women who are likely to be directly affected by welfare reform, those with at most a high school education. Mothers with a high school education or less are more likely than other employed women to work nonstandard hours and days, and they do so primarily because of job demands rather than preferences (Presser & Cox, 1997). If mothers who are not employed and are receiving welfare are generally offered these jobs without corresponding increases in child care, then employment constraints from lack of child care are likely to become greater. For policymakers, then, the relationship between employment and child care at nonstandard times calls the feasibility of welfare reform into question. For the mothers most affected by welfare reform, trying to remain permanently employed and maintain child care during late hours and weekends is likely to be complex and difficult at best.

In addition to the question of availability, future research needs to explore the consequences of nonstandard employment schedules. What are the repercussions for children and mothers when women have to work nondays or weekends and arrange child care with relatives or friends at these times? For single mother families, this is an especially troubling question, given the involuntary nature of these schedules, the decline in potential child care by relatives, the high cost of nonrelative care, and the fact that single mothers generally work longer hours than married mothers. In addition, the question of how much mothers' employment is limited because they are unable to arrange child care—and how this varies by marital status—emerges. In 1982, married women reported that child care limited their employment when they worked nondays substantially more often than when they worked fixed daytime shifts (Presser, 1986). We do not know to what extent the lack of commercial child care during nondays and weekends limits the employment of never and formerly married mothers, although their high rates of nonstandard schedules and of using commercial care (with its daytime hours) suggests that it may be great. Finally, even when mothers are able to arrange child care, the consequences for children are not known. If never and formerly married mothers are subsuming their child care arrangements to the demands of their employment schedules, is the care that they find less reliable or of lower quality than the arrangements found by mothers on fixed weekday schedules?

Recently, the Women's Bureau (1995) aptly referred to the need for child care during nonstandard times as "a sleeper issue relative to other work/family issues" (p. 25). The Bureau further indicated that it would take "a 'champion'—either from management, labor, or the community—to make the issue a priority" (p. 25). In 1996, for the first time at a national political convention, there was recognition of the fact that many parents with young children work late hours. Hillary Clinton (1996) remarked in her speech at the Democratic National Convention, "Right now there are mothers and fathers just finishing a long day's work, and there are mothers and fathers just going to work. Some to their second and third jobs of the day" (p. 1). While this public acknowledgment of the diversity of employment schedules by our country's First Lady is significant, the pervasive silence on this issue among public leaders remains.

Clearly, both researchers and policymakers need to explore further how employment schedules impact the abilities of single and married mothers to negotiate paid work with family demands. The results of this study, combined with the questions of child care availability and the social and economic consequences of nonstandard schedules, suggest that we continue to ask not only how and to what degree the competing demands of employment and family can be balanced, but also when and *for whom* such a balance can exist.

APPENDIX 4.A

Operational Definitions of Variables Used in Regressions

Variable	Definition
Dependent Variables	
Nonstandard hours	Whether respondent worked a shift most days last week with at least half of the hours falling after 4 p.m. and before 8 a.m., with rotating hours, or with irregular hours, compared to working a fixed daytime shift, 0-1
Nonstandard days	Whether respondent usually worked at least some of her days on the weekend or has workdays that vary, compared to working a fixed schedule during Monday through Friday, 0-1
Independent Variables	
Marital status	Married, spouse present, compared to never married or formerly married (separated, divorced, widowed), 0-1
Age	Age in years, 18-74[a]
Age squared	Squared age in years, 324-5,476
Years of school	Years of school completed, capped at 18, 0-18
Race-ethnicity	Four categories: non-Hispanic White, non-Hispanic Black, Hispanic, and non-Hispanic other race-ethnicity; non-Hispanic Whites are comparison group, 0-1
Number of children	Number of own children under 14 living in household, 1-7
Youngest child is under 5	Whether youngest own child is less than 5 years old, 0-1
Full time	Whether the number of hours worked at all jobs last week totals 35 or more per week, 0-1
Has more than one paid job	Whether employed in more than one job last week (sector, industry, occupation, and schedule data refer to job where respondent worked most hours), 0-1
Private sector or self-employed	Whether respondent works in the private sector or is self-employed, compared to working for the government, 0-1
Industry	Five groups: extractive and transformative, distributive services, producer services, social services, and personal services; distributive services are comparison group, 0-1
Occupation	13 categories: 7 detailed occupations and 6 grouped categories; secretaries are comparison group, 0-1

a. Some of these women are undoubtedly grandmothers who have adopted their grandchildren.

APPENDIX 4.B

Chi Squares for Models and Differences Between Chi Squares With and Without Industry and Occupation

Model	Never Married		Formerly Married		Currently Married	
Including Industry						
Nonstandard hours						
Full model[1]	67.503***	15 df	136.113***	15 df	590.243***	15 df
Model without industry[2]	43.691***	11 df	101.591***	11 df	525.703***	11 df
Difference	23.812***	4 df	34.522***	4 df	64.543***	4 df
Nonstandard days						
Full model	168.636***	15 df	262.343***	15 df	977.737***	15 df
Model without occupation	59.693***	11 df	84.636***	11 df	521.375***	11 df
Difference	108.943***	4 df	177.707***	4 df	456.362***	8 df
Including Occupation						
Nonstandard hours						
Full model[3]	117.288***	27 df	220.390***	27 df	838.692***	27 df
Model without occupation[4]	67.503***	15 df	136.113***	15 df	590.243***	15 df
Difference	49.785***	12 df	84.277***	12 df	248.449***	12 df
Nonstandard days						
Full model	253.838***	27 df	384.178***	27 df	1511.333***	27 df
Model without occupation	168.636***	15 df	262.343***	15 df	977.737***	15 df
Difference	85.202***	12 df	122.835***	12 df	533.596***	12 df
(N)	(573)		(1,425)		(6,838)	

NOTE: * $p < 0.05$; ** $p < 0.01$; *** $p < 0.001$.
1. Includes all variables except industry and occupation.
2. Includes all variables except occupation.
3. Includes all variables except occupation.
4. Includes all variables.

NOTES

1. We concentrate in this chapter on mothers, rather than on both mothers and fathers, since the increases in men's child care giving, although notable, remain small. That is, women still do most of the intellectual and emotional labor involved in balancing family and employment, and, whether as married or single mothers, they are more often the ones to adapt their employment to their family needs (Bielby & Bielby, 1992; Presser, 1984). Although the number of single father families has increased substantially in the past 20 years, they are still a small minority of single parent families (12% of children in single parent families lived with a single father in 1991; U.S. Bureau of the Census, 1992, Table 68). Moreover, single fathers are less likely to face the same difficulties balancing employment and family as single mothers because single fathers are much more likely than single mothers to cohabit. In 1990, between 29% and 45% of single fathers cohabited, depending on race-ethnicity, compared to only 5% to 7% of single mothers (McLanahan & Casper, 1995).

2. Kindergarten and grade school are not included as types of child care arrangements for this calculation.

3. In 1985, more than half of the jobs with nonstandard schedules were in the service sector, rather than in manufacturing industries as they had been in previous decades (Hedges & Sekscenski, 1979; Mellor, 1986). Earlier research on pay differentials for nonday or rotating shifts focused on jobs with characteristics more common to the manufacturing than the service sector, such as full-time status, and its generalizability to the present is therefore questionable. Moreover, manufacturing jobs tend to have higher benefits and higher rates of unionization than jobs in the service sector (Hedges & Sekscenski, 1979; Mellor, 1986; Smith, 1984).

4. The disorders include increased fatigue resulting from poor and insufficient sleep, increased digestive and appetite disorders, and increased neuroses (Carpentier & Cazamian, 1977; U.S. Congress, 1991).

5. The entire sample of women with children under 14, who are employed in civilian, nonagricultural occupations, is 9,511; the sample in our analysis is reduced to 9,307 because 204 women (2% of the initial sample) do not have complete employment schedule data.

6. We adapt a shift-work definition used by the Bureau of Labor Statistics (BLS) here. Like the BLS, we use self-definitions to identify those working rotating and irregular shifts. For those working fixed daytime, fixed evening, or fixed night shifts, we use the reported hours for beginning and ending work; the BLS uses self-definitions for fixed shifts. Also unlike the BLS, we do not differentiate those who work a split shift, a self-defined response category, because of small numbers and a predominance in daytime hours. Of the 9,511 employed women with children under 14, 109 reported working a split shift, 96 during the day, 10 during the evening, and 3 at night. We classified these women as working day, evening, and night shifts, respectively.

7. One of the response options offered by the CPS in the self-defined shift question is, "Irregular days as determined by employer." We differentiate this where possible as irregular day or irregular nonday.

8. Included with those on rotating shifts are four women (0.1% of the total sample) who worked 24-hour shifts.

9. This is a CPS response category, "days vary"; thus, which days are worked cannot be determined.

10. This is the case, for example, with occupational gender segregation; the different occupational distributions of women and men are the result of structured segregation (vs. individual "choice"; England, Farkas, Kilbourne, & Dou, 1988).

11. These detailed occupations are as follows: cashiers; secretaries, stenographers, and typists; receptionists; bookkeeping, accounting, and auditing clerks; data entry keyers; waitresses; cooks; nursing aides, orderlies, and attendants; maids; child care workers. The remaining occupational groups are as follows: managerial and professional specialty; other technical and sales occupations; other administrative support occupations; other service occupations; precision production, craft, and repair occupations; and operators, fabricators, and laborers. The 10 detailed occupations are the most common ones for never married mothers; they constitute 36.9% of this group, as compared to 28.5% of formerly married mothers and 26.3% of currently married mothers. The remaining shares fall into the six broader occupational groups. We chose the detailed occupations of never married mothers because they have the smallest sample size; 7 of these 10 occupations are among the 10 most common occupations of formerly and currently married mothers as well. Because we use only 10 detailed occupations, our standardization reflects much but not all of the differences in occupational distribution across the three groups of mothers. Our standardized rates are thus conservative estimates of the effect of occupation on the rates of nonstandard employment schedules. If we had performed similar standardizations for all 500 detailed occupations and not grouped any, we would likely have explained even more of the marital status differences in work schedule rates.

12. For the 5.5% of currently married mothers, the 6.6% of formerly married mothers, and the 5.6% of never married mothers who are multiple job holders, we use the characteristics of their principal job. That is, the private/government sector, industry, occupation, and schedule for these women refer to the job where they worked the most hours during the reference week.

13. This classification is based on one created by Singlemann and Tienda (1985); precise definitions for categorizing Census Bureau industries into these groups were provided by J. Singlemann (personal communication, June 16, 1994). Our definition differs in that we group extractive and transformative industries together, as there are too few never married mothers in extractive industries to include them separately in the regression.

14. We restrict the analysis to the six most common detailed occupations of never married mothers and group the remaining because of small sample sizes in the cells of less common detailed occupations.

15. Whether industry affects never married mothers' employment schedules the most and currently married mothers' schedules the least, however, cannot be determined with this analysis.

16. As with industry, whether occupation affects never married mothers' employment schedules the most and currently married mothers' schedules the least cannot be determined with this analysis.

17. Although an earlier study using the same data set did find that education significantly lowers the likelihood of working nonstandard schedules (Presser, 1995), the sample size in that study was 4 to 44 times as large as the three samples in our study, making statistical significance in general a more frequent occurrence.

18. The CPS asks the main reason for working nonstandard hours, but not the main reason for working nonstandard days. This analysis is therefore limited to hourly schedule. In addition, respondents were asked their main reason for working nonstandard hours only if they reported that they work nonstandard hours, restricting the samples to the 573 never married mothers, 1,425 formerly married mothers, and 6,838 currently married mothers who work other than fixed days.

19. Data not shown.

20. The CPS includes a school enrollment question but unfortunately asks it only of respondents under age 25. As a result, we cannot analyze more rigorously the extent to which school enrollment is a determinant of nonstandard schedules for these mothers.

REFERENCES

Bianchi, S. M. (1995). The changing demographic and socioeconomic characteristics of single parent families. *Marriage and Family Review, 20,* 71-97.

Bielby, W. T., & Bielby, D. D. (1992). I will follow him: Family ties, gender-role beliefs, and reluctance to relocate for a better job. *American Journal of Sociology, 97,* 1241-1267.

Brayfield, A. A., Deich, S. G., & Hofferth, S. L. (1993). *Caring for children in low-income families: A substudy of the National Child Care Survey, 1990* (Urban Institute Report 93-2). Washington, DC: Urban Institute Press.

Carpentier, J., & Cazamian, P. (1977). *Night work: Its effects on the health and welfare of the worker.* Geneva: International Labour Office.

Casper, L. M. (1993). Who's minding the kids? Child care arrangements: Fall 1991. U.S. Bureau of the Census, *Current Population Reports,* Series P70-36.

Clinton, H. (1996). Speech to the Democratic National Convention in Chicago. At http://www.dncc96.org/day2/speeches/t53.html on June 25, 1997.

Cotter, D. A., DeFiore, J., Hermsen, J. M., Kowalewski, B. M., & Vanneman, R. (1998). The demand for female labor. *American Journal of Sociology, 103,* 1673-1712.

Coverman, S., & Kemp, A. A. (1987). The labor supply of female heads of household: Comparisons with male heads and wives. *Sociological Inquiry, 57,* 32-53.

Cox, A. G. (1994). *The effects of occupation and family structure on employment schedules: A focus on single mothers.* Master's thesis, Department of Sociology, University of Maryland, College Park.

England, P., Farkas, G., Kilbourne, B., & Dou, T. (1988). Explaining occupational sex segregation and wages: Findings from a model with fixed effects. *American Sociological Review, 53,* 544-558.

Finn, P. (1981, October). The effects of shift work on the lives of employees. *Monthly Labor Review, 104,* 31-34.

Garfinkel, I., & McLanahan, S. S. (1986). *Single mothers and their children: A new American dilemma.* Washington, DC: Urban Institute Press.

Hedges, J. N., & Sekscenski, E. S. (1979, September). Workers on late shifts in a changing economy. *Monthly Labor Review, 102,* 14-22.

Johnson, B. L., & Waldman, E. (1983). Most women who maintain families receive poor labor market returns. *Monthly Labor Review, 106,* 30-34.

King, A. G. (1978). Industrial structure, the flexibility of working hours, and women's labor force participation. *Review of Economics and Statistics, 60,* 399-407.

Leibowitz, A., Waite, L. J., & Witsberger, C. (1988). Child care for preschoolers: Differences by children's age. *Demography, 25,* 205-220.

Lester, G. H. (1991). Child support and alimony: 1989. U.S. Bureau of the Census, *Current Population Reports,* Series P-60, No.173.

McLanahan, S., & Casper, L. (1995). Growing diversity and inequality in the American family. In R. Farley (Ed.), *State of the union: America in the 1990's: Vol. II. Social trends* (pp. 1-45). New York: Russell Sage.

Mellor, F. F. (1986, November). Shift work and flexitime: How prevalent are they? *Monthly Labor Review, 109:* 14-21.

Presser, H. B. (1984). Job characteristics of spouses and their work shifts. *Demography, 21,* 575-589.

Presser, H. B. (1986). Shift work among American women and child care. *Journal of Marriage and the Family, 48,* 551-563.

Presser, H. B. (1988). Shift work and child care among young dual-earner American parents. *Journal of Marriage and the Family, 50,* 133-148.

Presser, H. B. (1989a). Can we make time for children? The economy, work schedules, and child care. *Demography, 26,* 523-543.

Presser, H. B. (1989b). Some economic complexities of child care provided by grandmothers. *Journal of Marriage and the Family, 51,* 581-591.

Presser, H. B. (1995). Job, family, and gender: Determinants of nonstandard work schedules among employed Americans in 1991. *Demography, 32,* 577-598.

Presser, H. B., & Cox, A. G. (1997, April). The employment schedules of low-educated American women and welfare reform. *Monthly Labor Review,* pp. 26-35.

Saluter, A. F. (1993). Marital status and living arrangements: March 1992. U.S. Bureau of the Census, *Current Population Reports,* Series P20-468.

Singlemann, J., & Tienda, M. (1985). The process of occupational change in a service society: The case of the United States, 1960-1980. In B. Roberts, R. Finnegan, & D. Gallie (Eds.), *New approaches to economic life* (pp. 48-67). Manchester, UK: Manchester University Press.

Smith, J. (1984). The paradox of women's poverty: Wage-earning women and economic transformation. *Signs: Journal of Women in Culture and Society, 10,* 291-310.

Smith, S. J. (1986, November). The growing diversity of work schedules. *Monthly Labor Review, 109,* 7-13.

Sylvestri, G. T. (1995, November). Occupational employment to 2005. *Monthly Labor Review,* pp. 60-84.

U.S. Bureau of the Census. (1992). *Statistical abstract of the United States: 1992* (112th ed.). Washington, DC: Government Printing Office.

U.S. Congress. (1991). *Biological rhythms: Implications for the worker.* Office of Technology Assessment, OTA-BA-463. Washington, DC: Government Printing Office.

Wetzel, J. R. (1995). Labor force, unemployment and earnings. In R. Farley (Ed.), *State of the union: America in the 1990's: Vol. I. Economic trends* (pp. 59-105). New York: Russell Sage.

Women's Bureau. (1995). *Care around the clock: Developing child care resources before nine and after five.* Washington, DC: U.S. Department of Labor.

CHAPTER 5

Effects of Public and Private Policies on Working After Childbirth

SANDRA L. HOFFERTH

The increase in women's labor force participation over the past 50 years has been dramatic. Between 1940 and 1994, the participation rate of women in the U.S. labor force increased from 27% to 58%. Between 1970 and 1992 alone, the proportion of married mothers with preschool children in the labor force doubled from 30% to 62% (Bureau of Labor Statistics, 1995). However, the most dramatic increase of all has been in the labor force participation of mothers of infants. Using data from the Survey of Income and Program Participation (SIPP), O'Connell (1990) showed that whereas only about 14% of mothers with newborns who had their first baby in 1961-1965 were working by the time the child was 6 months old (increasing to 17% by the twelfth month), 44% of new mothers in 1981-1984 were working 6 months after childbirth, increasing to 53% by the twelfth month. By the mid-

AUTHOR'S NOTE: From "Effects of Public and Private Policies on Working After Childbirth," by Sandra L. Hofferth, November 1996, *Work and Occupations, 23*(4), pp. 378-404. © Copyright 1996 Sage Publications, Inc.

Helpful comments from Liset van Dijk, John Marcotte, and Duncan Chaplin are gratefully acknowledged.

1980s, this proportion had risen to 53% by the sixth month and 61% by the twelfth month (Joesch, 1994). In 1994, 56% of married mothers of infants were in the labor force (Bureau of Labor Statistics, 1995).

Over the same period, employers increased their family benefits, and numerous states passed parental leave legislation. There has been a dramatic growth in employer-provided benefits since the late 1970s. According to private surveys of employers, in 1978, only 110 employers provided child care support; by 1995, over 6,000 employers provided such assistance (The Conference Board, 1988; Families and Work Institute, personal communication, 1995).

This chapter examines the link between state and employer policies and the employment behavior of mothers of infants. We first discuss previous research on working after childbirth, the development and expansion of employer and state policies, and our framework for why such policies should affect maternal employment behavior. We then discuss the data, the variables, and the statistical methods and present the results.

Previous Research on Working After Childbirth

Several previous studies have looked at factors associated with the timing of maternal employment following childbirth. How quickly new mothers enter or reenter employment depends upon work patterns during pregnancy and financial need. Working during pregnancy predicted earlier entry into employment. Of those who worked sometime during pregnancy, 56% were back within 6 months (O'Connell, 1990). Of those who continued working until 1 month of a birth, 71% returned within 6 months. These figures are not surprising, because women who work during pregnancy and close to the time of the birth are more attached to their jobs than are those who do not work during pregnancy. They tend to be older, White, and more educated as well. In contrast to the characteristics of those who work during pregnancy, those who are most likely to be working soon after the birth are Black women, women with premarital first births, and teenagers (O'Connell, 1990). It is likely that these latter women depend on their own earnings to keep their families solvent. Clearly, financial need is an important factor in working soon after a birth. Another study of the determinants of women's employment after first childbirth, using the National Longitudinal Survey of Youth (NLSY), found that higher wage mothers worked sooner, but that those with higher other family incomes delayed their return to work longer after birth (Leibowitz, Klerman, & Waite, 1992). Because they affect the speed of working after childbirth differently, it is important to distinguish between the mother's earnings or human capital and other family income. Finally, little work has examined the impact of the availability of maternity leave and other benefits in determining how soon mothers work after childbirth. In the SIPP study (O'Connell, 1990), recipients of maternity leave benefits worked sooner than those who did not receive such benefits. That study did not ask, however, who had such benefits available but did not take advantage of them. Thus we cannot conclude that availability of benefits affects how soon mothers enter the workforce after childbirth.

Conceptual Framework

The theoretical model is based upon the new home economics framework of Becker (1965, 1991). This framework assumes that the goal of individuals and families is to maximize the consumption of goods and services, given resource constraints. It implies that the employment decision of a mother will be based upon a comparison of the value of her market time (her wage rate, net of child care expenses, and accumulated human capital—education, job skills, seniority, and experience; Desai & Waite, 1991; Joesch, 1994; Leibowitz et al., 1992) with the value of her time at home (the reservation wage).[1] The opportunity cost of not working is the wage forgone plus the depreciation of skills due to the time off from work and any future reduction in earnings due to this time out of work. The opportunity cost of working is the loss in investment in the home and child due to time spent outside the home. A mother will work outside the home when the value of her market time or earnings is greater than the value of her home time.

The relative costs and benefits of employment and time at home depend upon the ages of children (Leibowitz et al., 1992). Even if a new mother could find someone to care for her newborn, the cost of such care would be high (the opportunity cost of the father equals his net wage, for example). Thus, after having a baby, the value of a mother's home time is greater than her market wage, so she remains home. However, as the child ages, the need for her time and attention declines, alternative caregivers become feasible and affordable, and the value of her time at home may decline relative to the value of her time at work. Other factors that affect this decision vary from family to family, so two mothers with the same wage level will not necessarily return to work at the same time. For example, age and race may proxy tastes or preferences for working outside the home versus inside the home.

The process of entry into work after childbirth varies from mother to mother. After the birth, the value of the mother's home time gradually declines and the value of her market time increases. When the value of market time exceeds the value of home time, she may wish to return to the market for a few hours. Unfortunately, work often comes only in a fixed full-time schedule. If so, a mother may have to stay home until the market wage exceeds the reservation wage by enough to balance the substantial loss of home time and the cost of working full-time. Many mothers prefer to work part-time first when they enter the workforce after the birth of a child. For them, moving back into the workforce may occur in two stages—a return to a part-time schedule followed by a shift to full-time work. For some, the choices are part-time or no work; if they cannot work part-time, they will not work at all. Others will first work full-time either because they cannot find part-time work and they need the money, or because they are committed to their work. The availability of alternative schedules should be crucial in determining how quickly mothers return to work and whether they return part-time or full-time.

Previous research has found the opportunity structures and normative climates in communities to affect individuals' social, economic, and psychological costs of engaging or not engaging in certain behaviors (Billy & Moore, 1992). We were specifically interested in two important area characteristics: employment opportunities and the normative climate regarding the appropriate behavior of young mothers. The county unemployment rate in 1986 proxies the demand for labor in the local labor market prior to measurement of return to work.[2] We expected that areas of greater unemployment would have mothers who take longer in entering employment following childbirth because their employment opportunities would be limited. We used the 1987 county income per capita, a proxy for affluence of the area, and suburban residence as measures of a normative climate more favorable to mothers staying at home with young children. Because of the hypothesized greater value of home time to wealthier families and the ability of such families to afford one parent staying home, the higher the county income per capita, the more it may be accepted that mothers will remain at home during much of the first year after childbirth. Many families choose a suburban residence over an urban one because of a family-centered lifestyle; in such families, mothers should be more likely to stay home longer after childbirth.

Hypotheses Regarding the Effects
of Public and Private Policies

The availability, quality, and cost of substitutes for the mother's time, characteristics of the family and community, and public and private policies affect the value of both market and home time. They can act to alter entry into the workforce in two ways: they may reduce the cost and increase the benefit of working relative to staying home, thereby raising the effective wage, or they may reduce the cost and raise the benefit of staying home relative to going to work, thereby raising the reservation wage.

State Policies and Regulations. Access to state policies that reduce the cost of working may affect mothers' employment. These include higher expenditures for children's programs, which should reduce the price, increase the quality, and increase the availability of substitute arrangements and programs, thus making employment more attractive. Policies that reduce the cost of staying home should cause mothers to remain home longer. Such policies include the availability of state-mandated parental leave, with or without pay, and the availability of higher welfare benefits to those who are eligible (Moffitt, 1992). Finally, strict regulations have offsetting effects—they may increase quality but reduce supply and increase costs (Gormley, 1991; Hofferth & Chaplin, 1995; Phillips, Lande, & Goldberg, 1990).

Public and Private Sector Employer Policies. The second set of policies are employer benefits regarding work and family life. Mothers who have access to benefits through their employer that reduce the cost and increase the benefit of staying home will take longer to work following childbirth than those without access to such benefits. Parental leave is the clearest example. This relationship should be stronger if the leave is paid.

Mothers who have access to employer-sponsored benefits that help parents balance work and family life by reducing the cost and increasing the benefit of working will return sooner than those who do not have access to such benefits. Employers may offer workplace child care, part-time work, liberal unpaid leave, a flexible spending account to help the employee pay for care, flexible schedules, or a cafeteria benefit plan where one benefit the employee does not want can be traded for another that the employee does want. Having access to part-time work increases employment because mothers can gradually increase their labor market time as the value of their at-home time declines. A flexible schedule and liberal leave make the management of work and family life easier.

Although parents who have greater need (lower income) will work sooner than employees with higher incomes, if they have access to employer benefits they may work even sooner because the benefits of working are higher. That is, we hypothesize a significant interaction between income and the effect of benefit policies.

Characteristics of the Child Care Market. Finally, the characteristics of the local child care market—the availability, price, and quality of care in the area—may affect the rate of maternal employment after childbirth because they reduce the cost of working or increase the benefit of staying home. Mothers living in areas with a greater supply of child care centers and family day care are expected to work sooner, like mothers with access to other adults either in the home or nearby who could care for their child. Mothers who live in a community in which child care is less expensive will be likely to work sooner than mothers who live in an area in which child care is more expensive. Mothers living in areas of higher quality child care should work sooner than other mothers, because they would be less concerned about the quality of care their child would receive. All three factors reduce the cost and increase the benefit of working.

DATA

These hypotheses are examined on a sample of all mothers who had a birth in the year before the survey. Data come from the National Child Care Survey 1990, A Profile of Child Care Settings, and a contextual data file.

National Child Care Survey 1990

The National Child Care Survey 1990 (NCCS) is a nationally representative survey of households with children under age 13, funded by the National Association for the Education of Young Children and the Administration for Children, Youth, and Families (Hofferth, Brayfield, Deich, & Holcomb, 1991). A nationally representative survey of households with children under age 13 was fielded by Abt Associates from November 1989 through May 1990. Of the families surveyed, 1,679 of these families had a youngest child under age 3, 1,092 had a youngest child 3 to 5 years old, and 1,621 had a youngest child 6 to 12 years of age. Through random digit-dial techniques, 4,392 households in 100 primary sampling units (144 counties) representative of the United States were interviewed by phone using computer-assisted telephone interviewing methods. The response rate to the screener was 83%, and the response rate to the survey was 69%, making the overall response rate to the survey 57%. Based upon the Current Population Survey, weights were computed that adjust for differential response rates as well as differential coverage rates due to households without telephones. Because of concern for potential bias, estimates of key variables from the NCCS were compared with estimates from the 1988 and 1991 waves of the Survey of Income and Program Participation and from the 1988 Child Health Supplement to the National Household Interview Survey (Hofferth et al., 1991, Appendix B). Based upon these comparisons, the results of the NCCS appear to be unbiased.

For the present study, the 613 women who had borne a child within the year prior to the interview were selected. The NCCS obtained a detailed employment history for both parents over the year before the survey date. A 1-year period was selected to minimize reporting errors due to the length of period of recall. Respondents were asked to provide beginning and ending dates of all jobs held during this period. Because some jobs may have been in effect for several years, the incidence of missing values in the reported month and year were examined. The incidence of missing data was small, with the respondent less likely to provide the month of the event than the year. As expected, the more time that had passed since the event, the less likely the respondent was to report the month.

Finally, the NCCS asked a set of questions about employer benefits, including parental leave. Respondents who were employed or whose spouse was employed at the time of the survey were asked a series of questions about the availability of a variety of employer benefits at either their or their spouse's workplace.[3] These included child care at the workplace, a flexible (pretax) spending account, a cafeteria benefit plan, vouchers for child care, an information and referral system, flexible scheduling (flex-time), liberal unpaid leave, part-time work, and work at home. This analysis examines the effect of whether or not the mother reported access to an employer-provided benefit on employment behavior following childbirth.

A Profile of Child Care Settings

The objective of A Profile of Child Care Settings (PCS) was to obtain national estimates of the level and characteristics of early childhood programs available in 1989-1990 for young children through telephone interviews with a representative sample of early education and child care providers (Kisker, Hofferth, Phillips, & Farquhar, 1991). The sampling frame consisted of all regulated and nonregulated preschool programs and regulated family day care homes. A survey of providers was fielded by Mathematica Policy Research from October 1989 through February 1990. Using computer-assisted telephone interviewing methods, interviews were conducted with 2,089 center directors and 583 family day care providers in 144 counties representative of the United States. The response rates for the PCS study were high. Interviews were conducted with 89% of center programs and 87% of home-based providers eligible for the study. Comparisons with other data show the results to be representative of licensed and registered center-based and home-based care in the United States in 1990. The PCS survey obtained detailed information on general administrative characteristics, admission policies, enrollment size, fees and subsidies, staffing, curriculum and activities, health and safety, and operating experiences and expenses. Both the NCCS and the PCS share the same first-stage sample.

In the present study, the NCCS was the source of data on the employment history of mothers with children under 1 year of age in 1990. The PCS was the source of data on the availability and quality of the center-based and regulated family day care homes in each community in which these children lived.

Contextual Data File

Using data from the U.S. Bureau of the Census (1988), the median income per capita and unemployment rate in each of the 144 counties in the NCCS and PCS were compiled. To develop the lists of providers in each county from which the PCS obtained its sample required calling officials at the state and the county level. Information was compiled on state regulations regarding staff qualifications, group size, staff/child ratios, parental involvement, health and safety, space, liability insurance, and inspections for centers and family day care. The ratio of centers and family day care homes to 1,000 preschool children in the county was obtained from the actual count of programs. Finally, information on state policies regarding parental leave, welfare benefits, and state expenditures on children was obtained from published sources (Adams & Sandfort, 1992; Bond, Galinsky, Lord, Staines, & Brown, 1991; Center for Policy Alternatives, 1992; Committee on Ways and Means, 1992; Finn-Stevenson & Trzcinski, 1990).

METHOD

The Hazard Model

This analysis focuses on the decision to work or remain at home made by 613 mothers during the first year after the birth of a child. We modeled this process using a proportional hazards model. The hazard model allows us to estimate the rate at which mothers enter the workforce based upon their characteristics, those of their family, characteristics of the community, and public and private policies such as access to leave and child care.

From the date of birth of the youngest child and dates of employment in the last year, we calculated the length of time before mothers started working after a birth if mothers changed jobs or were not previously employed.[4] If they remained at the same job, we calculated length of leave from a separate question that asked mothers the amount of maternity leave they took. This allows us to establish the rate at which mothers entered or reentered the workforce. Similar to multiple regression analysis, the hazard model estimates the simultaneous influence of a number of covariates on the rate of entering employment. Unlike standard regression analysis, the hazard model can easily incorporate censored observations (i.e., mothers who, by the time data were collected, had not yet returned to work). Because our interest is in the effects of the covariates rather than in the functional form or actual value of the hazard, we used Cox's (1972) proportional hazards model. The advantage of the proportional hazards model is that the distribution of the hazard does not need to be specified. Because this model is in wide use today, only a brief description is presented here (see Menken, Trussell, Stempel, & Babakol, 1981, and Teachman, 1982, for detailed discussions).

The particular form used for the rate of working after childbirth is the following:

$$h_j(t;X) = h_o(t)\exp(XB), \text{ and } h_j(t;X)/h_o(t) = \exp(XB) \qquad (5.1)$$

where:

$h_j(t;X)$ is the hazard for a particular time t, a particular event j, and a particular set of covariates;

$h_o(t)$ is the baseline hazard function for a particular t and event j;

t indexes months since birth;

B is a vector of parameters;

and X is a vector of covariates such as family income and race.

The hazard at duration t is the product of an underlying hazard for a baseline or reference group and the covariates $\exp(XB)$. $\exp(XB)$ represents the ratio of the hazard of the category to the underlying hazard. If there are no co-variates, $XB = 0$ and the ratio of hazards equals 1. When covariates are cate-gorical, e^b for a category of a covariate is interpreted as the relative risk of the outcome for that category compared with the omitted category ($e^0 = 1$). When continuous, e^b represents the relative risk of the outcome for a one-unit change in the independent variable. Risk ratios are calculated and presented in tables along with the coefficients and standard errors.[5]

Evaluation of the Proportional
Hazards Assumption

The assumption of proportionality implies that the shift in the hazard rate due to covariates is proportional throughout the duration of observation (Allison, 1984; Yamaguchi, 1991). To establish whether this assumption holds, we conducted several tests. For those variables that we thought might vary over time in their effects, we plotted the log of length of time before working against the log ($-\log[S(t)]$) for several categories of our independent variables as a test for proportionality (Allison, 1984). The plots suggested de-parture from proportionality for working during pregnancy. Consequently, we included a term for the interaction between working during pregnancy and time in our model:

$$[XB]_2 = [XB]_1 + b(z) + c(zt) \tag{5.2}$$

where z is whether worked during pregnancy. In so doing, we control for whether the mother worked during pregnancy and permit the relationship be-tween working during pregnancy and time to employment after childbirth to vary over time.[6] The coefficients b and c proved to be highly significant in our analyses.

Separate Models

To test whether the assumption of similar coefficients for mothers who worked and who did not work during pregnancy was reasonable, we also di-vided the sample by whether the mother worked during pregnancy and com-puted separate hazard models for the two groups. This method allows both the baseline hazard rate and the coefficients to vary without restrictions across the two groups.[7]

Competing Risk Hazard Model

As discussed earlier, we expected that factors that affect whether a mother first works part-time might differ from factors that affect whether she first works full-time. This we modeled using a competing risk framework in which separate hazard models were created for first working part-time and for first working full-time after a birth.[8]

Suppose there are m different types of events, $j_1 \ldots {}_m$. If the occurrence of one type removes the individual from the risk of the other types of events, then each event can be considered a separate hazard model and the sum of the hazards of the separate events equals the hazard of any event occurring (Allison, 1984). To calculate this competing risk or *type-specific* hazard model, individuals are considered to be censored either at the end of observation with no events or at the point of any event other than the one being modeled. In the model for return to work, mothers, who by the survey date have not yet begun working for the first time after the birth are censored. In addition, mothers who first worked part-time after birth, are censored at that time in the model for first working full-time, and mothers who first worked full-time are censored at that time for first working part-time after the birth.

RESULTS

Survival Functions

Kaplan-Meier estimates of the survival function based upon the NCCS weighted to the U.S. population were calculated. About 64% of mothers who had a baby in the previous year were still at home at 3 months, 56% at 6 months, half at 9 months, and 48% at 1 year after birth (Figure 5.1). That is, 36% were working within 3 months, 44% within 6 months, half within 9 months, and 52% within 1 year of the birth.

Working During Pregnancy. In the NCCS, about half of mothers (53%) worked during pregnancy. Mothers who were employed during pregnancy moved into the labor force at a much faster pace than those who did not work during pregnancy. Of mothers who worked during pregnancy, 65% were back within 3 months, 73% within 6 months, and 83% within 1 year. Among mothers who did not work during pregnancy, 7% were back within 3 months, 16% within 6 months, and 24% within 1 year.[9]

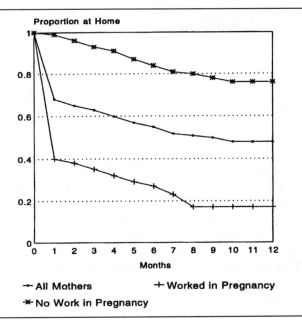

Figure 5.1. Survival Function for Return to Work by Work in Pregnancy

Summary Statistics. The means and standard deviations for all the variables used in the hazards models are presented in Table 5.1. These are not weighted, because our hazards models were conducted using unweighted data. There are a few differences between weighted and unweighted means. Because weights were used to correct for the underrepresentation of low-income families, the population has a slightly higher proportion of low-income families (15%) and Black families (16%) than the unweighted sample (13% and 12%, respectively). The population is slightly more Western and slightly less Midwestern than the sample.

Hazard Models

According to the theoretical framework, the value of the mother's time should be an important factor in the rapidity with which she entered the workforce following childbirth. The mother's wage is an indicator of the value of her time. Because not all mothers were employed at the time of the survey, a predicted wage was calculated for those with no wages based upon the ordinary least squares regression of the wages of mothers who reported wages at the survey on a series of background factors, including age, education, work experience, work experience squared, race, partner status, other household income, number of children, regional dummies, metro residence, per capita income in the county, and county unemployment rate.[10]

We first ran the models with and without employment during pregnancy to test its contribution. In the first column of Table 5.2, we present the model of working after childbirth for all mothers without any of the policy variables and excluding the variable "working during pregnancy." The second column adds working during pregnancy and the interaction between working during pregnancy and time. Columns 3 and 4 show the same model for mothers who worked and who did not work during pregnancy, respectively.

Column 1 shows that several background variables are associated with working soon after childbirth. As expected, younger, more educated mothers with fewer children and more job experience work sooner after childbirth than do other mothers. Each year of education increases the relative risk of working by 8%.[11]

Each year of age reduces the risk of working by 4%. Each additional year of work experience raises the risk of working by 16%. However, the negative coefficient on work experience squared suggests that the effect of tenure is nonlinear, declining at higher levels of experience. As expected, mothers living in families with higher income other than their own earnings did not return to work as rapidly after childbirth as mothers living in families with lower incomes. Each additional $1,000 in other family income reduced the risk of working by about 1%. The effect of the mother's wage on working is not statistically significant. Each additional child reduced the probability of working soon after childbirth by 14%. Finally, mothers living in areas of high unemployment did not work as quickly after childbirth as mothers living in areas of lower unemployment.

In the second column, working during pregnancy and the interaction between working during pregnancy and time are added. Working during pregnancy is highly related to working soon after birth. A mother who worked during pregnancy had a risk of returning more than 12 times that of someone who did not work during pregnancy. In addition, the large and significant interaction term coefficient suggests that the effect of working during pregnancy declines sharply over time.

Many of the effects of the other variables are no longer significant. This is because variables such as age, work experience, and number of children

TABLE 5.1 Descriptive Statistics for Variables Used in the Analysis

Variable	Mean	Standard Deviation
Control variable		
Black (non-Hispanic)	0.124	0.330
Hispanic	0.072	0.258
Education of mother (years)	13.311	2.208
Two parents (1 = yes)	0.865	0.342
Mother's hourly wage	11.770	9.541
Other family income than mother's (in thousands)	32.428	24.404
Age of mother	27.848	5.354
Mother's work experience (years)	7.631	5.358
Work experience squared	86.890	101.743
Number of children < 13	1.812	0.909
Northeast	0.202	0.402
West	0.176	0.381
Midwest	0.281	0.450
Central city	0.444	0.497
Suburb	0.307	0.461
Per capita income in county (in thousands)	15.587	3.854
Unemployment rate in county	6.994	2.966
Worked during pregnancy	0.563	0.496
Benefit availability		
State has parental leave law	0.305	0.461
Proportion whose employer offers:		
Liberal unpaid leave	0.215	0.411
Cafeteria benefit plan	0.049	0.216
Flexible spending account	0.091	0.288
Flex-time	0.157	0.364
Part-time work	0.274	0.446
Information and referral	0.062	0.241
Work at home	0.069	0.253
Workplace child care	0.078	0.269
Mother took maternity leave	0.083	0.276
Mother took paid maternity leave	0.020	0.141
Availability of substitutes		
Other adult in household	0.055	0.229
Relative lives nearby	0.514	0.500
Ratio of centers per 1,000 preschool children in county	5.475	3.278
Ratio of family day care homes per 1,000 preschool children in county	9.807	10.123
State expenditures per child on early childhood services	42.262	29.751

TABLE 5.1 Continued

Variable	Mean	Standard Deviation
Quality and price of child care in county		
Family day care—Child/staff ratio	5.468	1.703
Center—Child/staff ratio	8.596	1.195
Family day care—Provider trained?	0.548	0.341
Center—Provider trained?	0.787	0.117
Family day care—Group size	4.914	2.739
Center—Group size	15.976	2.327
Family day care—Average hourly fee	1.462	0.462
Center—Average hourly fee	1.611	0.485
Income		
Aid to Families with Dependent Children (1 = yes, 0 = no)	0.113	0.317
Poor (1 = yes, 0 = no)	0.125	0.331
Near poor (between 100% and 125% of poverty)	0.139	0.346
Maximum AFDC benefit for a family of three in state	405.677	115.127
State regulations		
Are family day care homes regulated?	0.949	0.219
Family day care—Is training required?	0.338	0.473
Center—Is training required?	0.855	0.353
Family day care—Child/staff ratio for 2-year-old	3.605	1.796
Center—Child/staff ratio for 2-year-old	7.376	2.927

affect whether a mother works during pregnancy (not shown). Once working during pregnancy is controlled, these variables are no longer significant. The remaining maternal characteristic that is significantly associated with return to work is other family income. The risk of returning to work, for mothers in families with higher other income, was significantly lower than the risk of mothers with low other income. Each $1,000 in other earnings reduced the risk of working by about 1%. Income had both a direct negative effect on working during pregnancy (not shown) as well as a direct negative effect on working in the year following a birth. Finally, both a higher per capita income in the county and a higher unemployment rate reduced the risk of working within the first year. Presumably, families that live in a more prosperous area may place a greater value on work at home than those in less prosperous

TABLE 5.2 Effects of Demographic Variables on Risk of Working in Year After Childbirth

	All Mothers				Worked During Pregnancy		Did Not Work During Pregnancy	
	Model 1	Risk Ratio	Model 2	Risk Ratio	Model 3	Risk Ratio	Model 4	Risk Ratio
Black	-.015 (.219)		.028 (.221)		.158 (.238)		-.290 (.626)	
Hispanic	.004 (.260)		-.006 (.260)		.056 (.279)		-.046 (.777)	
Education of mother	.080 (.040)*	1.083	.050 (.039)		.037 (.042)		.132 (.124)	
Two parents	-.077 (.224)		-.027 (.228)		.040 (.250)		-.820 (.599)	
Mother's wage	.001 (.011)		.002 (.010)		.004 (.009)		-.069 (.071)	
Other income	-.011 (.004)**	.989	-.008 (.004)*	.992	-.008 (.004)†	.992	.010 (.019)	
Age of mother	-.044 (.023)†	.957	-.017 (.022)		.005 (.025)		-.077 (.059)	
Work experience	.152 (.044)***	1.164	.040 (.042)		.049 (.046)		.054 (.116)	
Work experience squared	-.004 (.002)†	.996	-.001 (.002)		-.002 (.002)		-.000 (.006)	
Number of children	-.149 (.089)†	.862	.001 (.085)		.049 (.091)		-.218 (.258)	
Central city	.123 (.187)		.229 (.190)		.296 (.209)		-.497 (.491)	
Suburb	-.183 (.188)		-.152 (.189)		-.101 (.210)		-.837 (.463)†	.433
Per capita income	-.039 (.025)		-.050 (.025)*	.951	-.039 (.028)		-.098 (.071)	
Unemployment rate	-.064 (.029)*	.938	-.074 (.029)*	.929	-.050 (.032)		-.217 (.082)**	.805
Worked during pregnancy			2.543 (.324)***	12.712				
Worked during pregnancy × Time	-1.116		-1.116 (.256)***	.328				
N	541		541		320		221	
-2 log L	3,016		2,867		2,419		318	
Chi square (df)	59 (14)		208 (16)		14ns (14)		23† (14)	

NOTE: Standard errors in parentheses. ns = not significant.

† p < .10; * p < .05; ** p < .01; *** p < .001.

areas, and those in an area of high unemployment who did not work during pregnancy may not be able to work as soon after birth because they cannot find jobs.

The first two models include mothers who did not work during pregnancy as well as those who did. Model 3 shows the results just for mothers who worked during pregnancy. The only variable that remains significant after this adjustment is other family income. The risk of returning to work among mothers who worked during pregnancy was marginally lower for mothers in families with higher other family incomes. No other factors approach statistical significance. In Model 4, which only includes mothers who did not work during pregnancy, the only two variables related to work after childbirth are living in the suburbs and the unemployment rate. Mothers living in the suburbs entered the workforce after childbirth more slowly than mothers living in rural areas. This variable may proxy a greater value placed on work at home while children are very young. Finally, in areas with greater levels of unemployment, the rate of entry to work following childbirth was significantly reduced. This did not so affect mothers who worked during pregnancy, suggesting that the local labor market opportunity structure only affects those without prior attachment.[12] Even though there is little evidence that the models are significantly different, prior labor force attachment is so important that it reduces the significance of almost all the other variables. Consequently, we separated the sample by employment status during pregnancy and conducted separate analyses of the effects of policy variables. We focused on the effects of public and employer policies upon return to work after childbirth among mothers who worked during pregnancy: Because they already had a job, such mothers should be most affected in returning to work by such policies. A larger set of individual-level factors affect the decision to work after childbirth, but their influence is mediated by labor force attachment.

Effects of Policy Variables Among Mothers Who Worked During Pregnancy

Months from birth until return to work or censoring were regressed separately upon each set of policy variables separated by blank lines, controlling for the variables in Model 3, Table 5.2. Table 5.3 shows the coefficients for the policy variables entered a set at a time. The effects of the control variables are the same over all models; consequently, we have not presented their coefficients for each of the separate regressions.

TABLE 5.3 Effects of Policy Variables on Risk of Returning to Work, Mothers Who Worked in Pregnancy

	Parameter Estimate	Standard Error	Risk Ratio
State has parental leave law	.142	(.165)	1.153
Mother took maternity leave	−.073	(.261)	.930
Mother took paid maternity leave	.028	(.394)	1.028
Employer offers:			
Liberal unpaid leave	.216	(.181)	1.241
Cafeteria benefit plan	.119	(.335)	1.127
Flexible spending account	.218	(.255)	1.244
Flex-time	.067	(.220)	1.069
Information and referral	.120	(.291)	1.127
Work at home	.233	(.264)	1.263
Workplace child care	.180	(.220)	1.198
Part-time work	.478	(.168)	1.612**
Interactions:			
Liberal unpaid leave	.575	(.155)	1.777***
Liberal leave × Poverty	.088	(1.149)	1.092
Poverty status	.349	(.330)	1.417
Flexible spending account	.494	(.231)	1.638*
Spending account × Poverty	0	(0)	
Poverty status	.215	(.319)	1.240
Child care at workplace	.316	(.218)	1.371
Workplace child care × Poverty	.274	(1.100)	1.315
Poverty	.172	(.325)	1.188
Part-time work	.674	(.149)	1.962***
Part-time work × Poverty	−.307	(.680)	.735
Poverty	.366	(.360)	1.442
Availability:			
Other adult in household	.280	(.312)	1.324
Relative lives nearby that could care for child	.191	(.145)	1.211
Ratio of number of centers to number of preschool children in county	.009	(.026)	1.009
Ratio of family day care to number of preschool children in county	.003	(.008)	1.003
State expenditures per child	.0007	(.002)	1.001
Quality and price:			
Family day care child/staff ratio	−.020	(.065)	.980
Center child/staff ratio	−.013	(.078)	.987
Center teacher trained	.557	(.711)	1.745
Family day care teacher trained	−.035	(.309)	.966

TABLE 5.3 Continued

	Parameter Estimate	Standard Error	Risk Ratio
Center—group size	.023	(.041)	1.023
Family day care—group size	.017	(.054)	1.017
Family day care—average hourly fee	−.006	(.228)	.994
Center—average hourly fee	.013	(.270)	1.013
State regulations:			
Are family day care homes regulated?	.843	(.577)	2.323
Family day care—is training required?	−.013	(.148)	.987
Center—is training required?	−.273	(.235)	.761
Family day care—child/staff ratio for 2-year-old	.044	(.060)	1.045
Center—child/staff ratio for 2-year-old	−.016	(.030)	.984
Income:			
Aid to Families with Dependent Children (AFDC)	−.700	(.387)	.496[†]
Poor	−.039	(.336)	.962
Near poor	−.578	(.285)	.561*
Maximum AFDC benefit for family of three in state	.0005	(.0005)	1.001

NOTE: [†] $p < .10$; * $p < .05$; ** $p < .01$; *** $p < .001$.

None of the state policy variables was significantly associated with the risk of returning to work soon after childbirth (Table 5.3), and no interactions between state policy and poverty status were significant (not shown). It appears that state policies do not significantly affect maternal employment behavior.

Employer policies were significantly associated with return to work. As a group, the only significant policy was the availability of part-time employment, which was associated with a faster return. Because several employer policies were correlated,[13] we also entered them one at a time into the multivariate model. Policies that were individually associated with a faster return included the availability of liberal unpaid leave, a flexible spending account, part-time work, work at home, and child care at the workplace. Work at home was strongly associated with liberal unpaid leave, so when we entered these five simultaneously in a model, work at home was no longer significant in any model and was not included in the final set of employer variables.

None of the interactions between employer policies and poverty status was statistically significant. Although the coefficients were large for several interactions, standard errors were also large, indicating that we do not have a good estimate of their effects. Consequently, we cannot draw any conclusions about differential effects of employer policies on the return to work of poor mothers compared with nonpoor mothers.

Two of the other policy variables were significantly related to return to work after childbirth. Families receiving Aid to Families with Dependent Children (AFDC) and families with incomes above but close to the poverty level were less likely to return to work soon after a birth. With all the other variables in the model, only the poverty level continued to be significantly related to return to work and that variable was retained.

Our final model is shown in Table 5.4. In this model, only the policy variables are related to how quickly mothers return to work after childbirth. Having part-time work available increased the speed of return, as does liberal leave policy. Finally, mothers in near-poor families were less likely to return to work quickly than mothers in better-off families.

Competing Risk Model for Returning to Work Part-Time or Full-Time, Mothers Who Were Employed During Pregnancy

The models for return part-time and full-time are shown in Table 5.4, along with the model for all returns to work. None of the background factors was associated with return to work at all (Columns 1 and 2). As expected, several background variables affected part-time (Columns 3 and 4) and full-time (Columns 5 and 6) return in different ways. Higher other family income reduced the risk of returning to work full-time but had no effect on returning part-time. The mother's wage had a significant positive effect on return to work part-time. Mothers with higher expected earnings returned more quickly to work on a part-time basis than mothers with lower earnings. The effect was negative but not statistically significant for return to work full-time. Thus, as hypothesized, higher income suppressed returns and higher wages increased them, but the effects only appeared when part-time and full-time returns were separated. Higher income suppressed returns full-time and higher wages increased returns part-time. This makes sense. Mothers who do not need the money as much do not need to return full-time; they may decide to return part-time. Part-time (but not full-time) work is also attractive to mothers with higher wages. Finally, the larger the number of children, the

TABLE 5.4 Effects of Demographic Variables on Risk of Returning to Work at All, Full-Time, and Part-Time, Mothers Who Worked During Pregnancy

	All Returns		Return Full-Time		Return Part-Time	
	Coefficient (Standard Error)	Risk Ratio	Coefficient (Standard Error)	Risk Ratio	Coefficient (Standard Error)	Risk Ratio
Black	.223 (.246)		.476 (.261)		−.014 (.475)	
Hispanic	−.082 (.282)		−.173 (.328)		.355 (.450)	
Education	.005 (.042)		−.014 (.051)		.032 (.064)	
Two parents	.030 (.274)		.042 (.303)		.587 (.549)	
Mother's wage	.005 (.009)		−.002 (.012)		.027 (.010)**	1.028
Other income	−.007 (.005)		−.010 (.006)†	.990	.001 (.006)	
Age of mother	−.0001 (.026)		−.317 (.327)		.011 (.036)	
Work experience	.037 (.046)		.087 (.056)		−.012 (.073)	
Work experience squared	−.001 (.002)		−.002 (.003)		−.000 (.003)	
Number of children	.084 (.092)		−.046 (.113)		.284 (.134)*	1.329
Central city	.191 (.217)		.369 (.255)		−.207 (.340)	
Suburb	−.201 (.215)		−.008 (.250)		−.225 (.320)	
Per capita income	−.021 (.028)		−.035 (.032)		−.023 (.048)	
Unemployment rate	−.044 (.033)		−.054 (.038)		−.028 (.053)	
Flexible spending account	.284 (.234)		.475 (.255)†	1.608	−.510 (.472)	
Part-time work	.474 (.165)**	1.606	.071 (.190)		1.475 (.267)***	4.374
Child care at work site	.298 (.219)		.318 (.253)		.611 (.330)†	1.842
Liberal unpaid leave	.293 (.174)†	1.340	.499 (.198)*	1.647	−.169 (.278)	
Poor	.209 (.340)		−.092 (.403)		.864 (.536)	
Near poor	−.528 (.292)†	.590	−.639 (.327)†	.528	.323 (.412)	
N	320		320		320	
−2 Log L	2,390		1,808		926	
Chi squared (df)	43 (20)		41 (20)		55 (20)	

NOTE: † $p < .10$; * $p < .05$; ** $p < .01$; *** $p < .001$.

greater the risk of returning to work part-time. The costs of working full-time are higher for such mothers.

**Effects of Employer Policies in Competing
Risk Models, Mothers Who Were
Employed During Pregnancy**

At the bottom of Table 5.4 are shown the effects of the six basic policy variables found to be significantly associated with return to work in the basic model. For all returns, mothers who had access to part-time work or liberal unpaid leave returned to work more quickly. Mothers in families that were near poor returned to work less quickly than mothers in better-off families. Policy factors were differentially associated with whether the first return to work was part-time or full-time. Having access to a flexible spending account (from which to pay for child care) and having access to liberal leave were associated with first returning to work full-time. Having access to part-time work and to child care at the work site were associated with first returning to work part-time.[14]

Although in general, as income rises, the rapidity of returning full-time declines, there is an especially low rate of return to work among mothers in near-poor families, relative to mothers in higher- or lower-income families.

DISCUSSION AND POLICY IMPLICATIONS

In this study, we found that income and employer policies—family income and the mother's own wage, and having access to part-time work, flexible spending accounts, liberal leave policies, and child care at the work site—were related to maternal rate of return to working after childbirth. These factors operate by affecting the relative value of work outside the home versus work at home caring for a young child.

Clearly, family income is an important factor in returning to work. Mothers who could rely on substantial incomes of other family members while they were on leave did not return to work as quickly as mothers living in families in which other family members had lower incomes. Mothers in families just above the poverty line had a very low risk of returning to work early, and the effects were strongest for returning on a full-time basis. For them, the benefits of staying home exceed those of working. Other research has shown that working-class mothers often have less access to benefits such as a flexible spending account or unpaid leave and to certain types of child care subsidies than do higher-income mothers. Thus they may be doubly disadvantaged (Hofferth, 1995; Miller, 1992). In addition, there is no evidence that low-income parents are more likely to use these employer benefits if they are available. Net of other family income, mothers with higher earnings returned to part-time work more quickly than mothers with lower earnings, as expected. The benefits of working are higher for those with better wage opportunities, and first returning part-time is a way many mothers find attractive to maintain their human capital and still manage to care primarily for an infant at home.

There has been considerable discussion about the part that employer benefits can play in helping mothers manage work and family life. One important employer policy that was consistently associated with return to work was the availability of part-time work. Mothers working for employers offering part-time work returned to work, particularly to part-time work, much more quickly than mothers without access to such policies. Although part-time work offers substantial short-term advantages, in the long-term, part-time work may sidetrack mothers onto the "Mommy Track," with its lower promotion, pay, and benefit opportunities (Schwartz, 1989).

A second employer policy associated with a more rapid rate of return to work, particularly full-time work after childbirth, was access to a flexible spending account. With this account, employees can pay for child care in pre-tax dollars, thus reducing their tax burden. Unfortunately, such benefits are more often available to high rather than low-income families (Hofferth et al., 1991). In the present study, no poor mothers reported having access to a flexible spending account.

A third employer policy that was associated with a more rapid rate of return to work was liberal leave. Mothers were more likely to return, particularly full-time, if their employer had a liberal unpaid leave policy. In 1993, the Family and Medical Leave Act, which mandates that firms with 50 or more employees provide unpaid parental leave in all states, was passed and signed by President Clinton (Zuckman, 1993). Our research suggests that even if the newly available leave is unpaid, it adds additional flexibility to help employees return to their jobs at their own pace.

Finally, mothers were more likely to return on a part-time (but not full-time) basis if their employer provided child care at the work site. Given that child care at the work site is center-based care and most parents prefer informal care for infants, it is likely to attract only the part-time employee. Mothers who return full-time may have contracted with a full-time sitter before birth and neither need nor want full-time care at the work site.

CONCLUSIONS

The first study to examine the effects of public and private policies on the employment patterns of American mothers after childbirth finds that mothers who have access to employer-sponsored benefits return to work sooner. Those who have access to part-time work through their employer or to child care at the work site return to work part-time sooner, and mothers who have access to a flexible spending account or liberal unpaid leave return to full-time work sooner, than mothers who do not have access to such policies. Whereas such policies operate like the proverbial carrot—by encouraging commitment to their employer or by attracting new employees—mothers who are low income are compelled by their need for income to return to work sooner and have no choice but to work full-time. Income is a consistent predictor of when a mother returns. Without income replacement, mothers from low-income families will continue to return to work sooner than those from wealthier families. High wage mothers were also more likely to return to work part-time. The opportunity cost of not working is higher for them and they can afford to compromise by working part-time. In this study, there were too few mothers who received paid leave to draw any conclusions about the impact of income replacement on return to work.

Although the data did not permit us to estimate the impact of employer-sponsored child care at the workplace with any certainty, the effects were generally consistent with mothers taking such policies into account in their employment decisions following childbirth. Greater employer flexibility in work schedules in response to maternal needs and the availability of benefits such as child care or a flexible spending account at the workplace may help new mothers. Employers who have such policies may retain employees who return sooner after childbirth or attract employees to work for them because of their benefits.

NOTES

1. The value of home time, although not directly measured, depends upon other income sources, such as the income of the husband or partner and AFDC receipt, the number of parents, and the number and ages of children. For families with children, having a nonworking mother has tended to be a normal good (Mason & Kulthau, 1989), one that can only be afforded by higher-income families. More income also raises the demand for home-produced services and the value of the time of homemakers in producing them. Thus a higher other family income increases the value of the

mother's time at home relative to time outside the home. It is expected that a higher level of mother's hourly earnings and human capital will shorten her time to work following childbirth, whereas a higher level of other family income will lengthen it. A larger number of children also increases the value of home time and should lengthen the time it takes to enter or reenter the workforce.

2. Although the actual value of unemployment may vary from year to year, the relative ranking of communities on this measure is not likely to vary much over the course of 3 years.

3. In preliminary analyses, we separated the benefits into availability at spouse's, own, both, and neither workplace. Fathers' benefits are clearly underreported. Fathers are reported to have only about half the benefits mothers report, most likely because the mother is the respondent and simply does not know what the father has available. Consequently, fathers' benefits added only slightly to the model.

4. Defining the length of leave after childbirth is not straightforward. The National Child Care Survey (NCCS) collected an employment history for both parents for the year prior to the survey. Consequently, for children born during the year before the survey, information on all jobs their mother held during that first year is available. With these unique data, we can rather accurately characterize the employment patterns after birth of mothers who change employers. Whereas in most surveys (such as the National Longitudinal Survey of Youth), it is difficult to identify maternity leave if the mother stayed with the same employer, the NCCS obtained additional information to use to determine whether a mother who stayed with the same employer took leave and when she returned to work. The NCCS asked a set of direct questions about whether the mother was on leave at the time of the survey. If not, she was asked whether she took leave at the birth of her youngest child, how much leave she took, and whether and how she was paid during that time. Mothers who did not report any time between jobs or who did not report taking any leave were assigned 2 weeks of leave (half a month). It is unlikely that these women took no leave; they simply did not report it. Assigning 2 weeks' leave permits us to test for the dependence of variables on time using a log specification (Equation 5.1) while not altering our findings.

5. The SAS procedure PHREG was used to obtain regression parameters based on the Cox proportional hazards model (SAS Institute, 1991).

6. This is the same as stratifying by whether the mother worked during pregnancy (Allison, 1984).

7. Because parents were only asked about their access to employer policies that help manage work and family life at the time of the survey, and only if they or their spouse was employed, employment is confounded with access to benefits. We do not know whether mothers who are not employed have access to employers with the same types of benefits. Consequently, the effects of employer benefits were examined using a sample of mothers who were employed at the time of the survey. A substantial proportion of mothers change jobs; consequently, the employer providing benefits at the survey date may not be the same one for whom the mother worked during pregnancy. Thus we also examined the effects of employer benefits on a subset of mothers who at

the time of the survey had been working for the same employer since before the birth of their child. This provides the most rigorous test of the impact of parental benefits on return to work, although selection may be a problem. The results of both analyses are very similar to those of mothers who had worked during pregnancy.

8. This is comparable to competing risk studies of cohabitation versus marriage where the dependent variable is the first occurrence of living with a partner, with the competing risks being nonmarital cohabitation or first marriage (Axinn & Thornton, 1992). If the dependent variable is marriage, then individuals who cohabit first are censored as they are no longer eligible for a marriage without cohabitation. If the dependent variable is cohabitation, then individuals who marry first are censored as they are no longer eligible for cohabitation prior to marriage.

9. The proportion of mothers who worked during pregnancy is lower in our sample of mothers of all parities than in a sample of first-time mothers such as that of O'Connell (1990) because labor force participation rates are lower for mothers than for nonmothers. According to Survey of Income and Program Participation (SIPP) data (O'Connell, 1990), 64% of mothers who had a first birth between 1981 and 1984 worked during pregnancy.

The same SIPP study shows that, of women with a first birth in 1981-1984, 44% were working within 6 months, and 53% by the twelfth month. We divided our sample by parity and conducted separate life tables for each parity. Our results show that first-time mothers enter the workforce more quickly than later parity mothers. About 42% of first-time mothers are working by 3 months, 51% by 6 months, 58% by 9 months, and 61% by 12 months (not shown). In contrast, among women with a second birth, 36% are back within 3 months, 44% by 6 months, 47% by 9 months, and 48% by 12 months. Of mothers with a third birth, 25% are working within 3 months, 28% within 6 months, and 34% within 12 months. Sample sizes are too small to calculate life tables for higher parity mothers.

10. Regional dummies were used as instruments for the wage equation as they are associated with wages but not with working after childbirth. The R^2 for the equation is .29. We did not correct for self-selection into the labor force. Mroz (1987) found no evidence that the failure to control for self-selection yields biased results. Leibowitz et al. (1992) also found no evidence for selection bias in the wage equation.

11. Calculated as (Relative risk − 1) × 100. This represents the percentage increase (or decrease) in risk of returning to work associated with a change in the dependent variable or the given category compared with the omitted category.

12. Thanks to an anonymous reviewer for this interpretation.

13. The policies affecting schedules—part-time work, flex-time schedules, liberal unpaid leave, and work at home—were strongly correlated.

14. There is some question as to why there is any variation in access to part-time work among those who return part-time. That is, logically, everyone who returns part-time has part-time work available. However, when we examined our data, we found that what mothers apparently consider part-time work and what we defined as

part-time work were not the same. We did not define *part-time* in the question about access to part-time work; we coded work of 1 to 34 hours per week as part-time, consistent with U.S. Department of Labor practice. Yet 40% of mothers working under 35 hours per week at the time of the survey said that they did not have access to part-time work. When we examined the hours mothers worked, we found that mothers who had access to part-time work in fact worked fewer hours (mean = 32) than mothers who did not have access to part-time work (mean = 40). Apparently many mothers have a higher hours threshold for work to be considered part-time work than do statistical agencies.

REFERENCES

Adams, G., & Sandfort, J. (1992). *State investments in child care and early childhood education.* Washington, DC: Children's Defense Fund.

Allison, P. D. (1984). *Event history analysis: Regression for longitudinal event data.* Beverly Hills, CA: Sage.

Axinn, W., & Thornton, A. (1992). The relationship between cohabitation and divorce: Selectivity or causal influence? *Demography, 29*(3), 357-374.

Becker, G. (1965). A theory of the allocation of time. *The Economic Journal, 75*(299), 493-517.

Becker, G. (1991). *A treatise on the family* (Rev. ed.). Cambridge, MA: Harvard University Press.

Billy, J. O., & Moore, D. E. (1992). A multilevel analysis of marital and nonmarital fertility in the U.S. *Social Forces, 70,* 977-1011.

Bond, J., Galinsky, E., Lord, M., Staines, G., & Brown, K. (1991). *Beyond the parental leave debate.* New York: Families and Work Institute.

Bureau of Labor Statistics. (1995). *Marital and family characteristics of the labor force from the March 1994 Current Population Survey.* Washington, DC: U.S. Department of Labor.

Center for Policy Alternatives. (1992). *Family leave laws in the states.* Washington, DC: Author.

Committee on Ways and Means. (1992). *Overview of entitlement programs, 1992 Green Book.* Washington, DC: Government Printing Office.

Conference Board. (1988, April 1). *BLS data on employer-supported child care.* Memo.

Cox, D. R. (1972). Regression models and life tables. *Journal of the Royal Statistical Society,* Series B34, 187-220.

Desai, S., & Waite, L. J. (1991, August). Women's employment during pregnancy and after the first birth: Occupational characteristics and work commitment. *American Sociological Review, 56,* 551-566.

Finn-Stevenson, M., & Trzcinski, E. (1990). *Public policy issues surrounding parental leave: A state-by-state analysis of parental leave legislation*. Unpublished manuscript, Bush Center, New Haven, CT.

Gormley, W. T., Jr. (1991). State regulations and the availability of child-care services. *Journal of Policy Analysis and Management, 10*(Winter), 78-95.

Hofferth, S. (1995). Caring for children at the poverty line. *Children and Youth Services Review, 17*(1-2), 1-31.

Hofferth, S. L., Brayfield, A., Deich, S., & Holcomb, P. (1991). *The National Child Care Survey, 1990*. Washington, DC: Urban Institute.

Hofferth, S. L., & Chaplin, D. (1995). *State regulations and child care choice*. Revised version of paper presented at the Annual Meeting of the Population Association of America, April 1994.

Joesch, J. M. (1994). Children and the timing of women's paid work after childbirth: A further specification of the relationship. *Journal of Marriage and the Family, 56*(May), 429-440.

Kisker, E., Hofferth, S., Phillips, D., & Farquhar, E. (1991). *A profile of child care settings: Early education and care in 1990*. Washington, DC: Government Printing Office.

Leibowitz, A., Klerman, J. A., & Waite, L. J. (1992). Employment of new mothers and child care choice: Differences by children's age. *Journal of Human Resources, 27*(1), 112-133.

Mason, K., & Kuhlthau, K. (1989). Child care ideals among mothers of preschool children. *Journal of Marriage and the Family, 51*(3), 593-603.

Menken, J., Trussell, J., Stempel, D., & Babakol, O. (1981). Proportional hazards life table models: An illustrative analysis of sociodemographic influences on marriage dissolution in the United States. *Demography, 18,* 181-200.

Miller, B. (1992). *The distribution of family oriented benefits* (Issue Brief 130). Washington, DC: Employee Benefit Research Institute.

Moffitt, R. (1992). Incentive effects of the U.S. welfare system: A review. *Journal of Economic Literature, 30*(March), 1-61.

Mroz, T. A. (1987). The sensitivity of an empirical model of married women's hours of work to economic and statistical assumptions. *Econometrica, 55*(4), 765-799.

O'Connell, M. (1990). Maternity leave arrangements: 1961-85. In *Work and family patterns of American women,* Current Population Reports, Special Studies Series P-23, No. 165. Washington, DC: Government Printing Office.

Phillips, D., Lande, J., & Goldberg, M. (1990). The state of child care regulation: A comparative analysis. *Early Childhood Research Quarterly, 5*(2), 151-179.

SAS Institute. (1991). *SAS/STAT software: The PHREG procedure.* Cary, NC: Author.

Schwartz, F. (1989). Management women and the new facts of life. *Harvard Business Review, 67,* 65-76.

Teachman, J. (1982). Methodological issues in the analysis of family formation and dissolution. *Journal of Marriage and the Family, 44,* 1037-1053.

U.S. Bureau of the Census. (1988). *County and city data book.* Washington, DC: Author.

Yamaguchi, K. (1991). *Event history analysis.* Newbury Park, CA: Sage.

Zuckman, J. (1993, February 6). As family leave is enacted, some see end to logjam. *Congressional Quarterly, 51*(6), 267-269.

CHAPTER 6

Returning to Work

*The Impact of Gender, Family,
and Work on Terminating a
Family or Medical Leave*

JOANNE C. SANDBERG

DANIEL B. CORNFIELD

A s fewer households have a nonemployed adult available to care for infants and ill and aging family members, employees are increasingly caught between the conflicting demands of work and family. At times even the most finely tuned strategies that workers draw upon are unable to meet the competing needs of their families and employers. Since the implementation of the Family and Medical Leave Act (FMLA) in 1993, a new strategy has become available to employees on a widespread basis (Brannen, 1996). Eligible employees[1] may take up to 12 weeks of leave per year. Their health benefits are to continue during their leaves, and they are guaranteed the same jobs or comparable jobs upon their return.[2] Their leaves may be taken to care for newborns, newly adopted children, newly placed foster children, for their own serious health conditions, or for serious health conditions of family members.

Little research has addressed the constraints faced by individual families as they take family and medical leaves. In this chapter, we examine the impact of gender and family and work obligations and resources on leave-taking and, specifically, on leave-takers' reasons for returning to work. Our study of leave-takers, which draws on the FMLA data set made available by the Commission on Family and Medical Leave, is one of the first multivariate and national studies of leave-taking behavior. As such, we intend to illuminate, and draw policy-relevant inferences about, how gender, family, and work constraints and opportunities influence employee decisions regarding when to return to work from a leave.

The push to pass the FMLA was due, in part, to changes in employment rates and demographic patterns over the past few decades. The increase in labor force participation rates among married women, particularly those with children living at home, and relative stability in those of men, creates conflicting obligations for many workers. Furthermore, there are fewer households with children that have a married couple present. Single, divorced, and widowed mothers, a group whose employment rates have increased, also juggle the demands of work and family, as do an increasing, but limited, number of single fathers. In addition, an increase in life expectancy means that more adults may need to care for their aging parents during some period of their lives (U.S. Bureau of the Census, 1996).

These changes have resulted in a workforce in which employees often provide a significant amount of care for infants and ill family members. For some, this results in the decision to take a leave from work. Taking a leave from work to care for family members has two components: The worker must choose to take a leave (and be able to do so); and, the worker must also decide when to return to the workplace. It is the latter decision that forms the focus of this chapter. The decision to return to work after a leave does not occur in a vacuum. This decision is made as employees negotiate their need to return to work within the context of family demands or personal health problems.

In our study, we analyze the impact of gender and family and work obligations and resources on work-related constraints that influence men's and women's decisions to return to work following family and medical leaves. In order to discern how gender mediates employee decisions to return to work following leaves, we examine the effects of family obligations and resources as well as workplace opportunities and constraints separately for women and men. This approach illuminates how workplace and domestic conditions influence the multiple pressures that women and men experience as they negotiate their return to work following a leave.

LEAVE-TAKING BEHAVIOR

Researchers have begun to explore leave-taking behavior. There are now several studies that document the prevalence of employer family-leave policies (Catalyst, 1986; Galinsky, Bond, & Friedman, 1993; Makuen, 1988), the frequency with which employees take advantage of family leave, and the length of leave taken following the birth or adoption of a child (Catalyst, 1986; Pleck, 1988, 1993). There are also a few studies that explore the prevalence of leave-taking to care for elders (Scharlach & Boyd, 1989). There are, however, far fewer studies that provide an understanding of how decisions are made regarding family leaves.

The increased rate of employment among mothers of young children has prompted interest in women's work behavior following the birth of a child. There are several studies that use nationally representative samples to explore this topic. Garrett, Lubeck, and Wenk (1991) and Joesch (1994) drew upon national probability samples to explore women's return to or entrance to paid employment after childbirth. Their data do not, however, allow them to distinguish between factors that influence return from leave and those that influence labor force participation more generally. Garrett and her colleagues (1991) explored personal, family, and economic variables and found that among women who quit their jobs, remaining on the job until the child was born, being Black, having a higher household income, being married, having a higher level of education, and being younger increased the speed with which they reentered the workforce. To examine the timing of women's return to work after having a child, Joesch (1994) drew upon the new home economics model that highlights the costs of staying home versus the costs of returning to paid employment. She found that working during pregnancy had the greatest impact on the likelihood of working following the birth of a child. When work status during pregnancy was controlled, neither education nor number of children significantly influenced women's rate of participation following the birth of a child. However, the respondents' federal tax rate and being a homeowner increased women's hazard of paid employment. Race was not significant. Hofferth (Chapter 5 in this volume), using a nationally representative sample, examined the impact of state and local employer policies, including paid and unpaid leave, on the timing of women's return to paid employment following the birth of a child. She found that state policy did not significantly influence the likelihood that women who worked during pregnancy would return to work following the birth of a child. She did find, however, that employer "family-friendly" policies, including liberal unpaid leave, increased the likelihood that a woman would return to work following the birth of a child.

There has also been increased interest in men's leave-taking behavior (Essex & Klein, 1991; Hyde, Essex, & Horton, 1993; Pleck, 1988, 1993). Pleck (1993) proposed that men who take family leaves return to work after only a short time due to men's understanding of fatherhood, which emphasizes earning wages over providing extensive day-to-day care; the negative attitudes of coworkers and/or bosses toward men taking prolonged leaves; and the relative ease of taking short, informal leaves, such as using vacation days. Hyde et al.'s (1993) study suggests that more generous employers' leave policies and reduced pressure from coworkers and supervisors significantly increases men's length of leave. While these studies illuminate factors that affect the length of men's leaves, they are limited by relatively small sample sizes and geographical restrictions.

Other studies have explored both male and female leave-taking behavior to care for newborns. Bond, Galinsky, Lord, Staines, and Brown (1991) studied employer and employee experiences in four states following the enactment of state legislation that required companies to provide maternity and paternity leave. They found that, among female leave-takers who returned to work following the birth of a child, women with lower household incomes tend to return to work sooner than their more affluent counterparts. The study also provided mixed support for the hypothesis that legislation giving male workers the right to take parental leave enables or encourages men to take longer leaves.

Gender-neutral policies often do not result in gender-neutral practices (Bergmann, 1997; Fried, 1996; Gewirtz, 1995; Haas, 1992, 1993; Hochschild, 1997). In her ethnographic case study of a single corporation, Fried (1996) found that none of the men upper management interviewed availed themselves of their employer-provided entitlement to a parental leave; the few women in upper management who did take leaves limited the lengths of their leaves. She also found that, among nonmanagement women, professional women took longer unpaid leaves than nonprofessional women, presumably due to differences in finances. Even Sweden's liberal gender-neutral leave policy has not resulted in equal division of use of leave time among working couples after the birth of a child. Haas (1992, 1993) concluded that biological (men's inability to breast-feed), social-psychological, and economic factors and differences in social support influenced the pattern of men using a relatively small proportion of leave time available to a couple during an infant's first year.

The information on leave-taking behavior to care for elderly relatives is even more sparse. Numerous studies, particularly in the medical literature, have explored the gendered nature of care giving (Matthews, 1995; Stone, Caffarata, & Sangl, 1987), the impact of employment on eldercare responsibilities (Brody & Schoonover, 1986), the percentage of workers using leaves for eldercare (Scharlach & Boyd, 1989), and the gender and status of workers using "family days" (Gewirtz, 1995). Studies that focus on the factors that influence the length of leaves taken by men and women to care for elderly relatives appear to be in short supply.

The Commission on Family and Medical Leave (1996) and MacGonagle, Connor, Heeringa, Veerkamp, and Groves's (1995) Final Report to the Commission provide pioneering bivariate analyses of employee leave-taking experiences since the implementation of FMLA. They explored female and male workers' experiences with FMLA leaves and drew upon the national probability sample that forms the basis of the multivariate analysis in our study. Although the Commission's analysis did not focus on gender, they noted a few relevant findings. Women are more likely than men to take a leave, but men are more likely than women to take leaves for their own health. The Commission's report also revealed that although women, on average, take longer leaves than men, men take longer leaves for their own serious health conditions than do women.[3] A multivariate analysis, however, would provide a more nuanced understanding of the processes that influence leave-taking behavior.

Previous research based on national probability samples has not fully illuminated the gendered nature of leave-taking behavior because of its restricted focus on the behavior of women (e.g., Garrett et al., 1991; Hofferth, Chapter 5 in this volume; Joesch, 1994). Studies based on more limited samples, such as those limited by region or by work site, are less generalizable across geographic regions and employers (e.g., Bond et al., 1991; Fried, 1996; Gewirtz, 1995). Furthermore, very little research has explored the behavior of workers taking leaves to care for ill family members. This study, which draws upon a national probability sample to explore both men's and women's decisions to return to work following leaves for their own health or to care for newborn children or ill family members, therefore addresses a critical gap in our understanding of leave-taking behavior.

To understand leave-taking behavior adequately, we must first explore the gendered nature of expectations and experiences that influence men's and women's choices. There is reason to expect that men and women respond differently to workplace pressures to return to work. Despite changes in women's labor force participation rates, children continue to see differences in the activities of men and women. The majority of child care, be it performed by parents or paid help, is done by women. Women, even when working full-time, usually perform the majority of the domestic labor. Reverse situations, in which men perform the majority of the child care and/or domestic tasks, are still relatively rare. It is still generally expected that one of the major ways that men care for their families is through financial support. Although many men and women now expect fathers to be actively involved in their children's day-to-day lives, there is little societal support for men who would choose to be stay-at-home fathers, not engaged in paid labor (Gerson, 1993).

The process of socialization may result in women and men identifying with the caretaker role to different degrees. Even men who provide care for elderly relatives often do not think of themselves as caretakers, and are often not perceived by others as caretakers (Gewirtz, 1995; Matthews, 1995). Since men are more likely to perceive themselves as providers and less likely to think of themselves as caretakers, they may respond differently to workplace and domestic pressures that may potentially influence their decisions to return to work following a leave.

Employee decisions to return to work may also be influenced by the unequal division of labor in the household. While some studies indicate that men may be increasing their proportion of domestic labor (at least among certain cohorts), women continue to perform the majority of child care and household tasks. Women, in general, spend more time on child care, household chores, and caring for elderly relatives than men (Coltrane, 1996; Coverman & Sheley, 1986; Gerson, 1993; Hochschild, 1989; Stoller, 1990; Stone et al., 1987). This holds true even among dual-income households. Because women perform so much of the domestic labor, it may be reasonable to expect that women who work outside the home experience greater conflict between the demands of their paid employment and their unpaid "second shift" than men (Hochschild, 1989). Furthermore, since more men than women have spouses who are not in the paid labor force, men are more likely to have a spouse who can handle the demands of caring for family members without the constraints of paid employment (Galinsky et al., 1993).

Numerous studies have shown that both employers and employees express, directly or indirectly, their understandings of gender at the workplace, through assignment of job tasks, assumptions regarding desire to travel, and topics of conversation, for example (Fried, 1996; Hossfeld, 1990; Kanter, 1977; Markham, Bonjean, & Corder, 1986). The messages conveyed by employers and employees can place slightly different expectations, and therefore slightly different pressures, on female and male employees. There are additional work-related concerns that might also influence decisions regarding returning to work. One relates to pressure from bosses and coworkers. As Pleck (1993) pointed out, one of the reasons men take short paternity leaves and often do not identify them as such is that they receive limited support from coworkers and employers for taking lengthy, formal leaves. Hochschild's (1997) work provides support for this as well. Women and men, in general, face different expectations. The Catalyst (1986) study found that employers were less supportive of men taking paternity leaves than women taking maternity leaves, even among companies that provided formal, unpaid paternity leave. It should also be remembered that men are less likely to expect themselves to take formal or extended family leaves. Therefore men who do not consider taking a leave or who use a limited amount of vacation time following the birth of a child may not feel constrained by the pressures from coworkers and supervisors since they are not challenging the norms. However, the apparently limited number of men who do want extended, formal family leaves may feel significant pressure to limit their absence.

Employer expectations and employee behaviors are influenced by status as well as gender (Fried, 1996; Gewirtz, 1995). Women in top managerial positions and men of different statuses are expected not to take advantage of family-friendly policies. Upper-status women are expected to show commitment to their jobs through long hours at the work site regardless of family needs. While mid- to lower-status women also face pressure to demonstrate that they can be "counted on," management often considers those women to be the employees who would be expected to take advantage of family leave benefits. The status of female employees influences whether their supervisors or coworkers think it is "appropriate" for them to use "family-friendly" policies; however, the status of men has limited impact on others' expectations.

Both men and women who want extended leaves may feel strong economic pressures to return to work. Although the FMLA requires that covered employees be eligible to take up to 12 weeks of family or medical leave a year, it does not stipulate that the leave be paid. As a result, leave-takers with limited financial resources often return to work more quickly than their more affluent coworkers (Bond et al., 1991).

We expect that employees whose terms of employment are covered by a union contract would feel less pressure to return to work. It seems reasonable to assume that the workplace culture would be influenced by the union and would emphasize the importance of workers' rights, one of these rights being the right to take a family or medical leave. This attitude might reduce the workplace pressure experienced by workers who want to extend their leaves.

Previous research provides mixed support for the position that employee status, employer size, and unionization influence benefits. A 1993 study by Galinsky et al. indicated that employees were more likely to have better flex- and leave-time benefits if they were managers and professionals, have higher hourly wages, be more educated, and be nonminority. Size of employer did not, however, influence the availability of flex time or leave benefits. Their study concurs with Glass and Fujimoto's (1995) analysis, which indicated that the number of employees did not influence parental or maternity leave benefits during a period prior to implementation of the FMLA, although it did have a positive effect on vacation leave, sick leave, disability leave, and leave benefits in general. Other benefits, such as the number of dependent care programs and the amount of traditional benefits received were influenced by workplace size (Galinsky et al., 1993). Furthermore, Glass and Fujimoto (1995) found that women who were covered by union contracts were more likely to have better leave opportunities, including maternity leave or parental leave, during that time period. Although these studies were conducted before implementation of the FMLA, they do reflect that particular employee and employer characteristics may reflect the availability of family-work benefits to employees.

Because men and women are socialized differently, perform different amounts of domestic labor, and are often treated differently at the workplace, it is expected that domestic and workplace constraints and opportunities affect women's and men's leave-taking decisions differently.

GENDERED REASONS FOR RETURNING TO WORK

We expect that men's and women's reasons for terminating their leaves and returning to work not only differ, but are constrained by different configurations of work-related and family obligations and resources. As we have seen, women generally perform more domestic chores than their spouses, even when both work full-time. Furthermore, when the pressures become greatest, it appears that women often take on more of the caretaking responsibilities than men. Stone et al. (1987) found that husbands and wives quit work at roughly the same rates to care for spouses. Daughters, however, were more likely than sons to quit work to become caregivers. Enright's (1991) study indicated that husbands who care for brain-impaired wives receive more paid and unpaid assistance than working women. This may be largely due to men's greater ability to pay for outside services. Men are less likely to perceive themselves as caretakers and are more likely to emphasize their economic contributions and work identity.

The FMLA data set that constitutes the empirical basis of our study provides five useful self-reported reasons for why a leave-taker returned to work: (a) could no longer afford time off from work; (b) exhausted leave time; (c) felt pressured by coworkers and/or bosses to return to work; (d) too much work to do at work; and (e) wanted to return to work. The first four reasons index workplace constraints on the decision to return to work; the fifth reason indexes a nonconstrained "volitional" reason for returning to work. In light of the greater work-and-family cross-pressures felt by working women than by working men, women workers are more likely than men workers to feel pressured by the workplace to return to work. Therefore, *our first hypothesis is that women leave-takers are more likely than men leave-takers to return to work for the first through fourth reasons, and that men are more likely than women to terminate their leaves and return to work for the fifth reason.*

Notwithstanding this hypothesized gender difference in return reasons, it is likely that men's and women's return reasons—whatever they are—respond to different sets of family and work constraints and resources. Family constraints are those stemming from the size, dependence level, and composition of the leave-taker's family that influence the amount of responsibility for family members that fall on the individual leave-taker. These constraints and resources include marital status, number of children, caring for a baby (or newly adopted child or new foster child) or ill family member (or, in a few instances, non-family member) on a daily basis, and taking a leave for one's own health or to care for another person. Work constraints and resources are those that derive from the leave-taker's employer and employment conditions and that influence an employee's leave eligibility and leave-benefit generosity, and the socioeconomic resourcefulness of the individual leave-taker. These constraints and resources include whether a respondent's terms of employment are covered by a union contract, whether the employee works at an FMLA-covered work site, duration of employment, hours worked per week, employee status, payment during leave, and knowledge and eligibility for individual coverage under the FMLA.

Given the higher level of women's involvement in the household division of labor, and the emphasis on breadwinning in the concept and practice of fatherhood, we present four hypotheses that reflect our expectation that gender significantly influences the relative effects of workplace and family conditions on return-to-work decisions. The unequal distribution of domestic labor, even among dual-income couples, results in greater work-family conflict for women. We therefore propose hypothesis 2a: *Women's decisions to terminate their leaves are significantly influenced by workplace policies and conditions.* Since men are usually less responsible for caring for newborns and ill relatives than women, and because work is more generally considered the default position, hypothesis 2b is: *Men's reasons to terminate their leaves are minimally responsive to workplace policies and conditions.*

Hypotheses 3a and 3b are closely related to the preceding argument. Since women generally have more responsibility for the care of infants or ill family members, family concerns are likely to influence women's return-to-work decisions. We therefore posit hypothesis 3a: *Women's reasons for returning to work following a leave are significantly influenced by family obligations and/or resources.* Given that men usually have less responsibility for family caretaking responsibilities, hypothesis 3b is: *Men's reasons for returning to work following a leave are minimally influenced by family obligations and/or resources.* As previously discussed, research on caregiving is consistent with these hypotheses.

ANALYSIS OF REASONS FOR RETURNING TO WORK

In order to test our hypotheses, we use the FMLA data set to examine the impact of gender, work, and family on reasons for terminating a leave and returning to work. The data set permits us to examine the effects of gender on, and gender differences in the determinants of, reasons for returning to work.

Sample

The FMLA data set is a national telephone survey of employees conducted by the University of Michigan Survey Research Center for the U.S. Commission on Family and Medical Leave. The survey was restricted to residents of the United States who were at least 18 years old at the time of survey and who had worked for pay at some point between January 1, 1994 and the time of the survey, approximately 18 months later. Only leave-takers were used for our analysis.

Initially, 8,492 households were interviewed to determine which household members would be eligible for inclusion in the full survey and to enable the oversampling of leave-takers. The respondents chosen to complete the interview reflect the demographic characteristics of the paid workforce, with an oversampling of leave-takers and leave-needers. Respondents were asked the following:

Since January 1, 1994, (have you, has relationship) taken a leave from work to care for a newborn, newly adopted or new foster child or for (your/their) own serious health condition, the serious health condition of (your/their) child, spouse, or parent that lasted *more than 3 days* or required an overnight hospital stay? (MacGonagle et al., 1995, Appendix III, p. 2)

The phrasing of the question ensures that leaves that met the restrictions of the FMLA were included. The wording is also helpful because it encourages employees to think of periods away from work that they might not have thought of as leave time otherwise, such as vacation days taken to care for a newborn or an ill family member. The Survey Research Center completed 2,254 telephone surveys. Although the number of completed interviews of leave-takers was 1,218, our sample is limited to 937. The sample was reduced primarily because of the restricted number of individuals who were asked the dependent variables. Only 1,007 respondents were asked the first two dependent variables, if they had returned for work for financial reasons or just because they wanted to go back. One hundred five were not asked the dependent variables because they were still on their only leave taken during that leave period, making questions about returning from their leave inappropriate. Thirty additional respondents were not asked those questions because, although they had taken more than one leave, they were currently on leave and their current leave was longer than any other leaves taken. Those who took more than one leave were instructed to think only of their longest leave when giving their responses. Thirty-six more were excluded from the analysis because they did not return to work after their leave. Thirty-seven more cases were lost because the remaining three dependent variables were asked only of those who returned to the same work site, excluding those who took on different jobs. In addition, cases in which there were missing data for variables other than income were also excluded from the analysis.

Variables

The five reasons for returning to work discussed above are the dependent variables in our analysis. Leave-takers who had already returned to work were asked all of the following questions: Did you return to work because you: (a) "couldn't afford financially to take any more time;" (b) "used up all the leave time you were allowed;" (c) "felt pressured by your boss and/or coworkers to come back;" (d) "had too much to do to stay away longer;" and (e) "just wanted to get back to work?" (MacGonagle et al., 1995, Appendix III, p. 9). The respondents could respond "yes" to any or all of the questions. We use logistic regression to analyze individual differences in the odds of answering "yes" to these questions because each question is coded dichotomously.

In order to test each hypothesis previously discussed, we use three sets of independent variables, in addition to gender (female = 1). The first set consists of variables that index *family* constraints and opportunities and provide some indication of the responsibilities that workers continue to bear and the resources that they can draw upon on a regular basis: *married* (yes = 1); the *number of children* under the age of 18 living with the respondent; whether or not the respondent *cares for an ill person*[4] (yes = 1) or *a baby,* newly adopted child, or new foster child (yes = 1) on a daily basis; and whether the respondent took a leave for the respondent's *own health* or to care for someone else (own health = 1).

The second set of independent variables consists of *workplace* characteristics that may constrain the decision to return to work: whether or not respondent's terms of employment was covered by a *union contract* (yes = 1); whether or not the respondent is a *salaried employee* (yes = 1); whether or not the respondent took a fully *paid leave* (yes = 1); whether or not the respondent worked for the *same employer* for at least one year[5] (yes = 1); whether or not the respondent's *employer was covered by the FMLA* at the time of the survey[6] (yes = 1); and *FMLA coverage* status of respondent's leave (not covered or respondent did not know if it was covered = 0; respondent knew that leave was covered by FMLA = 1).

The third set of independent variables consists of *controls* for respondent socioeconomic status and demographic background and the length of respondent's leave that constrain the formulation and implementation of family strategies and may influence leave-taking behavior. A set of dummy variables was used to indicate race and ethnicity: non-Latino/a *African American* (yes = 1); *Latino/a* (yes = 1); *Other* (non-White, non-African American, and non-Latino) (yes = 1); the omitted benchmark group is non-Latino/a White. *Age* is expressed in years. *Education* is a 6-point scale that ranges from 1 to 6. We use the logarithmic value of the respondent's 1994 *household income.* A dummy variable, *imputed income,* is included because approximately 19% of women and 18% of men in the sample have imputed income values.[7] *Leave length* in days was logged to reduce skewness.

Descriptive statistics for all variables by gender are presented in Table 6.1. The table indicates that there are significant differences between the means

TABLE 6.1 Means and Standard Deviations of All Variables by Gender

Variables	Men Mean	(N = 398) S.D.	Women Mean	(N = 539) S.D.
Return Reasons				
Could not afford to take any more time off***	.354	.479	.527	.500
Used up leave time***	.178	.383	.269	.444
Felt pressured by boss or coworkers**	.173	.379	.241	.428
Too much to do to stay away longer	.289	.454	.336	.473
Just wanted to***	.646	.479	.486	.500
Family				
Care for:				
ill person	.058	.234	.078	.268
baby**	.078	.268	.132	.339
Leave for own health	.648	.478	.627	.484
Number of children	1.050	1.281	1.019	1.063
Married***	.741	.439	.642	.480
Work				
Unionized*	.234	.424	.178	.383
Same employer	.897	.304	.911	.285
FMLA-covered employer	.734	.443	.753	.432
Salaried employee	.412	.493	.373	.484
FMLA leave	.090	.287	.106	.308
Paid leave***	.593	.492	.471	.500
Controls				
African American	.080	.272	.106	.308
Latino/a	.063	.243	.078	.268
White, non-Hispanic	.809	.394	.772	.420
Other ethnicity	.048	.213	.043	.202
Education	4.060	1.284	.045	.150
Age***	40.236	12.513	37.250	11.726
Household income	51340.93	73446.65	47678.77	65058.53
Leave length*	26.764	44.508	32.568	42.095
Household income imputed	.181	.385	.191	.394

NOTE: * Gender difference in means is significant, $p \leq .05$
      ** Gender difference in means is significant, $p \leq .01$
     *** Gender difference in means is significant, $p \leq .001$

for male and female respondents. Women's return-to-work decisions are more likely to have been influenced by issues of affordability, lack of additional leave time, and pressure from bosses and coworkers than men's. Men, however, are more likely than women to return to the workplace because they want to return.

There are significant differences in family, workplace, and control variables as well. Women, on average, are more likely to be unmarried and to care for a baby (or newly adopted child or foster child) on a daily basis than men. A greater percentage of male leave-takers are covered by union contracts and receive full pay during their leaves than women. This latter finding may be the result of men relying primarily on paid leaves (by using formal paid leaves or using vacations days for informal leaves), returning to work before their leave days become unpaid (Haas, 1992, 1993; Pleck, 1993). Finally, women tend to be younger and to have taken longer leaves than men.

Results

The results of the logistic regressions for the whole sample in Table 6.2 support the first hypothesis. The dependent variables in these equations are the five reasons given by the respondents for returning to work, and the independent variables include gender, family, work, and control variables. In Equations 1 through 4, the statistically significant ($p \leq .05$) coefficients for gender indicate that women are more likely than men to have returned to work for each of these workplace-related reasons: because they could not afford to stay away longer, they had used up their leave time, they felt pressured by coworkers and bosses to return to work, and they had too much work to do to stay away longer. The significant gender coefficient in Equation 5 indicates that men are more likely than women to have returned to work because they wanted to return to work.

In order to examine hypotheses 2a, 2b, 3a, and 3b, we estimated equations for all five dependent variables separately for women and men. This allows us to analyze the impact of work and family constraints and opportunities on men's and women's reasons for returning to work. With the exception of the equation that explored the impact of work and family variables on the odds of men returning to work because of pressure from boss or coworkers, all of the models are statistically significant ($p \leq .05$). This lack of significance for the one model indicates that pressure from bosses and coworkers on men's return-to-work decisions may operate relatively independently of the workplace and family constraints and opportunities that we are able to identify. We conducted t tests of the gender difference of the coefficients of those vari-

TABLE 6.2 Logistic Regression of Return Reasons on Gender and Family, Work, and Control Variables, Whole Sample ($N = 937$)

	(1) Could Not Afford More Time Off		(2) Used Up Leave Time		(3) Pressured by Boss/Coworkers		(4) Too Much to Do		(5) Just Wanted To	
Variables										
Gender	1.736***	(.552)	1.513*	(.414)	1.441*	(.365)	1.452*	(.373)	.529***	(−.638)
Family										
Care for:										
ill person	1.878*	(.630)	1.936*	(.661)	2.257**	(.814)	1.874*	(.628)	.879	(−.129)
baby	.772	(−.258)	.913	(−.092)	1.090	(.086)	.949	(−.052)	1.245	(.219)
Leave for own health	.609**	(−.497)	.542***	(−.612)	1.321	(.278)	.956	(−.045)	1.759***	(.565)
Number of children	1.100	(.095)	1.053	(.051)	1.060	(.059)	1.081	(.078)	.958	(−.043)
Married	.907	(−.097)	1.355	(.303)	1.257	(.229)	1.139	(.130)	.882	(−.126)
Work										
Unionized	.807	(−.215)	1.274	(.243)	1.013	(.013)	.775	(−.255)	.797	(−.227)
Same employer	.597*	(−.516)	.773	(−.257)	.597*	(−.517)	.851	(−.162)	1.412	(.345)
FMLA-covered employer	.728	(−.318)	1.118	(.112)	.708	(−.346)	.409***	(−.895)	1.005	(.005)
Salaried employee	.808	(−.214)	1.019	(.019)	1.009	(.009)	1.879***	(.631)	1.242	(.217)
FMLA leave	1.270	(.239)	1.136	(.128)	1.214	(.194)	1.149	(−.139)	1.055	(.054)
Paid leave	.270***	(−1.309)	.804	(−.218)	.514***	(−.665)	.865	(−.145)	1.875***	(.629)
Constant	2.970		−.849		−0.573		−2.047		−.061	
−2 Log L	1,062.090		945.654		915.175		1,070.678		1,209.901	
Model Chi-square (20 df)	228.778***		66.132***		53.857***		98.214***		78.149***	

*$p \le .05$; **$p \le .01$; ***$p \le .001$.

NOTE: Each equation controls for African American, Latino/a, Other ethnicity, Education, Age, Household income, Leave length, and Income imputed, not shown to preserve space.

ables whose coefficients are significant in both Tables 6.3 and 6.4. Of those tested, no significant differences are found. Although significant differences are not found between the coefficients of men and women who return from leave, the variation in patterns of significance is suggestive.

We find support for hypothesis 2a, which explores the effect of workplace variables on women's return-to-work choices. As Table 6.3 indicates, women who work for an FMLA-covered employer are less likely to return to work for financial reasons, because they felt pressured by bosses and coworkers, and because they had too much work to do to stay away longer. The decreased economic, interpersonal, and workload pressure may be a result of the FMLA, and/or a reflection of increased benefits and greater flexibility often associated with larger workplaces.

Table 6.3 also suggests that having a fully paid leave decreases women's likelihood of returning to work for financial reasons and because of pressure from bosses or coworkers; having a fully paid leave increases the likelihood that they will return to work because they want to return. Women who are fully paid during their leave are less likely to experience a financial crunch than those receiving no pay or partial pay (although some women may return because they had used up all of their paid leaves).

There is moderate support in Table 6.4 for hypothesis 2b, that men's work opportunity constraints and opportunities have a limited impact on their return-to-work decision. The work variables have no strong pattern of association with men's reasons for returning to work. As with women, having a fully paid leave decreases men's likelihood of returning to work for financial reasons and due to the pressure of coworkers. It is probable that having a fully paid leave affects men's decisions for the same reason that it does women's decisions. A fully paid leave does not, however, significantly influence the likelihood that men will return to work just because they want to return. Working for the same employer for at least one year significantly decreases the odds of men's returning to work for financial reasons and increases the likelihood that they will return just because they want to go back. Duration of employment apparently does have some effect, possibly due to assurances that they will maintain their job due to provision of the FMLA, or individual company's leave policies.

The findings in Table 6.3 reflect support for hypothesis 3a, that family variables have an impact on women's reasons for returning to work. Caring for an ill person on a daily basis increases the odds that a woman will return to work for financial reasons, due to pressure from a boss or coworker, and because there is too much work to do. Caring for a baby does not have the same effect, suggesting that formal and informal workplace policies meet the

TABLE 6.3 Logistic Regression of Return Reasons on Gender and Family, Work, and Control Variables, Women Leave Takers (N = 539)

Odds Ratios (Regression Coefficients)

Variables	(1) Could Not Afford More Time Off		(2) Used Up Leave Time		(3) Pressured by Boss/Coworkers		(4) Too Much to Do		(5) Just Wanted To	
Family Care for:										
ill person baby	2.332*	(.847)	1.616	(.480)	3.597***	(1.280)	2.074*	(.730)	0.823	(−.194)
	.630	(−.462)	.943	(−.059)	1.214	(.194)	.829	(−.187)	1.495	(.402)
Leave for own health	.670	(−.401)	.531**	(−.634)	1.251	(.224)	.927	(−.075)	1.449	(.371)
Number of children	1.233*	(.210)	1.120	(.114)	.968	(−.033)	1.023	(.023)	.873	(−.136)
Married	.816	(−.203)	1.350	(.300)	1.424	(.353)	1.139	(.130)	.917	(−.086)
Work										
Unionized	.700	(−.356)	1.110	(.104)	.996	(−.004)	.959	(−.042)	.992	(−.009)
Same employer	.851	(−.162)	.970	(−.031)	.600	(−.511)	.765	(−.268)	.826	(−.192)
FMLA-covered employer	.556*	(−.587)	.914	(−.090)	.587*	(−.533)	.375***	(−.981)	1.169	(.157)
Salaried employee	1.056	(.054)	1.151	(.141)	.756	(−.280)	1.785*	(.579)	1.223	(.201)
FMLA leave	1.299	(.262)	1.300	(.263)	.977	(−.023)	.916	(−.087)	.703	(−.352)
Paid leave	.276***	(−1.287)	.874	(−.135)	.547*	(−.604)	.912	(−.092)	2.500***	(.916)
Constant	5.076		−.572		.891		−4.837		−.232	
−2 Log L	617.907		591.640		553.897		610.987		692.194	
Model Chi-square (19 df)	127.774***		36.057*		41.638**		77.009***		54.601***	

* $p \leq .05$; ** $p \leq .01$; *** $p \leq .001$.
NOTE: Each equation controls for African American, Latino/a, Other ethnicity, Education, Age, Household income, Leave length, and Income imputed, not shown to preserve space.

TABLE 6.4 Logistic Regression of Return Reasons on Family, Work, and Control Variables, Men Leave Takers (N = 398)

Odds Ratios (Regression Coefficients)

Variables	(1) Could Not Afford More Time Off		(2) Used Up Leave Time		(3) Pressured by Boss/Coworkers		(4) Too Much to Do		(5) Just Wanted To	
Family										
Care for:										
ill person	1.545	(.435)	2.826*	(1.039)	1.247	(.221)	1.412	(.345)	.757	(−.279)
baby	1.338	(.291)	.815	(−.204)	1.183	(.168)	1.714	(.539)	.709	(−.343)
Leave for own health	.491*	(−.710)	.586	(−.535)	1.404	(.340)	.897	(−.109)	2.351**	(.855)
Number of children	.978	(−.023)	1.061	(.059)	1.207	(.188)	1.159	(.147)	1.038	(.037)
Married	1.336	(.290)	1.075	(.073)	1.057	(.056)	1.004	(.004)	.847	(−.166)
Work										
Unionized	.879	(−.129)	1.293	(.257)	.998	(−.002)	.491*	(−.711)	.711	(−.341)
Same employer	.458*	(−.782)	.518	(−.657)	.512	(−.670)	.835	(−.180)	2.396*	(.874)
FMLA-covered employer	.918	(−.085)	1.678	(.518)	.954	(−.047)	.438**	(−.825)	.840	(−.174)
Salaried employee	.608	(−.497)	.893	(−.113)	1.759	(.565)	1.989*	(.688)	1.176	(.162)
FMLA leave	1.450	(.371)	.998	(−.002)	1.772	(.572)	1.660	(.507)	1.494	(.402)
Paid leave	.207***	(−1.576)	.800	(−.224)	.400**	(−.915)	.671	(−.399)	1.528	(.424)
Constant	1.776		−.613		−2.149		−.463		−.414	
−2 Log L	416.015		343.237		339.592		426.701		479.934	
Model Chi-square (19 df)	101.425***		30.044*		27.511		51.858***		37.506**	

* $p \le .05$; ** $p \le .01$; *** $p \le .001$.
NOTE: Each equation controls for African American, Latino/a, Other ethnicity, Education, Age, Household income, Leave length, and Income imputed, not shown to preserve space.

needs of parents with newborns better than those who have to provide ongoing care for ill family members. This is consistent with other studies that have shown that employer policies and resources often do not adequately provide for the needs of workers who regularly provide care for elderly relatives (Abel, 1991; Gewirtz, 1995), and the unexpected bouts of illness that they may experience.

Consistent with hypothesis 3b, men's reasons for returning to work are virtually unresponsive to family variables. The results for men in Table 6.4 show that taking a leave for one's own health decreases the odds of returning to work for financial reasons and increases the odds of returning because one wants to return. This indicates that having daily caregiving responsibilities for other household members places few constraints on men's reasons for returning to work.

Discussion

Our findings indicate a gendered pattern in the determinants of leave-takers' reasons for returning to work. Consistent with our first hypothesis, women are more likely than men to terminate their leaves in response to pressures from work; men are more likely to terminate their leaves because they "wanted to." Since men, in general, do not face the same expectations and ongoing responsibilities for the day-to-day care of newborns and ill family members, they are less likely to feel the same degree of conflict between work and family responsibilities as female employees. Men, therefore, are more likely to return to work because that is the expectation that they, and others, hold. Women, shouldering the greater responsibility for the ongoing care of family members, are more likely to return to work as a result of conflicting demands.

Our second and third hypotheses on the relative importance of work and family for women's and men's reasons for returning to work received some support. As expected, both work and family variables influenced women's reasons for returning to work. Working for an FMLA-covered employer and having a fully paid leave reduces the constraints of work on a woman's reasons for returning to work. Although a family-friendly leave policy does not guarantee a family-friendly work culture, company policy and education can reduce work-family stress at the workplace ("An Evaluation of Johnson and Johnson's Work-Family Initiative," 1993). In addition to the financial and legal opportunities these conditions provide, the results suggest that employers covered by the FMLA and those that provide paid leave may foster an environment more supportive of leave-takers by promoting general support for employee leave-taking or making appropriate arrangements so that other employees feel less burdened in the leave-taker's absence. Family obligations, in particular, caring for an ill person, significantly increase the constraints of work on a woman's reasons for returning to work. In contrast, the impact of work and family variables on men's reasons for returning to work were, as expected, more limited and less patterned than the findings for women. Our findings indicate that workplace policies and benefits and family obligations have a greater and more patterned impact on women's reasons for returning to work than they do on men's reasons. Because women often shoulder the burden of caregiving responsibility, employer policies that ease the work-family conflict have the greatest impact on women.

CONCLUSION

The passage of the Family and Medical Leave Act marks a new era in employee rights and opportunities. Covered employees are no longer required to choose between their families and their jobs. It is, however, important to note that the Commission on Family and Medical Leave (1996) estimates that only approximately 55% of employees are covered under this legislation. Furthermore, although passage of the FMLA has significantly increased the number of male and female employees eligible for family leave, the percentage of employees eligible for paid parental or personal leave has not significantly increased (Mitchell, 1997). Any discussion of the significance of the Family and Medical Leave Act should bear these facts in mind.

The gendered pattern of findings in our study of leave-takers' reasons for returning to work suggests three avenues for future research on the interplay between leave policy and the work-family struggle. First, our findings show that, for women leave-takers, a combination of public and private policies reduces the constraints of work on women's reasons for returning to work. Although we are unable to disentangle the effects of the FMLA and better job benefits generally associated with larger employers, working for employers who are covered by the FMLA and who provide their employees with fully paid leaves reduces the conflicts that female leave-takers experience as they make return-to-work decisions. At the same time, the right to take an extended leave may be sharply curtailed by financial realities, particularly in lower-income households (Bond et al., 1991; Bookman, 1991). Employer provision of paid family and medical leave would make the right to take a 12-week leave when needed a genuine, rather than theoretical, possibility for those at the lower end of the pay scale. More research is needed to identify which private policies best complement the FMLA to enable workers to reconcile work-family conflicts and to enable employers to develop sound human resource management policies.

Second, the conflicting pressures that employees experience between home and work seem to be particularly acute for those who care for ill family members regularly. Employees who regularly care for those who are ill face greater conflicts than similar employees with infants when negotiating their return to work. It therefore appears that employer policies and attitudes do not adequately reflect the needs and concerns of workers caring for sick family members. This may be due, in part, to the often unexpected nature of these leaves. Leave policies need to be devised that are more reflective of the demands placed on employees who must regularly care for ill family members. Increased employer sensitivity to these issues would also be beneficial since changes in company policy can positively influence employee perceptions and experiences in the workplace ("An Evaluation of Johnson and Johnson's Work-Family Initiative," 1993).

Finally, our findings suggest that men's decisions to return to work are not equally responsive to the work and family constraints that influence women's decisions. Our analysis indicates that men leave-takers tend to return to work when they want to, and are less responsive to work and family constraints. This suggests that gender-neutral policies do not necessarily result in gender-neutral behavior. As Bergmann (1997) notes, family-friendly policies do not necessarily lead to gender equality and can, in fact, reinforce gendered division of labor. Future research ought to examine more closely men's leave-taking behavior in order to illuminate how public and private leave policy can be developed to encourage more men to confront the work-family struggle.

NOTES

1. To be eligible, an employee must work at a covered work site (a public or private agency employing at least 50 employees within a 75-mile radius), have worked for the employer at least 12 months, and have averaged at least 25 hours per week during the previous 12 months.

2. There are a few restrictions on this. Salaried employees whose compensation places them in the top 10% of employees within a 75-mile radius of the work site may be denied the guarantee of returning to the same or a comparable job if the employer can demonstrate that they are "key" employees whose absence would cause undue hardship to the employer. Such employees must be notified of their "key" status shortly after they inform their employer of their intent to take a leave (Commission on Family and Medical Leave, 1996).

3. The Commission used slightly different criteria for distinguishing those taking medical leaves from those taking family leaves than we did. While they apparently considered those taking maternity-related disabilities (such as toxemia) to be on family leave, we considered those workers to be on medical leave (Commission on Family and Medical Leave, 1996, Appendix A).

4. In the limited number of cases ($n = 12$) in which the respondent cared for more than one person on a daily basis, only the first person listed by the respondent was used to create the variables, cares for ill person or cares for baby. No cases were coded "1" for both variables. This decision was based on the assumption that the person needing the most care was listed first.

5. The respondents were asked if they had worked for their employer for at least one year at the time of the survey. It is therefore possible that they had not been with their employer at the time the leave was taken. It is therefore a conservative measure of work tenure.

6. Although the employees were asked if they had worked at least 25 hours per week, the approximate number necessary to be covered by the FMLA, this variable was not included in the analysis. There were too few men in the subsample who worked less than 25 hours to be able to perform the analysis.

7. Household income was originally coded in two ways. The responses of those who gave dollar values were used as given (with \$999,999 as the amount reflecting having earned at least \$999,999). Second, those who initially refused to state their income were asked multiple questions regarding whether their household income was greater or less than particular amounts. Among respondents who refused to give an exact amount but answered at least one question that somehow limited the range of their income, we imputed a value based on the median income of those who did give precise amounts and fell within each specific range option. We assigned the median household income value of the entire subsample who gave precise income values to respondents who refused to give any information about income. A dummy variable that reflects whether or not (yes = 1) respondent's household income was imputed was included in all of the equations. The regression coefficient for this dummy variable was statistically insignificant ($p > .05$) in all equations.

REFERENCES

Abel, E. K. (1991). *Who cares for the elderly? Public policy and the experience of adult daughters.* Philadelphia: Temple University Press.

Bergmann, B. R. (1997). Three perspectives on policy: Work-family policies and equality between women and men. In F. D. Blau & R. G. Ehrenberg (Eds.), *Gender and family issues in the workplace* (pp. 277-279). New York: Russell Sage.

Bond, J. T., Galinsky, E., Lord, M., Staines, G. L., & Brown, K. R. (1991). *Beyond the parental leave debate: The impact of laws in four states.* New York: Family and Work Institute.

Bookman, A. (1991). Parenting without poverty: The case for funded parental leave. In J. S. Hyde & M. J. Essex (Eds.), *Parental leave and child care: Setting a research and policy agenda* (pp. 66-89). Philadelphia: Temple University Press.

Brannen, K. C. (1996). Job-protected leave for family and medical reasons. In P. J. Dubeck & K. Borman (Eds.), *Women and work: A reader* (pp. 274-277). New Brunswick, NJ: Rutgers University Press.

Brody, E. M., & Schoonover, C. B. (1986). Patterns of parent-care when adult daughters work and when they do not. *The Gerontologist, 126*(4), 372-381.

Catalyst. (1986). *Report on a national study of parental leaves.* New York: Author.

Coltrane, S. (1996). *Family man: Fatherhood, housework and gender equity.* New York: Oxford University Press.

Commission on Family and Medical Leave. (1996). *A workable balance: Report to Congress on family and medical leave policies.* Washington, DC: U.S. Department of Labor, Women's Bureau.

Coverman, S., & Sheley, J. F. (1986). Change in men's housework and child-care time, 1965-1975. *Journal of Marriage and the Family, 48,* 413-422.

Enright, R. B., Jr. (1991). Time spent caregiving and help received by spouses and adult children of brain-impaired adults. *The Gerontologist, 3*(3), 375-383.

Essex, M. J., & Klein, M. H. (1991). The Wisconsin parental leave study: The role of fathers. In J. S. Hyde & M. Essex (Eds.), *Parental leave and child care: Setting a research and policy agenda* (pp. 280-293). Philadelphia: Temple University Press.

An evaluation of Johnson and Johnson's Work-Family Initiative. (1993). New York: Families and Work Institute.

Fried, M. (1996). *Caregiving choices, company voices: Workplace cultures and parental leave at Premium, Inc.* Unpublished doctoral dissertation, Brandeis University.

Galinsky, E., Bond, J. T., & Friedman, D. E. (1993). *The changing workforce: Highlights of the national study.* New York: Families and Work Institute.

Garrett, P., Lubeck, S., & Wenk, D.-A. (1991). Childbirth and maternal employment: Data from a national longitudinal study. In J. S. Hyde & M. Essex (Eds.), *Parental leave and child care: Setting a research and policy agenda* (pp. 24-38). Philadelphia: Temple University Press.

Gerson, K. (1993). *No man's land: Men's changing commitments to family and work.* New York: Basic Books.

Gewirtz, M. L. (1995). *Employers' perspectives regarding eldercare initiatives: The experience at Travelers.* Unpublished doctoral dissertation, Boston University.

Glass, J., & Fujimoto, T. (1995). Employer characteristics and the provision of family responsive policies. *Work and Occupations, 22*(4), 380-411.

Haas, L. (1992). *Equal parenthood and social policy: A study of parental leave in Sweden.* Albany: State University of New York Press.

Haas, L. (1993). Nurturing fathers and working mothers: Changing gender roles in Sweden. In J. C. Hood (Ed.), *Men, work and family* (pp. 238-261). Newbury Park, CA: Sage.

Hochschild, A. R. (1997). *The time bind: When work becomes home and home becomes work.* New York: Henry Holt.

Hochschild, A. R., with Machung, A. (1989). *The second shift.* New York: Avon Books.

Hossfeld, K. J. (1990). "Their logic against them": Contradictions in sex, race, and class, in Silicon Valley. In K. Ward (Ed.), *Women workers and global restructuring* (pp. 149-178). Ithaca, NY: ILR Press, School of Industrial and Labor Relations, Cornell University.

Hyde, J. S., Essex, M. J., & Horton, F. (1993). Fathers and parental leave: Attitudes and experiences. *Journal of Family Issues, 14*(4), 616-641.

Joesch, J. M. (1994). Children and the timing of women's paid work after childbirth: A further specification of the relationship. *Journal of Marriage and the Family, 56,* 429-440.

Kanter, R. M. (1977). *Men and women of the corporation.* New York: Basic Books.

MacGonagle, K. A., Connor, J., Heeringa, S., Veerkamp, P., & Groves, R. M. (1995). *Commission leave survey of employees on the impact of the family and medical leave act.* Ann Arbor: University of Michigan, Institute for Social Research, Survey Research Center.

Makuen, K. (1988). Public servants, private parents: Parental leave policies in the public sector. In E. F. Zigler & M. Frank (Eds.), *The parental leave crisis: Toward a national policy* (pp. 195-210). New Haven, CT: Yale University Press.

Markham, W. T., Bonjean, C., & Corder, J. (1986). Gender, out-of-town travel, and occupational advancement. *Sociology and Social Research, 70,* 156-160.

Matthews, S. H. (1995). Gender and the division of filial responsibility between lone sisters and their brothers. *Journal of Gerontology, 50B*(5), S312-S320.

Mitchell, O. A. (1997). Work and family benefits. In F. D. Blau & R. G. Ehrenberg (Eds.), *Gender and family issues in the workplace* (pp. 259-279). New York: Russell Sage.

Pleck, J. H. (1988). Fathers and infant care leave. In E. F. Zigler & M. Frank (Eds.), *The parental leave crisis: Toward a national policy* (pp. 177-210). New Haven, CT: Yale University Press.

Pleck, J. H. (1993). Are "family supportive" employer policies relevant to men? In J. C. Hood (Ed.), *Men, work and family* (pp. 217-237). Newbury Park, CA: Sage.

Scharlach, A. E., & Boyd, S. L. (1989). Caregiving and employment: Results of an employer survey. *The Gerontologist, 29,* 382-387.

Stoller, E. P. (1990). Males as helpers: The role of sons, relatives and friends. *The Gerontologist, 30*(2), 228-235.

Stone, R., Caffarata, G. L., & Sangl, J. (1987). Caregivers of the frail elderly: A national profile. *The Gerontologist, 27,* 616-626.

U.S. Bureau of the Census. (1996). *Statistical abstract of the United States* (116th ed.). Washington, DC: Government Printing Office.

PART III

Later in the Life Course

These chapters explore key work and family issues that arise later in the life course, that is, as children reach middle childhood, adolescence, and young adulthood. Thus we turn from exclusive focus on managing the day-to-day demands of coping with work and family to the issues of how time needs to be allocated slightly later in the life course in order to maximize child well-being. Parcel, Nickoll, and Dufur are directly concerned with child outcomes themselves. Although many of the remaining chapters certainly bring evidence to bear on the issue of adult well-being, which has implications for children, they do not study child outcomes explicitly. Second, the Parcel et al. chapter treats maternal and paternal work equally in studying the effects of parental working conditions on child outcomes. This is a particularly welcome innovation given the importance of fathers to families and the relative infrequency with which maternal inputs and paternal inputs into child well-being are considered evenhandedly. Theoretically, the chapter draws on both James Coleman's notions of family social capital and Mel Kohn's ideas on work and personality to argue that parental work should affect child cognition. Using a sample of 1,067 9- to 12-year-olds of employed and nonemployed mothers from the 1992 National Longitudinal Survey's child-mother data set, the authors found that the most important determinants of reading and mathematics achievement were characteristics of the children and parents themselves. Maternal mental ability had positive effects while child's low birth weight had negative effects; higher numbers of siblings showed negative effects on scores, while boys scored higher on the mathematics test but lower on the reading test than girls. Maternal work characteristics were not generally important, although children's reading achievement was higher when mothers were highly educated and did not work; in addition, mothers with complex work who worked high part-time hours had children with stronger reading achievement than mothers who did not have this combination of work advantages. Paternal part-time and paternal overtime work hours were helpful to math scores.

Johnson and Mortimer are interested in how adolescents view future work and family roles, and whether these sets of attitudes differ by gender. They also investigate what difference these attitude sets might make for early adult status attainment and family formation, outcomes that clearly have important implications for well-being in later adulthood. They posit an amalgamation hypothesis wherein young women are likely to combine aspirations for both paid employment and family formation, and contrast this view with others suggesting that female goals for achievement might compete with those supporting family formation. They argue that among males the goals for achievement and family formation might be more loosely coupled, or that males might follow the traditional model of these values being closely associated, based on the thinking that career success facilitates family formation. The authors use data from the Youth Development Study, a prospective longitudinal study of ninth graders in St. Paul, Minnesota, public schools. Analysis focused on data from 1991, when respondents were in 12th grade, and 1995, 4 years after graduation. Gender differences in work aspirations were not significant, suggesting that both male and female adolescents aspire to high work involvement; females were, however, more likely to aspire to family formation than males, thus suggesting support for the amalgamation perspective among young women. They did, however, anticipate sacrificing paid work involvement to the needs of family. In terms of behavior, young women also acquire family roles more quickly than men. Achievement and family orientations in adolescence predicted early adult behaviors; for example, those who aspired to early marriage were more likely to marry early. Sequencing strategies—for example, completing schooling before marriage—foster attainment. Young women clearly did amalgamate expectations for paid work involvement with those for family formation.

Roberta Iversen and Naomi Farber bring evidence to bear on the important issue of intergenerational value transmission regarding work and welfare. They study a randomly selected subsample of 50 respondents from a larger set of 74 interviews with young Black women, ages 13 to 24, who were interviewed in Milwaukee, Wisconsin, between 1987 and 1989. Twenty-four of the 50 were teen mothers, and 26 were nonparent peers. The authors are concerned with four questions: What values about welfare and work did respondents and their families hold? How were these values transmitted across generations? What implications did variations in transmission have for respondents' socioeconomic outcomes? Were these values, processes, and outcomes different by teen-parent status? The authors found almost universal dislike for welfare receipt and particular respect for education and training as mechanisms toward employment and self-sufficiency. Intergenerational value transmission processes include direct verbal messages; offering of tangible support, such as child care, financial help, or transportation, to allow the respondent to obtain training; and examples of other family members who were self-sufficient, in some cases despite clear obstacles. Self-sufficiency among the teen mothers and nonparent peers was more likely when respondents reported that value transmission was multifaceted; more peers than teen mothers reported multifaceted value transmission. Iversen and Farber argue that social policies need to encourage the accumulation of social capital via multifaceted value transmission regarding work and self-sufficiency, and that although such value transmission within families needs to be supported, additional nonfamilial support might also be useful. Their contribution to the theme of time allocation revolves round the concept of family social capital. Investments in the nature and strength of family social capital in one generation can pay off in the self-sufficiency of the next generation. Although these payoffs are potentially long term, the richness of Iversen's and Farber's evidence makes a compelling case for these investments' potential effectiveness.

CHAPTER 7

The Effects of Parental Work and Maternal Nonemployment on Children's Reading and Math Achievement

TOBY L. PARCEL

REBECCA A. NICKOLL

MIKAELA J. DUFUR

FOUNDATIONS OF THE STUDY

Researchers and parents continue to express concern that maternal employment may have deleterious effects on child well-being. Rates of maternal employment rose sharply during the 1980s, especially employment among mothers of young children. The U.S. Bureau of the Census (1987, 1993) reported that for mothers with children under 6, 54% worked in 1986 and close

AUTHORS' NOTE: An earlier version of this article was presented at the annual meetings of the American Sociological Association, 1996, New York City. Preparation of this article was supported in part by the College of Social and Behavioral Sciences and the Center for Human Resource Research at The Ohio State University. We appreciate comments by Doug Downey and Elizabeth Menaghan on an earlier draft.

to 60% worked in 1992. Past studies on the effects of maternal employment on children's cognition have examined *either* the impact of employment status (Easterbrooks & Goldberg, 1985; Farel, 1980; Gold & Andres, 1978; Milne, Myers, Rosenthal, & Ginsburg, 1986) *or* the effects from different working conditions on child well-being (Parcel & Menaghan, 1994b). A particular focus in past research has been to study whether maternal employment when children are young is problematic, with several studies suggesting that dangers have been overgeneralized (see Parcel & Menaghan, 1994a, for key findings and review). Relatively neglected, however, has been analysis of the implications of maternal work for older children. In this study, we consider *both* maternal employment status and work characteristics for employed mothers as determinants of reading and math outcomes among 9- to 12-year-olds. We build on past research and incorporate theory from Kohn's (1977) work on jobs and personality and Coleman's (1988) ideas about social capital in the family.

Several strands of literature combine to suggest it is important to study the effects of maternal employment status on child well-being. In their study of nonemployed wives, Bird and Ross (1993, p. 913) conceptualize the full-time housewife as a "unique occupation." They argue that many of the negative aspects of being a housewife are associated with the lack of pay, with no opportunity to receive a raise or get a promotion except indirectly through a household member. In addition, a housewife cannot benefit from the psychological support employment can provide to buffer the effects of stress in other aspects of life (Hoffman, 1989). Bird and Ross (1993) also report that housewives felt less fulfillment and more routinization from their work, as well as a lower sense of personal control in their work than paid workers. Glass (1992) found that wives employed full-time were younger, more highly educated, had higher incomes, and had fewer children than married housewives. However, mothers who worked full-time reported more stress about not spending enough time with their children, which could offset the positive psychological effects of employment (Hoffman, 1989). These findings suggest that the effects of mothers' work may vary according to the amount of time she spends at work or the kind of work performed.

Children of nonemployed mothers will likely spend more time at home instead of in child care and so may have more opportunities to be influenced by the home environment and their mothers' background characteristics. However, Greenstein (1995) found that, compared to children of nonemployed mothers, the 4- to 6-year-old children of "advantaged mothers," or those with the education and income to provide cognitively stimulating home environments, did not fare worse on standardized tests of verbal ability when their mother worked in the first 4 years of their lives. Because even younger children who stand to gain the most cognitively from maternal nonemployment do not suffer adverse effects when their mothers work, we hypothesize that maternal nonemployment per se will generally not be an asset to older children's cognitive outcomes. Because of the added earnings and the greater chance for mothers to exercise their own cognitive skills that maternal employment brings to the family, we believe children will generally benefit from having a mother who works outside the home. However, as past research suggests, the positive effects of maternal employment may depend on the complexity of the work performed by the mother and her level of work hours (Parcel & Menaghan, 1994a, 1994b).

Past studies have shown that although maternal employment status alone is insufficient to explain differences in children's cognitive achievement, it may be a contributing factor (Hoffman, 1989). Kalmijn (1994), in studying high school and college outcomes, found that children of nonemployed mothers fared about the same as children of the average employed mother but fared worse than children of managerial and professional women. However, previous research does not explicitly consider both employment status and work characteristics in their effects on cognition in older children. Our study will address this limitation and add to the understanding of how parents' employment or nonemployment affects their children. Given that past research demonstrates that employed and nonemployed mothers differ in terms of skills and resources, we examine employment status in our model. However, we also consider work characteristics for those mothers who are employed, as well as for their spouses.

SOCIAL CAPITAL IN THE FAMILY

Theory also suggests that maternal employment status is relevant to child well-being. Coleman (1988) stresses the importance of the social capital available within families as an influence on children's outcomes. Social capital is embedded in social structure and refers to relations among actors. These relations may constitute social resources upon which actors can draw. Social capital is often specific to certain activities and can take many forms, such as obligations, expectations, information channels, and norms. Within a family, social capital includes the relationships among parents, children, and other family members; its amount is influenced by the strength of the bonds among family members. Because parents build social capital with their children through their interactions, attention, and physical presence, mothers' employment outside the home may limit the development of social capital. Indeed, Coleman feels that a family in which "both parents work outside the home, can be seen as structurally deficient, lacking the social capital that comes with the presence of parents during the day" (p. S111). If a family lacks social capital, children will have reduced opportunities to benefit from parental human capital. For instance, poorly educated and/or financially unstable parents may not possess a great deal of human capital. However, if they spend time interacting with their children, playing with them, or helping them with homework, they will establish strong bonds with their children so the children may have access to whatever human capital the parents do possess, including ties to the community or personal resources such as self-esteem. Analyses of the effects of social capital for older children are particularly compatible with work by Crane (1991a, 1991b) and Massey, Gross, and Eggers (1991), suggesting that social capital influences adolescent outcomes such as premarital pregnancy and educational attainment.

As Parcel and Menaghan's (1994a, 1994b) work has shown, maternal nonemployment during children's first few years does not have uniformly positive effects on children's cognition, thereby discounting the idea that maternal employment per se impairs social capital in families. For instance, the effect of nonemployment during the first year of a child's life only benefited those children whose mothers later worked in low complexity jobs. Early nonemployment had a negative effect on children whose mothers later worked in high complexity jobs, a near zero effect for mothers working in average complexity jobs, and a positive effect for those in low complexity jobs. Therefore, although relationships in families may be an important aid for children's cognitive achievement, maternal employment does not uniformly result in lower cognitive outcomes for children.

JOBS AND PERSONALITY

Given that many parents do work outside the home, how do their jobs influence their children? One likely mechanism is for parental work to affect parents' psychological states, which in turn affect parenting. For both men and women, occupational characteristics affect adult psychological functioning (Kohn & Schooler, 1973, 1982; Lennon & Rosenfield, 1992; Link, Lennon, & Dohrenwend, 1993; Miller, Schooler, Kohn, & Miller, 1979). Jobs that encourage self-direction at work increase ideational flexibility and encourage *personal* self-direction, but jobs that limit self-direction promote conformist values. Kohn and Schooler (1983) show that occupational complexity as well as opportunity for autonomy and self-direction are the occupational characteristics that have the greatest influence on adult men's personalities. Miller et al. (1979) found that women's occupational conditions affected their intellectual flexibility as well as their general psychological functioning, but psychological functioning did not, in turn, affect working conditions. Amount of job control also affects levels of psychological distress (Lennon & Rosenfield, 1992; Link et al., 1993). Lennon and Rosenfield found that mothers experienced less distress when they had more job control and autonomy, and that job control offsets the negative impact of high family demands even with children present in the family. Link et al. assessed direction, planning, and control over others' work and found them to be important predictors of distress levels. Thus perceptions of control over one's job play an important role in the psychological well-being of individuals, which may link to parenting and child well-being.

Some researchers have investigated how job conditions indirectly influence parental child-rearing values through personality. Kohn (1977) argued that parents of different social classes raise their children in different ways, largely due to differences in parenting values. These parental values arise from how each social class experiences life, or the social structural conditions its members face (Spade, 1991). Parcel and Menaghan (1994a) argue that parents encourage in their children those values they internalize from their own working conditions. This suggests an intergenerational link for the influence occupational conditions have on parents and ultimately on their children. Individuals who perform high complexity work are more likely to value self-direction and the internalization of this concept by their children, whereas individuals who perform low complexity work are more likely to instill values of conformity to established norms in their children. Routinized work also diminishes individuals' intellectual flexibility, which in turn affects the amount of intellectual stimulation the child experiences at home; such stimulation, in turn, could affect child cognition.

Parents who value self-direction tend to value supportive behavior toward their infants and, in turn, provide more supportive home environments in terms of maternal warmth and involvement with the child, emotional responsiveness, and time spent reading to the child (Luster, Rhoades, & Haas, 1989). Previous research suggests that parents who do complex work may encourage high cognitive achievement in their children (Parcel & Menaghan, 1990, 1994a; Piotrkowski & Katz, 1982). Therefore, we expect parents in our sample whose occupations require self-direction and intellectual flexibility to encourage greater cognitive skills in their children than parents working in highly routinized jobs.

OTHER WORK CHARACTERISTICS

As implied by Coleman's (1988) arguments, the extent of parental employment may have implications for children's cognitive outcomes. Parcel and Menaghan (1994a) found that both mother's and father's overtime hours negatively affected young children's verbal facility. Parents who work overtime hours may not spend as much time interacting or playing with their children as do parents who work 35 to 40 hours per week. Just as overtime hours may have negative effects on children, paternal part-time hours may negatively affect children's cognitive achievement due to lower paternal self-esteem if the father cannot find steady full-time employment or was fired.

However, as Leibowitz (1977) argues, the amount of time parents spend with children is often difficult to calculate. Rather, the types of activities in which parents and children participate, not the amount of time alone, provide more reliable measures of parental time spent with children. Parental characteristics such as cognitive skills and education may largely set the tone, at least early in a child's life, for the types of activities in which children participate at home. Parents who value self-direction and independent thinking encourage these skills, which in turn encourage their children's cognitive achievement.

Mothers' and fathers' earnings also influence children's outcomes. Higher earnings provide more resources for engaging in cultural events or from which parents can provide educational resources for their children. Higher earnings resulting from maternal employment tend to have positive effects on children's cognition in the second and later years of a child's life (Blau & Grossberg, 1990). Lower earnings can cause psychological distress among family members or cause them to work several jobs. This can result in a poor atmosphere for children to build social capital with their parents and gain access to parental human capital resources, ultimately impairing their cognitive achievement. We therefore predict that higher maternal and paternal hourly wages will have a positive effect on children's cognitive outcomes.

FATHERS' INVOLVEMENT

Paternal characteristics are important to consider in tandem with maternal characteristics. Paternal values and human capital likely influence children throughout the socialization process. In addition, if the spouses of employed mothers increase their share of child care, they will have greater interaction with their children and more opportunities to teach values. Paternal involvement in children's lives could offset some of the resource dilution that may occur when mothers work outside the home. Nugent (1991), in his study of Irish working-class fathers (married to both employed and nonemployed mothers), found that fathers' involvement during the first year of the child's life had an independent positive effect on the cognitive functioning of the infants at 1 year of age.

CHILD CHARACTERISTICS

In our model, we control for low birth weight and child health problems. Severe health problems limit the extent to which children can attend school and participate in activities, whereas low birth weight may place children at a higher risk for impaired cognitive development. Because the Peabody Individual Achievement Tests (PIAT) are administered to the child by an interviewer the child does not know, the testing conditions may cause anxiety in the child. Past research supports the hypothesis that children who are shy may feel especially anxious during the tests, which could affect their performance (Parcel & Menaghan, 1990, 1994a). We expect that children who seemed shy or anxious at the time of the cognitive testing will score lower on the tests and therefore control for shyness and anxiety as observed by the interviewer. We also control for gender, because the cognitive development of boys may lag behind that of girls in reading achievement (Blake, 1989) but be accelerated in mathematics.

FAMILY CHARACTERISTICS

We control for parental age because older parents may possess personal resources or coping skills gained from their greater experience with the stresses and demands of life than younger parents possess. Older parents have had more opportunities to establish themselves in a career or strengthen their own sense of control over their lives before having children. We expect older parents of 9- to 12-year-olds to have more personal resources apart from human capital resources they already possess from which children could benefit. In addition, we expect that parents with high levels of education and cognitive skills will encourage cognitive development in their children. As Leibowitz (1977) found, more highly educated mothers were more likely to participate

TABLE 7.1 List of Variables

Variable	*Description*
PIAT Math	Measured in 1992. This test taps math achievement from recognizing numerals to trigonometry concepts.
PIAT Reading	Measured in 1992. This portion of the test taps reading using measures of reading recognition and pronunciation ability from preschool to high school levels.
Occupational complexity	Measured in 1992 for mothers and 1991 for spouses. This 19-item scale ($\alpha = .94$) was developed by Parcel by first matching data from the *Dictionary of Occupational Titles* (U.S. Department of Labor, 1977) to 1970 U.S. Census occupational codes and then performing factor analysis on the data. The scale measures three aspects of jobs including the education/training levels required for the work; the direction, control, and planning of activities; and the complexity of working with people and data. Our scale uses 1980 census occupational codes for mothers and 1970 codes for spouses. Nonemployed mothers received a missing value for this variable.
Usual work hours per week	Measured in 1992 for mothers and 1991 for spouses. For mothers, dummy variables capture no work hours, low part-time hours (1 to 20), high part-time hours (21 to 34), full-time hours (35 to 40), and overtime hours (41+). For spouses, a dummy variable represents part-time (1 to 34), full-time (35 to 40), and overtime (40+) hours. For both parents, full-time hours are the reference group.
Maternal nonemployment	Measured in 1992. Mothers who reported no work hours were coded 1 and all employed mothers were the reference group.
Hourly wages	Measured in 1992 for mothers and 1991 for spouses. For both parents, this is captured by average hourly wage. For fathers, this measure was constructed by dividing average annual earnings by average hours worked.
Marital status	A dummy variable measuring mothers who were married or not married in 1992. Not married is the reference group.
Parental education	Measured in 1992 for mother and spouse. Mother's education level is captured by years of education minus the mean maternal education level to get a deviation from the mean. Spouse's education is measured by number of years.
Parental age	Measured in 1992 for mother and mother's spouse.
Maternal cognitive skills	Measured by the mother's percentile score on the Armed Forces Qualifying Test (AFQT) given in 1980. This test measures paragraph comprehension, word knowledge, arithmetic ability, and numeric operational skills.

TABLE 7.1 Continued

Variable	Description
Maternal self-esteem	Measured in 1987 using a 10-item Rosenberg self-esteem scale ($\alpha = .78$).
Maternal ethnicity/race	Measured as a dummy variable capturing Black, White, Mexican Hispanic, and other Hispanic groups.
Additional siblings	This is measured in 1992 as the number of siblings the child had.
Child gender	A dummy variable with female as the reference group.
Child health problems	Measured in 1992. A dummy variable with no health problems that limit the child's participation in activities and school as the reference group.
Shyness and anxiety	Assessed by the interviewer at the start of the 1992 interview. The scale ranges from 1 = *not at all shy/anxious* to 5 = *extremely shy/anxious*.
Low birth weight	A dummy variable distinguishing between children whose birth weight was below 5.5 pounds and weight of 5.5 pounds or more as the reference group.
Grandmother's education	The child's maternal grandmother's level of education.

NOTE: PIAT = Peabody Individual Achievement Test

in activities with their children that encouraged the development of verbal skills, such as reading to their children, instead of activities such as watching television, which may not involve interaction.

We expect children in families where the mother is married to have higher cognitive skills than children from single-parent families. Having two parents present in the home provides greater opportunity for parent-child interactions and a greater base of parental resources from which the child may draw. In addition, marital dissolution causes added emotional and often financial stress on family members, which could hamper children's cognitive development.

We predict that, following the resource dilution hypothesis, greater numbers of siblings in the family will negatively affect children's cognitive outcomes (Blake, 1989; Desai, Chase-Lansdale, & Michael, 1989; Downey, 1995; Herr, 1985). Researchers have argued that additional children dilute the amount of time (Leibowitz, 1977) and the emotional and financial resources parents can spend on each child. Blake (1989) and Herr (1985) found that having a larger number of siblings generally had a negative effect on a child's educational attainment. We therefore control for the number of siblings in 1992.

INTERACTIONS

A key finding from earlier research is that the effects of parental work on child well-being can vary depending on parental or child background or on family circumstances (Parcel & Menaghan, 1994a, 1994b). To test Parcel and Menaghan's (1994a) finding that maternal cognitive skills were more effective in encouraging children's cognitive skills when the mother reinforced her skills on the job, we evaluate whether Armed Forces Qualifying Test (AFQT) scores interact with occupational complexity. We expect complex work to increase the effect of mothers' cognitive skills. We also test for an interaction between another measure of maternal resources, education, and maternal employment status. Following Kohn's (1977) theory about how work helps individuals exercise their cognitive skills, we expect nonemployment to hinder the cognitive development of children of mothers with low levels of education more than that of children of highly educated mothers. Poorly educated mothers who do not work may not engage in activities on their own or with their children to practice their cognitive skills.

We test for an interaction between maternal work characteristics such as complexity and work hours to examine whether extent of employment has different implications for cognitive outcomes depending on the type of work the mother does. We expect higher levels of work hours to be more beneficial if the mother does complex work, because the benefits of work complexity would be reinforced via longer job hours.

We also test for interactions between work and family variables. Because the number of siblings a child has dilutes the child's access to the parent's human capital resources, maternal employment may have a more negative effect on cognition with larger numbers of children in a family. To determine whether spouse's work characteristics have more positive effects when mothers are not employed, we test for an interaction between spouse's occupational complexity and maternal employment status. Conversely, mother's work characteristics may be more important for children's cognitive outcomes when the mother is not married and she is the sole breadwinner, so we test for an interaction between marital status and maternal employment. If

TABLE 7.2 Means, Standard Deviations, and Correlations for Variables in the Model (*N* = 1,067)

Variable	Mean	Standard Deviation
PIAT Math 1992	100.436	12.723
PIAT Reading Recognition 1992	103.885	14.418
Child characteristics		
Male	.521	.500
Low birth weight	.060	.238
Number of siblings 1992	1.455	1.035
Shy at interview 1992	1.668	.864
Health problems 1992	.056	.230
Parental characteristics		
Mother		
Grandmother's education	10.675	2.692
Non-White	.287	.453
AFQT percentile score 1980	39.597	26.558
Self-esteem 1987	.012	.563
Age 1992	31.832	2.181
Education 1992	12.136	1.721
Married 1992	.654	.476
Spouse		
Age 1992	35.025	3.997
Education 1992	12.358	2.713
Maternal work characteristics 1992		
Occupational complexity	−3.145	10.637
Hourly wages	8.35	11.185
Nonemployed	.227	.419
Employed mothers' hours		
Average hours	34.824	10.927
1 to 20	.161	.323
21 to 34	.153	.317
34 to 40	.568	.436
Over 40	.118	.284
Spouse work characteristics 1991		
Occupational complexity	−3.541	7.652
Hourly wages	13.489	6.125
Work hours		
Average hours	45.219	9.507
Under 35	.044	.156
35 to 40	.526	.381
Over 40	.430	.377

NOTE: PIAT = Peabody Individual Achievement Test; AFQT = Armed Forces Qualifying Test.

TABLE 7.3 1992 PIAT Math and Reading: Impact of 1992 Family Background,
Child, and Work Characteristics ($N = 1,067$, standard errors in
parentheses)

Variable	PIAT Math		PIAT Reading	
	b	β	b	β
Grandmother's education	.124	.026	−.038	−.007
	(.144)		(.162)	
AFQT score 1980	.138**	.287	.177**	.326
	(.018)		(.020)	
Maternal self-esteem 1987	−.396	−.018	−.974	−.038
	(.651)		(.733)	
Mother's age 1992	−.180	−.031	.049	.007
	(.175)		(.196)	
Mother's education 1992	.218	.030	.165	.020
	(.241)		(.317)	
Spouse's age 1992	.059	.019	−.031	−.009
	(.091)		(.102)	
Spouse's education 1992	.277**	.059	.261*	.049
	(.133)		(.149)	
Non-White	−2.640**	−.094	−1.405	−.044
	(.908)		(1.020)	
Male	1.877**	.074	−2.595**	−.090
	(.693)		(.913)	
Low birth weight	−4.174**	−.078	−3.808**	−.063
	(1.461)		(1.647)	
Married 1992	−.226	−.008	1.886**	.062
	(.882)		(.879)	
Number of siblings 1992	−.294	−.024	−1.384**	−.099
	(.429)		(.387)	
Child health problems 1992	−4.603**	−.083	−3.921**	−.063
	(1.509)		(1.695)	
Child shyness 1992	−1.727**	−.117	−2.053**	−.123
	(.407)		(.457)	
Mother's work 1992				
Hourly wages	−.032	−.029	−.014	−.011
	(.031)		(.035)	
Hours worked[a]				
Nonemployed	−1.018	−.034	.052	.002
	(1.836)		(1.380)	
1 to 20	1.314	.033	1.174	.026
	(1.134)		(1.269)	
21 to 34	.406	.010	−.002	−3.689E-5
	(1.160)		(1.385)	
35 to 40[b]	—	—	—	—

TABLE 7.3 Continued

Variable	PIAT Math		PIAT Reading	
	b	β	*b*	β
Over 40	.009	2.087	−1.266	−.025
	(1.269)		(1.421)	
Occupational complexity	.021	.018	−.029	−.021
	(.034)		(.057)	
Spouse's work 1991				
Hourly wages	.252**	.121	.101	.043
	(.066)		(.074)	
Hours worked				
Less than 35	4.373*	.054	−.773	−.008
	(2.287)		(2.567)	
35 to 40[b]	—	—	—	—
Over 40	2.545**	.075	1.210	.032
	(.962)		(1.076)	
Occupational complexity	−.084	−.050	−.010	−.005
	(.051)		(.064)	
Maternal nonemployment				
• Married	3.142*	.085		
	(1.713)			
Nonemployed • Education			1.078**	.070
			(.522)	
Nonemployed • Male			−3.303*	−.072
			(1.835)	
Maternal complexity • High				
part-time hours			.216**	.062
			(.106)	
Male • Maternal complexity			.137*	.076
			(.073)	
Spouse's complexity				
• Maternal complexity			−.235**	−.064
			(.118)	
Constant		93.072		99.862
Adjusted R^2		.240		.255

NOTE: Only significant interaction effects included for each model.

a. *F* tests showed the set of dummy variables to be insignificant at *p* < .10.

b. no data on reference group for categorical variable.

PIAT = Peabody Individual Achievement Test, AFQT = Armed Forces Qualifying Test.

* *p* < .10; ** *p* < .05, one-tailed test.

children of nonemployed mothers fare better on average on cognitive tests than children of employed mothers, regardless of work characteristics, then mothers' time out of the home may, as Coleman (1988) suggests, hinder children's access to social capital. However, we expect children of mothers who are employed to fare better than children of nonemployed mothers on cognitive tests if their mother performs complex work and does not work overtime hours.

In addition, we test for interactions between child gender and maternal work characteristics. Because research shows that boys lag behind girls in reading achievement (Blake, 1989), maternal employment may prove an additional hindrance to boys' reading achievement. To test this hypothesis, we test an interaction between extent of maternal employment and child gender. We expect higher levels of work hours to have a more negative effect on boys' reading achievement than lower levels. Because boys might be more negatively affected by maternal employment than girls, we test for an interaction between child gender and maternal nonemployment. Finally, we also test for an interaction between child gender and maternal occupational substantive complexity to determine whether working in a more complex occupation has more positive effects for boys than for girls.

SAMPLE, MEASUREMENT, AND METHODS

We use the Merged Child-Mother Data from the 1992 wave of the National Longitudinal Survey of Youth (NLSY). The NLSY is an ongoing national survey begun in 1979 by the National Opinion Research Center in Chicago and the Center for Human Resource Research at Ohio State University. The original multistage stratified area probability sample of 12,686 youths who were 14 to 21 years old in 1979 (the Youth cohort) overrepresents Blacks and Hispanics. Reinterviews occurred each year, and in 1986, new funding allowed data collection on the children of the mothers in this cohort, including assessments of the children's cognitive outcomes (*NLS Handbook 1994*). For the NLSY Child-Mother Data, the unit of observation is each of the biological children born between 1979 and 1992 of NLSY cohort women. The Child-Mother Data links information about the mother's background, health, attitudes, and occupational conditions to information about the child's health, child care situation, family history and composition, and scores on assessment tests. The longitudinal nature of the NLSY, as well as the 91.8% retention rate of respondents, make the data set ideal for studying intergenerational linkages between family behaviors and child outcomes (*NLS Handbook 1994*).

Our sampling frame consists of 9- to 12-year-old children of employed and nonemployed mothers in 1992. This age group is particularly important to study because at this age, children have had some formal schooling but have not yet entered the often tumultuous adolescent years. Children of these ages are learning how to compare their abilities with those of other children in school and also how to measure the amount of their efforts, skills, and motivation necessary to achieve rewards. Entwisle, Alexander, Pallas, and Cadigan (1987) describe this as "developing an academic self-image," a process that begins when children enter first grade and presumably continues throughout the rest of their formal schooling. Kagan (1978, p. 103) argues that during the few years before a child enters puberty, the child gains "several new and profound intellective capacities," such as the ability to deal with hypothetical situations. Children ages 9 to 12 have more experience with formal school than do first graders, but they are still learning how to manage teachers' requirements as well as their own strengths and shortcomings. Children's patterns of academic achievement during these years may set the tone for achievement during adolescence and beyond, which emphasizes the importance of understanding how parents' work and absence from the home can affect children's cognition.

If a mother had more than one child aged 9 to 12 in 1992, we randomly selected one child for our sample to avoid overrepresenting mothers with high fertility. Our sample includes only those children who resided with their mother in 1992, because maternal employment or nonemployment may not affect a child as strongly if the child does not reside with the mother. Children who reside with guardians other than their mothers face additional barriers to building social capital with their mothers that are beyond the scope of this study.

The NLSY sample of mothers in 1992 ($N = 3,326$), when weighted, is representative of American mothers ages 27 to 34 on January 1, 1992, and their children are representative of American children born to such a sample of women (Baker, Keck, Mott, & Quinlan, 1993). Our analyses use sampling weights to make the original sample of mothers generalizable to a nationally representative sample. Our sample ($N = 1,067$), however, is limited in its representativeness by the fact that the mothers who had children ages 9 to 12 in 1992 were early and on-time childbearers who had their children when they were 15 to 25 years old. They likely have fewer educational and occupational skills than later childbearers.

Table 7.1 presents a description of variables and their measurement. We will briefly highlight some of the main variables of interest. We use the Mathematics and Reading Recognition assessments from the PIAT as measures of children's reading and math achievement in 1992. The PIATs measure academic achievement and were given to all children whose age on the PPVT-R (a test of verbal ability administered to all children) was 5 and older. The math portion of the PIAT taps the child's math achievement from recognizing numerals to advanced trigonometry concepts. The test is widely used because of its high test-retest reliability and concurrent validity. The reading recognition test correlates moderately well with the math test and has fairly high test-retest reliability. It measures word recognition and pronunciation skills from the preschool to high school levels; word recognition and pronunciation are crucial skills for reading achievement (Baker, Keck, Mott, & Quinlan, 1993).

We use a 19-item-based occupational complexity scale (see also Parcel, 1989) that taps the direction, control, and planning of jobs, the education and training required by a job, and the complexity of working with people and data, including verbal and numeric aptitude. This scale ($\alpha = .94$) ranges from –26.56 to 27.34 for our sample. Examples of occupations with high complexity scores include foreign language teacher (27.34) and computer systems analyst (18.39). Occupations with low substantive complexity include waitress (–12.85) and maid (–23.48). Nonemployed mothers receive a missing value for occupational complexity.

Regarding work hours, we contrast nonemployed mothers with all mothers who were employed (the reference group) in 1992. For the mothers who were employed, we distinguished between low part-time hours (1 to 20), high part-time hours (21 to 34), full-time hours (34 to 40, the reference group), and overtime hours (more than 40 hours per week). Nonemployed mothers received missing values for the work hours variables. For spouses, we distinguished between part-time hours (less than or equal to 34), full-time hours (35 to 40, the reference group), and overtime hours (greater than 40 hours per week.) Unmarried mothers received missing values for all spouse work variables and married mothers with unemployed spouses received missing values for spouse's occupational complexity and 1991 hourly wages.

The NLSY only gathered data about *maternal* resources such as locus of control, self-esteem, and cognitive ability. We measure maternal cognitive skills by the percentile score on the Armed Forces Qualifying Test given in 1980, which assesses paragraph comprehension, word knowledge, arithmetic reasoning, and numeric operations. Our measure of maternal 1992 education is the number of years of education minus the mean level of education for our sample, which centers our measure of education on the mean.

Our study uses regression analysis to test our hypotheses. Missing data are handled using the mean substitution method, which assigns the mean value for a variable to cases that have missing data for that variable. This strategy provides a more conservative test and reduces the number of missing cases in a regression.

SAMPLE CHARACTERISTICS

Table 7.2 displays means and standard deviations of variables in the model. The low percentile score on the AFQT test and the low maternal occupational complexity score reflect the lower levels of skills possessed by this sample of mothers. The mean substantive complexity score for employed mothers was -3.145. This negative score indicates that this sample of mothers held below average complexity occupations compared to a self-weighted sample of occupations. About 24% of employed mothers held occupations with above average complexity (greater than one standard deviation from the mean for this sample), and 28% held occupations with below average complexity (lower than one standard deviation from the mean score for this sample).

Of the entire sample, 77% of the mothers worked during 1992 and close to one half of all mothers worked full-time. Mothers' spouses worked on average 45 hours per week in 1991, with 43% working overtime hours. The average hourly wage for spouses in 1991 was $13.49. Mothers averaged $8.35 per hour in 1992. Mothers were between 27 and 35 years old in 1992 and averaged 12 years of education; 65.4% of the mothers were married.

In the regression models, we initially progressively entered variables as follows: (a) the most exogenous family background characteristics; (b) the most exogenous child characteristics; (c) current mother, spouse, and child characteristics; and (d) mother and spouse current working conditions. Findings suggested that the final models represented key findings well, so only those are presented here. Regression coefficients are significant for one-tailed tests $p < .10$ and $p < .05$.

PIAT MATH

Table 7.3, Panel 1, presents results from the PIAT Math model. We found that scores were higher when mothers had higher AFQT scores and fathers were more educated; we also found that boys scored higher than girls. Low birth weight, maternal non-White race, child health problems, and child shyness have negative effects. Spouse's part-time and overtime hours had positive effects on PIAT math when compared to full-time hours. Spouse's hourly wages also positively influenced math scores.

As noted above, we tested for interactions between maternal hours and maternal complexity, being male and maternal nonemployment, and being male and maternal hours, none of which had significant effects on math scores. The interaction between maternal nonemployment and mother being married had a positive effect on math scores, whereas the interaction between maternal nonemployment and number of siblings had a negative effect on math achievement. Below we discuss these interactions more fully.

PIAT READING RECOGNITION

Table 7.3, Panel 2, displays results from the PIAT Reading Recognition model. Children with mothers who had higher AFQT, whose fathers were more educated, and whose mothers were married had higher scores, whereas boys, those with low birth weights, those with more siblings, and those who had health problems and who are shy had lower scores. Contrary to expectations, there were no direct effects of either maternal or paternal work on Reading Recognition scores.

An interaction between maternal AFQT and maternal occupational complexity did not have significant effects on reading scores. The interaction between maternal nonemployment and maternal education as well as the interaction between being male and maternal complexity both had positive effects on reading achievement. In addition, the interaction between maternal high part-time hours and maternal occupational complexity had a positive effect on reading scores. The interaction of maternal nonemployment and being male as well as the interaction between maternal nonemployment and spouse's occupational complexity had negative effects on reading scores. We now discuss these interactions more fully.

ASSESSING INTERACTIVE EFFECTS

For PIAT Reading, the interaction between being male and maternal occupational complexity had a positive effect on test scores. The more complex the mother's occupation was, the greater the benefit to male children. Because boys lag behind girls in reading achievement, they especially may need to take advantage of maternal cognitive skills reinforced by complex work. This explanation is also supported by the results from the interaction between maternal nonemployment and being male, which had a negative effect on reading scores. The mother's staying home instead of working more negatively affected boys than girls in terms of reading. In addition, maternal complexity had more positive effects on reading achievement when the mother worked 21 to 34 hours per week versus 35 to 40 hours per week. Thus children benefit in terms of reading if the mother works a moderate number of hours but performs complex tasks while at work.

We also tested for an interaction between maternal nonemployment and spouse's occupational complexity to determine if spouse's work has more positive effects on reading scores of children whose mothers are not employed. We expected spouse's work characteristics to be more important determinants of children's cognitive achievement in the absence of any maternal work characteristics. Results show that this interaction negatively affected reading achievement. As spouse's job complexity increased, maternal nonemployment had more negative effects on reading achievement compared to maternal employment. This suggests that at high levels of spouse's job complexity, mothers' work may be necessary to reinforce any positive effects children receive from having fathers who do complex work. Finally, although maternal nonemployment and maternal average education did not have direct effects on PIAT reading or math, their interaction was significant and positive for reading scores.[1]

Two of the hypothesized interactions were significant in the PIAT Math model. The interaction between maternal nonemployment and being married had a positive effect on math outcomes. Children benefited more directly from living with two parents when a mother did not possess her own set of work characteristics, and being married became less important to children's math achievement if the mother held her own job.

CONCLUSIONS

Our most important finding may be a negative one: Parental work does not have strong direct effects on cognitive outcomes of 9- to 12-year-old children. In contrast, the most important predictors of PIAT scores were the personal characteristics of children as well as maternal cognitive ability and spouse's education. The standardized coefficients in the final model show that mothers' AFQT score was the strongest predictor of PIAT scores overall. As expected, boys scored better on math tests than did girls, and non-Whites scored worse on math than Whites. Low birth weight can profoundly affect children's cognitive development, even 10 years later.

The effects of several characteristics differed between the reading and math models. Being non-White directly affected math scores but not reading. Being male was important for both PIATs, but the effect was positive for math scores and negative for reading scores. Mothers' being married and number of siblings were determinants of reading and math achievement. Finally, maternal work characteristics were not important for math or reading, but spouses' hours worked and hourly wages affected the math outcome.

We used Coleman's (1988) ideas about social capital in the family to consider how parents' work affects children. Our results indicate that the effects of work on 9- to 12-year-olds' cognition are conditional. In other words, we do not find support for the idea that children experience negative outcomes in terms of cognitive achievement, presumably associated with decreased social capital in a family, if both parents work outside the home. Among our sample of 9- to 12-year-olds, maternal employment status as well as occupational characteristics provide neither direct advantages nor disadvantages in terms of reading and math achievement. Building social capital may not be a result of the sheer amount of time parents spend in the home, as then maternal nonemployment should be a distinct advantage for children. A parent who spends more time in the home does not necessarily spend those hours in interactions with children, thereby limiting the chance to build social capital.

Instead, if the child is male, maternal nonemployment may actually decrease the development of social capital in the family because it results in lower reading scores for boys. In addition, mothers who perform complex work provide an advantage to their sons in terms of reading achievement, indicating that more complex work may facilitate building social capital with boys. Our results also show, however, that if mothers do perform complex tasks at work, high part-time hours provide more benefits to 9- to 12-year-olds' reading achievement than do full-time hours, suggesting that high levels of work hours, or full-time work, at very challenging jobs may sap mothers' time or energy spent with children building social capital. This may be especially true if the mother is a single parent or if she has sole responsibility for housework and child care as well. However, what parents do with their children, the affection they show toward them, and the experiences they bring to the interaction may have more of an influence on the amount of social capital in a family than just parental presence in the home.

POLICY IMPLICATIONS

This study provides findings compatible with earlier analyses suggesting that the dangers of maternal work have been overgeneralized (Parcel & Menaghan, 1994a, 1994b). There are no consistent advantages in child cognition to maternal nonemployment. We do see advantages in children's reading achievement when their mothers are highly educated and do not work. These mothers may be spending additional time with children in ways that facilitate reading achievement. We also know that mothers with complex work who work high part-time hours have children with stronger reading achievement than those mothers who do not experience this combination of work advantages. It may be that complex work in moderation allows mothers the time and energy to transfer the benefits of their work situation to their children.

It is also useful to compare these findings with those generated in studies of younger children. Parcel and Menaghan (1994a, 1994b) found that overtime hours for both mothers and fathers were detrimental to children's vocabulary development among 3- to 6-year-old children of working mothers. We see that in this study of older children, including those of nonworking mothers, the findings differ depending on whether we consider maternal or paternal hours, and on whether we consider reading or math achievement. First, maternal work hours at any level have neither positive nor negative effects on PIAT reading scores. This means that mothers who work overtime are not disadvantaging their children in terms of reading achievement. The same is true for fathers. Thus, although parents of young children should consider the implications of parental overtime work for their children's vocabulary development, by the time children reach 9 to 12 years of age, such concerns are no longer relevant. Second, maternal work hours appear irrelevant to children's math achievement. Third, both paternal part-time and overtime work, relative to paternal full-time work, are associated with higher levels of math achievement, findings that are also duplicated in bivariate correlations (data not shown). Clear explanations for these positive effects remain elusive. It may be that overtime work is acting as a proxy for paternal ability or motivation, concepts unmeasured in our analysis; professional fathers who work long hours may have children who score higher on tests of math achievement. Regarding low work hours, those fathers may be spending time with their children in ways that facilitate math achievement. Clearly, these hypotheses need additional research, particularly because both paternal low work hours and paternal overtime work hours have positive effects relative to paternal full-time work. It is heartening, however, to find that low paternal work hours can have some positive effects on child well-being, especially because earlier research provides contrasting evidence for younger children (Parcel & Menaghan, 1994b). Finally, children's math achievement is positively affected by paternal wage levels.

These findings also provide guidance for policy makers in firms and for lawmakers concerned with support to both parents and industry. Firms that provide opportunities for part-time work for parents during parts of the family life cycle may have a competitive advantage over firms with more rigid policies. Laws acknowledging that many workers are fulfilling both family and work roles during portions of their lives may also be important. In addition, it has been helpful that this analysis has evenhandedly considered the effects of both maternal and paternal work roles and their implications for child cognition. Just because maternal paid employment has increased in recent years does not mean that paternal working conditions are irrelevant to child well-being; indeed, Kohn and his colleagues argue for clear connections, and our evidence provides some empirical support. Accordingly, policies need to be framed in ways that allow parents of either sex to take advantage of work schedule flexibility. Under these conditions, we can be most optimistic regarding the compatibility of work and family with reference to implications for child cognition.

NOTE

1. Maternal education * maternal nonemployment is not significant for reading scores without maternal occupational complexity in the model.

REFERENCES

Baker, P. C., Keck, C. K., Mott, F. L., & Quinlan, S. V. (1993). *NLSY child handbook, revised edition: A guide to the 1986-1990 National Longitudinal Survey of Youth child data*. Columbus: Center for Human Resource Research, Ohio State University.

Bird, C. E., & Ross, C. E. (1993). Houseworkers and paid workers: Qualities of the work and effects on personal control. *Journal of Marriage and the Family, 55*, 913-925.

Blake, J. (1989). *Family size and achievement*. Berkeley: University of California Press.

Blau, F. D., & Grossberg, A. J. (1990). *Maternal labor supply and children's cognitive development* (NBER Working Paper No. 3536). Cambridge, MA: National Bureau of Economic Research.

Coleman, J. (1988). Social capital in the creation of human capital. *American Journal of Sociology, 94,* S95-120.

Crane, J. (1991a). Effects of neighborhoods on dropping out of school and teenage childbearing. In C. Jenkes & P. E. Peterson (Eds.), *The urban underclass* (pp. 299-320). Washington, DC: Urban Institute.

Crane, J. (1991b). The epidemic theory of ghettos and neighborhood effects on dropping out and teenage childbearing. *American Journal of Sociology, 96*(5), 1226-1259.

Desai, S., Chase-Lansdale, P. L., & Michael, R. T. (1989). Mother or market? Effects of maternal employment on the intellectual ability of 4-year-old children. *Demography, 26,* 545-561.

Downey, D. B. (1995). When bigger is not better: Family size, parental resources, and children's educational performance. *American Sociological Review, 60,* 746-761.

Easterbrooks, M. A., & Goldberg, W. A. (1985). Effects of early maternal employment on toddlers, mothers, and fathers. *Developmental Psychology, 21*(5), 774-783.

Entwisle, D. R., Alexander, K. L., Pallas, A. M., & Cadigan, D. (1987). The emergent academic self-image of first graders: Its response to social structure. *Child Development, 58,* 1190-1206.

Farel, A. M. (1980). Effects of preferred maternal roles, maternal employment, and sociodemographic status on school adjustment and competence. *Child Development, 51,* 1179-1186.

Glass, J. (1992). Housewives and employed wives: Demographic and attitudinal change, 1972-1986. *Journal of Marriage and the Family, 54,* 559-569.

Gold, D., & Andres, D. (1978). Developmental comparisons between ten-year-old children with employed and nonemployed mothers. *Child Development, 49,* 75-84.

Greenstein, T. N. (1995). Are the "most advantaged" children truly disadvantaged by early maternal employment? *Journal of Family Issues, 16*(2), 149-169.

Herr, D. (1985). Effect of sibling number on child outcomes. *Annual Review of Sociology, 11,* 27-47.

Hoffman, L. W. (1989). Effects of maternal employment in the two-parent family. *American Psychologist, 44*(2), 283-292.

Kagan, J. (1978). *The growth of the child: Reflections on human development.* New York: Norton.

Kalmijn, M. (1994). Mother's occupational status and children's schooling. *American Sociological Review, 59,* 257-275.

Kohn, M. L. (1977). *Class and conformity, a study in values* (2nd ed.). Chicago: University of Chicago Press.

Kohn, M. L., & Schooler, C. (1973). Occupational experience and psychological functioning: An assessment of reciprocal effects. *American Sociological Review, 38,* 97-118.

Kohn, M. L., & Schooler, C. (1982). Job conditions and personality: A longitudinal assessment of their reciprocal effects. *American Journal of Sociology, 87,* 1257-1286.

Kohn, M. L., & Schooler, C. (1983). *Work and personality: An inquiry into the impact of social stratification.* Norwood, NJ: Ablex.

Leibowitz, A. (1977). Parental inputs and children's achievement. *Journal of Human Resources, 12,* 242-251.

Lennon, M. C., & Rosenfield, S. (1992). Women and mental health: The interaction of job and family conditions. *Journal of Health and Social Behavior, 33,* 316-327.

Link, B. G., Lennon, M. C., & Dohrenwend, B. P. (1993). Socioeconomic status and depression: The role of occupations involving direction, control, and planning. *American Journal of Sociology, 98,* 1351-1387.

Luster, T., Rhoades, K., & Haas, B. (1989). The relation between parental values and parenting behavior: A test of the Kohn hypothesis. *Journal of Marriage and the Family, 51,* 139-147.

Massey, D. S., Gross, A. B., & Eggers, M. L. (1991). Segregation, the concentration of poverty, and the life chances of individuals. *Social Science Research, 20,* 397-420.

Miller, J., Schooler, C., Kohn, M. L., & Miller, K. A. (1979). Women and work: The psychological effects of occupational conditions. *American Journal of Sociology, 85,* 66-94.

Milne, A. M., Myers, D. E., Rosenthal, A. S., & Ginsburg, A. (1986). Single parents, working mothers, and the educational achievement of school children. *Sociology of Education, 59,* 125-139.

NLS handbook 1994: The National Longitudinal Surveys. (1994). Columbus: Center For Human Resource Research, Ohio State University.

Nugent, J. K. (1991). Cultural and psychological influences on the father's role in infant development. *Journal of Marriage and the Family, 53,* 475-485.

Parcel, T. L. (1989). Comparable worth, occupation labor markets, and occupational earnings: Results from the 1980 census. In R. Michael, H. Hartmann, & B. O'Farrell (Eds.), *Pay equity: Empirical inquiries* (pp. 134-152). Washington, DC: National Academy of Sciences.

Parcel, T. L., & Menaghan, E. G. (1990). Maternal working conditions and children's verbal facility: Studying the intergenerational transmission of inequality from mothers to young children. *Social Psychology Quarterly, 53*(2), 132-147.

Parcel, T. L., & Menaghan, E. G. (1994a). Early parental work, family social capital, and early childhood outcomes. *American Journal of Sociology, 99*(4), 972-1009.

Parcel, T. L., & Menaghan, E. G. (1994b). *Parents' jobs and children's lives.* New York: Aldine.

Piotrkowski, C. S., & Katz, M. H. (1982). Indirect socialization of children: The effects of mother's jobs on academic behaviors. *Child Development, 53,* 1520-1529.

Spade, J. Z. (1991). Occupational structure and men's and women's parental values. *Journal of Family Issues, 12*(3), 343-360.

U.S. Bureau of the Census. (1987). *Statistical abstract of the United States: 1986* (107th ed.). Washington, DC: U.S. Government Printing Office.

U.S. Bureau of the Census. (1993). *Statistical abstract of the United States* (113th ed.). Washington, DC: U.S. Government Printing Office.

U.S. Department of Labor. (1977). *Dictionary of occupational titles 4th edition.* Washington, DC: U.S. Government Printing Office.

CHAPTER 8

Work-Family Orientations and Attainments in the Early Life Course

MONICA KIRKPATRICK JOHNSON
JEYLAN T. MORTIMER

Industrialization dramatically altered the relationship between work and family. Men increasingly performed work outside the home for pay, separated from the family labor of women based at home. Men were expected to hold jobs and provide income to support their families. Although the labor force participation of women has varied substantially by race and class in the United States (Goldin, 1990), women's primary role was that of homemaker, responsible for home management and child care.

The structure of work and family has undergone substantial change in recent decades, rendering the idealized breadwinner/homemaker family increasingly rare. Women's labor force participation has risen dramatically (Goldin, 1990). Concurrently, men's labor force participation has declined (Oppenheimer, 1994). Family formation has been postponed to later periods of the life course. Contemporary young couples are marrying several years

AUTHORS' NOTE: This research was supported by a grant, "Work Experience and Mental Health: A Panel Study of Youth," from the National Institute of Mental Health (MH42843), Jeylan T. Mortimer, Principal Investigator.

later than their counterparts in the 1950s and 1960s; first marriage ages are now more comparable to those before the turn of the 20th century (Ahlburg & De Vita, 1992). Couples are also delaying childbearing and having fewer children (Ahlburg & De Vita, 1992). Marriage rates fell 30% between 1970 and 1990; divorce rates over this same period rose 40% (Ahlburg & De Vita, 1992). Marital instability, coupled with the growing proportion of births to unmarried mothers, has contributed to a rise in single-parent homes (Bumpass, 1990). By 1991, only about one third of families consisted of a married couple with children; only one fifth of married couples fit the image of the "traditional family" by having two or more children, a breadwinner husband/father, and a homemaker wife/mother (Ahlburg & De Vita, 1992).

In contemporary marriages, both the husband and the wife are likely to be "providers." The proportion of dual-worker families in the United States increased from approximately 10% in 1940 to approximately 40% in 1991 (Ahlburg & De Vita, 1992). In addition to their roles as providers in dual-parent families, however, women still shoulder the predominant responsibility for child rearing and household labor. At the same time, women's greater earning power provides the economic wherewithal for independent living, for remaining single or for supporting oneself and children following divorce. Women are increasingly responsible for the economic support of their families as single parents.

To understand these changes in work and family, and to be able to anticipate future trends, it is important to examine individual-level orientations and attitudes. Motivations for behavior and individuals' interpretations of their own circumstances are critical in understanding these macrolevel social trends. To illustrate this point, marriage delay could be linked to disparate individual goals. Are young people today delaying marriage because they are having difficulty finding suitable marriage partners? Are they less interested in marriage altogether? Or is a continuing interest in marriage coupled with a purposeful delay to pursue activities that are incompatible with early marriage?

Marriage market models of marital behavior often make the assumption that being unmarried is perceived as an undesirable state, similar to being unemployed. For example, according to Lichter, McLaughlin, Kephart, and Landry (1992),

> Shortages of potential marital partners with complementary traits necessarily diminish prospects for assortive mating, which in turn affect the timing of first marriage. Nonmarriage in the marriage market is the conceptual

equivalent of unemployment in a labor market, and it occurs when there are mismatches between the demand for and supply of potential partners. (p. 782)

While this quote implies that being unmarried is problematic, individuals may not consider it this way. Knowledge of intentions and motivations can help us to understand the role of individual agency and the dynamics underlying observed macrolevel change. Thus, the plans and goals of young people provide a valuable perspective on the probable future direction of work and family arrangements. While this is not to say that structural forces are irrelevant, it recognizes that individuals' choices shape future structures.

In this chapter, we examine the work and family orientations of adolescents, and the influence of their attitudes and values on attainment and family formation processes in the first 4 years after leaving high school. Adolescents' perspectives on the future—their educational and occupational aspirations, their anticipated family involvements, and their ideas about the compatibility of future work and family roles—may reflect basic assumptions and values that shape their behaviors and influence choices with lifelong consequences. Studying adolescents enables us to learn how today's young people view their future work and family lives, and how these orientations influence their early attainment and family formation.

To place this analysis in its historical context, let us first consider how adolescents' orientations may have changed in recent decades. The "traditional" work-family model assumed that being a good provider was a necessary condition for being a good husband, and a good man in general (Gerzon, 1992). A male's occupational role was not seen as conflicting with, but contributing to family well-being. In fact, the "good provider" was characterized by his drive for occupational success (Bernard, 1981). Hence, with respect to individual orientations and goals, an interest in career advancement would be compatible with strong family orientations. For young men, one would expect family and work goals to be positively related. Those who anticipated high family involvement would also expect to have a high level of investment in paid work.

In contrast, for women, achievement outside the family was thought to detract from being a good wife and mother under the "traditional" work-family model. Achievement-oriented women were subject to considerable conflicts and feelings of guilt and self-doubt. Hence for females, a strong orientation toward the family would be incompatible with high achievement ambitions, and to the extent that young women wanted families, they had to forgo careers. For young women, then, one could expect family and work goals to be negatively related.

Studies of adolescents and young adults in the 1960s and 1970s support this model of so-called traditional work-family orientations. For example, among females, an orientation toward dating and early marriage was found to be negatively related to achievement orientations and educational aspirations (Marini, 1978). The anticipation of early marriage may have deflected girls from career preparation. Traditional attitudes toward the role of women were also associated with higher fertility expectations and lower educational aspirations, especially among females (Crowley & Shapiro, 1982).

Because females' status was largely derived from that of their husbands, not from their own occupational attainments, females' educational and occupational aspirations were only weakly associated with one another (Marini, 1978). Educational attainment influenced female stratification largely because it affected their position in the marriage market. For males, in contrast, educational attainment was important because of its influence on occupational achievement. Educational and occupational aspirations for males, therefore, were strongly associated (Marini, 1978). In view of the family's dependence on the male breadwinner for its economic viability, it is not surprising that plans for marriage and desired family size were positively related to the value adolescent boys placed on occupational stability (Herzog & Bachman, 1982).

With changes in the structure of both families and labor force participation, individual orientations and goals may be changing. As contemporary young women look toward their futures, they see expanding opportunities in the labor market. Many young women today have had employed female role models in their mothers, other relatives, and neighbors. The extent of maternal full-time labor force participation is positively related to daughters' commitment to their own careers (Curry, Trew, Turner, & Hunter, 1994; Johnson, 1996).

Even by the late 1970s and early 1980s, females' aspirations had risen to be comparable to those of males in terms of educational attainment and occupational prestige (Danzinger, 1983; Fiorentine, 1988; Shapiro & Crowley, 1982). Young women today are becoming more career oriented, with high educational and occupational aspirations and greater extrinsic ambitions (Dennehey & Mortimer, 1993; Marini, Fan, Finley, & Beutel, 1996).

Given the economic role many young women now anticipate performing, one might expect that they would have less incentive to enter marriage, would expect fewer children, and would be generally less "family oriented." This argument has been offered as one explanation for such macrolevel trends as declining marriage rates, increasing divorce rates, and declining rates of childbearing (for a review, see Oppenheimer, 1997). This "independence hypothesis" purports that as women have become more economically independent, marriage has become less necessary and less desirable. Moreover, high rates of divorce could make young career-oriented women less confident about the likelihood of their being able to achieve a stable, happy marriage and family life. That is, a "retreat from marriage" has occurred, with women leaving marriages or giving up the goal of marriage altogether.

Accordingly, one might hypothesize that contemporary young women's educational and work-related achievement orientations would continue, like their predecessors', to be negatively related to family orientations, but for different reasons than previously. Instead of relinquishing career goals to focus on their families, young women today may be lessening family involvement so as to be able to focus on their career achievement.

Alternatively, and in contradiction to the independence hypothesis, young women may be increasingly seeking the rewards offered from *both* family and employment roles. Instead of viewing employment and family as a trade-off, contemporary young women may typically desire to "have it all." Consistent with this, Fiorentine (1988) argues that a model of *masculinization*, in which females have attached greater importance to educational and occupational attainment at the expense of family and nurturing roles, does not accurately reflect recent changes in females' orientations toward work and family. Instead, Fiorentine proposes, a process of *amalgamation* has occurred, by which females are giving increasing emphasis to status attainment goals while still maintaining the value they previously placed on family and nurturing roles.

Our review of the evidence indicates that the amalgamation model has more empirical support than the retreat-from-marriage or masculinization thesis. Recent studies have found that females still expect to marry and have children at an earlier age than males (Dennehy & Mortimer, 1993; Spade & Reese, 1991) and place greater importance than males on their future familial roles as spouse and parent (Dennehy & Mortimer, 1993). In fact, from the mid-1970s to the early 1990s, researchers found no decline in the importance adolescent females attached to having a good marriage and family (Schulenberg, Bachman, Johnston, & O'Malley, 1995). Among today's college students, females overwhelmingly desire to combine a strong commitment to paid work with family roles, taking primary responsibility for child rearing and household management (Erwin, 1995).

Whereas employment has been necessary for women in single-parent and working-class families for a long period of time, young women of all economic strata may increasingly view their economic role as an integral part of their familial roles as wife and/or mother. Those women who anticipate high work involvement accept an important economic role in the family as well. Female undergraduate students anticipating careers are more likely than other female students to think that both parents' incomes are necessary to support a family (Curry et al., 1994). Much like the traditional male family role, these women see their provider role as a part of their responsibilities to their families.

Studies of job values have found similar evidence of amalgamation. Consistent with the fact that the traditional family's status and economic well-being rested more squarely on the male breadwinner's shoulders, young women in a previous era considered the extrinsic job rewards of money, advancement, prestige, and security of lesser importance than did males. However, among repeated cross-sections of high school seniors from 1976 to 1991, Marini and her colleagues (1996) found that females have converged with males in the value they place on extrinsic job rewards, while continuing to place greater importance on the social and altruistic rewards of work than males.

Much of the literature concerning the linkages of work and family focuses on the problematic character of time allocation on a daily basis, deriving from the simultaneous incumbency of work and family roles (Greenhaus & Beutel, 1985; Hofferth, Chapter 5 in this volume; Lambert, 1990; Lamphere, Zavella, & Gonzales, 1993; Trappe, Chapter 1 in this volume). But adolescents' achievement and family-related orientations provide a glimpse of time management strategies over a much longer term, through the early life course. That is, over the life span, preferences and values concerning the timing of marriage and parenthood, and the time allotted exclusively to parenting, constrain the time available to devote to human capital investment through education and employment.

In order to achieve both their family and their attainment goals, it may be that young women are shifting their attention to the *timing* of these pursuits: sequencing their investments in work and family as an alternative to choosing one over the other, or to pursuing them simultaneously. Delaying marriage and childbearing in order to pursue higher education and to invest in their early work role may be a long-term strategy in the interest of both career and family attainments.

More adolescents are now anticipating delaying marriage, with the trend stronger for females than males (Schulenberg et al., 1995). In fact, much of the reduction in the marriage rate may be due to delayed marriage instead of a "retreat" from marriage altogether (Oppenheimer, 1997). Women who are more "career oriented" expect to marry at later ages and view having children later as more acceptable than those who are less career oriented. Women preparing for nontraditional occupations also anticipate spending less time out of the labor force with young children than women preparing for more traditional female occupations (Baber & Monaghan, 1988). The importance of timing to career-oriented women is also revealed in their concern with establishing their careers "as soon as possible" (Curry et al., 1994).

To suggest that females' work and family orientations are now positively interrelated does not imply that they perceive little or no conflict between these two roles. In fact, the sequencing strategy is a plausible response to anticipated conflict. Do young women anticipate conflict in achieving their goals, which increasingly involve both arenas? Are they planning to combine employment and family roles *despite* anticipated conflict, or do they believe they have arranged their future plans in ways that will alleviate anticipated conflict?

For young men, changes in the labor market and in families may have different implications than for young women. Young men, particularly those at lower socioeconomic levels, may be anticipating less favorable occupational opportunities than their fathers had. Moreover, given widespread sharing of the provider role, they (and others) may no longer perceive the status of their families to be as dependent on their achievement in work. To the extent that "success" in work and family is decoupled for men, they may have less interest in family life altogether.

But like their contemporary female counterparts, males do not appear to have become any less interested in family life. From the mid-1970s to the early 1990s, male adolescents' commitment to having a good marriage and family life, like that of females, remained highly stable (Schulenberg et al., 1995).

Yet with women's changing labor market participation and increasing expectations for egalitarian marital roles, young men may no longer see marriage as supportive of their careers. They may be less likely than young men in prior generations to anticipate having a full-time homemaking spouse to support them in their career achievement. High achievement ambitions may no longer seem as nicely compatible with family life. Thus, while young men may still desire to have families, family goals may not be so closely tied to their achievement ambitions. In this case, the work-related and family orientations of young men would now be only weakly related.

But despite these changing circumstances, there is reason to believe that young men's orientations are remaining quite traditional in character. As might be expected given their advantageous position in the traditional family, males continue to lag behind females in gender role attitude change (Komarovsky, 1973). Males are significantly more likely than females to have traditional orientations toward work and family roles and the division of household labor (Spade & Reese, 1991; Willetts-Bloom & Nock, 1994). Despite women's growing financial contributions to their families, males have also been resistant to taking on new household roles (Gager, 1995; Hochschild, 1989; Machung, 1989).

Furthermore, researchers have found that young men's interest in a nonemployed spouse far exceeds young women's desire to be homemakers (out of the labor force). Many young men are also unsure of their feelings about their future spouse working (Spade & Reese, 1991). High levels of male uncertainty may indicate an acceptance of an employed wife "if she wants to," without expecting an economic contribution from her. In this way, the male still sees himself as "breadwinner," ultimately responsible for the financial well-being of the family. If these more traditional views prevail, young males would be likely to retain achievement and family attitudes that are positively interrelated.

There has been no recent study that compares the *interrelations* of achievement and family orientations of males and females in a contemporary cohort of young people. Our study examines the linkages of a broad range of orientations toward education, employment, and family. We seek to determine the ways in which adolescents view their future family and work roles, in tandem, and whether these constellations of attitudes differ for males and females.

In addition, we examine the predictive capacity of these orientations for the early adult attainment and family formation processes that shape life trajectories (Featherman, 1980). While status attainment researchers customarily study achievement aspirations, and investigations of family formation focus on family orientations, we examine the influences of these aspirations and orientations across these arenas. Through this approach, it is our aim to understand more fully the social psychological sources of attainment across family and work domains (Mortimer, 1996).

HYPOTHESES

The Linkages of Work and Family Attitudes

According to the independence hypothesis, females' goals for achievement in school and work should be negatively related to their family goals. Those who attach greater importance to educational and occupational attainment should be less likely to plan to marry or have children; they should place little importance on their family roles. The amalgamation hypothesis, in contrast, predicts that females who attach greater importance to educational and occupational attainment will also attach high levels of importance to their family roles. The sequencing framework, consistent with this latter hypothesis, predicts that females who attach greater importance to educational and occupational attainment will plan later marriages.

According to the decoupling hypothesis, males' goals for achievement in school and work should be only weakly related to their family goals. The traditional hypothesis, on the other hand, predicts that males' goals for achievement in school and work will remain solidly positively related to their family goals.

Early Attainments and Family Formation

Whereas there is much controversy about the extent to which attitudes predict behavior in general (Schuman, 1995), there is considerable evidence that prior attitudes and values do predict behavior in the work realm (Mortimer & Lorence, 1979, 1995), and some evidence that they are predictive in the family realm as well (Pimentel, 1996).

If, in fact, young adults act on their motivations and beliefs, predictions about the effects of prior orientations on attainments and family formation should be relatively straightforward. Consistent with the extensive literature on status attainment, achievement aspirations should positively influence educational persistence for both males and females (Sewell & Hauser, 1975). Whereas aspirations should eventually also influence occupational attainment, this would not likely occur while young people are still attending school, as the kinds of jobs held while in postsecondary institutions will differ from those obtained when education is complete. Thus, for both males and females in this early stage of the attainment process, achievement orientations should exert a positive influence on educational persistence and the time invested in part-time work, which tends to support postsecondary schooling (Mortimer & Johnson, 1998). Achievement orientations should have a negative influence on investments in full-time work during this life stage, as full-time work conflicts with educational investment.

According to the independence hypothesis, females' achievement orientations should have a negative influence on entry into marriage and parenthood. Under the amalgamation hypothesis, females' achievement orientations would also be expected to be negatively related to family formation, not because of a retreat from marriage but in the interest of compatible sequencing.

Young women who merely delay marriage and parenthood to pursue educational and occupational goals should not yet have entered these family roles during the years immediately following high school. If women expect to be increasingly taking economic responsibility for their families, strong family orientations would be expected to be positively related to postsecondary educational achievement (and part-time work) in the interest of human capital formation and earnings potential.

For contemporary young males, it would be compatible with the decoupling hypothesis to find that achievement orientations have little or no influence on family formation. Conversely, family orientations should have little or no effect on educational persistence or time invested in work. In contrast, the traditional hypothesis predicts that family orientations have a positive influence on investment in schooling and part-time work (at this early life stage), since such investment would promote earning capacity and, therefore, family economic welfare and stability. Achievement orientations would thus be consistent with delayed marriage.

In summary, our study addresses broad issues of structural change and individual agency with crucial implications for future social change. For example, if, as contemporary young women become more oriented to achievement in the labor force, they become less interested in family, recent changes in family forms may become more pronounced. However, if young women only wish to delay marriage to pursue higher education and work, marriage-based family forms will persist, and perhaps even be strengthened. Education, and especially age at marriage, tend to be positively associated with marital stability (Huber & Spitze, 1988; Martin & Bumpass, 1989). Women's economic contributions to their families may also enhance marital stability, as economic strain increases marital conflict and increased income has a stabilizing effect on the family (Conger, 1996). Finally, a delay in marriage may help alleviate the stress that arises when the demands of work, in establishing one's career, and the demands of family, in the early child-rearing years, peak simultaneously.

DATA AND MEASURES

To address these questions, we used data from the Youth Development Study (YDS), a prospective longitudinal study of adolescents in St. Paul, Minnesota. The panel of adolescents was chosen randomly from a list of enrolled ninth graders in the St. Paul public schools. Consent to participate was obtained from 1,010 parents, who represented 64% of all eligible invitees. Eligibility was defined by enrollment in the district at the time of data collection and by the absence of disabilities that would prevent the child from filling out a questionnaire. The analysis in this chapter utilized data from the fourth year of the study (1991), when the respondents were in the 12th grade, and the eighth year of the study (1995), 4 years after most had graduated from high school. Panel retention through the fourth wave was 93%; retention through the eighth wave was nearly 78%.

Because of a concern that participants in this kind of study may select themselves on the basis of high socioeconomic background, a probit analysis of the decision to participate was conducted, using information from the 1980 Census reported at the tract level to characterize the neighborhoods of all eligible families. These were the most recent Census data available when data collection began in 1988. The contextual dimensions constituted the independent variables in the equation, along with age, gender, and the school in which the child was enrolled; the decision to participate was the dependent variable. This analysis is reported elsewhere (Finch, Shanahan, Mortimer, & Ryu, 1991); it is important to note that no socioeconomic contextual variables (e.g., race, family composition, median household income, parents' education and occupational level) proved to be statistically significant predictors of participation in the study. We conclude that the sample is representative of the general population of ninth graders attending the St. Paul public schools. A comparison of the St. Paul population to the U.S. population at large (Mortimer, Finch, Shanahan, & Ryu, 1992) suggests that although no one community can be considered representative of the nation, the findings of this study are not likely unique to St. Paul.

We considered family and achievement plans, as well as job values measured in the senior year. In the domain of family, we asked about expectations for marriage, the anticipated age at marriage, expected family size, and the anticipated importance of marriage and parenthood. Measures are shown in Table 8.1. Since the anticipated importance of marriage and parenthood were highly correlated ($r = .68$), we constructed an index of family importance by averaging the responses to each. We also asked about plans for employment after marrying, for the respondents themselves and for their future spouses. For those who planned employment after having children, we asked how much time they anticipated taking out of the labor force after the birth of a child. In addition, we asked whether respondents anticipated that marriage and children would interfere with their career plans.

In the domain of achievement plans, we considered educational plans and aspirations, and occupational aspirations. To create a construct measuring achievement aspirations, we added these responses, weighted by lambda

(Text continued on page 228)

TABLE 8.1 Measures

Importance of career, marriage, and parenthood:	1 = not at all important
	2 = somewhat important
	3 = very important
	4 = extremely important
Index of importance of family: Average of the importance of marriage and parenthood	$\alpha = .802$
Marriage Age:	_____ years
Expectation of spouse working:	1 = expecting that a spouse will not work after marriage
	2 = expecting that a spouse will work after marriage but not after having children
	3 = expecting that a spouse will work after marriage but unsure whether a spouse will work after having children
	4 = expecting that a spouse will work after marriage and after having children
Timing of return to work after having children: When my child (or my youngest child) is	1 = less than a year old
	2 = about 1 or 2 years old
	3 = in nursery school
	4 = in kindergarten
	5 = in elementary school
	6 = in junior high school or later
	7 = never (expected not to work after having children)
Interference of marriage and parenthood with career plans:	0 = expecting interference neither from marriage nor parenthood
	1 = expecting interference from marriage or parenthood, but not both
	2 = expecting interference from both marriage and parenthood
Educational aspirations and plans:	1 = less than high school graduate
	2 = high school graduate
	3 = junior college degree
	4 = 4-year college degree (B.A., B.S.)
	5 = master's degree
	6 = Ph.D. or professional degree
Occupational aspirations:	*1980 Census of Population: Alphabetical Index of Industries and Occupations* three-digit classification and assigned occupational prestige scores (Stevens & Hoisington, 1987).

TABLE 8.1 Continued

Achievement aspirations: weighted sum of:	*Lambda coefficients from confirmatory factor analysis:*
educational aspirations	1.000
educational plans	1.002
occupational aspirations	0.840
	$\alpha = .800$

Intrinsic and extrinsic work values:
weighted sum of:

1 = not at all important
2 = somewhat important
3 = very important
4 = extremely important

Lambda coefficients from confirmatory factor analysis:

Intrinsic indicators:

	(1.000)
A chance to learn a lot of new things at work.	(1.008)
A job where I have a lot of responsibility.	(0.912)
A job that uses my skills and abilities.	(0.988)
A chance to make my own decisions at work.	(0.794)
A chance to work with people rather than things.	(0.866)
A chance to be helpful to others or useful to society.	range = 5.57-22.27
	$\alpha = .824$

Extrinsic indicators:

Good pay.	(1.000)
A job that people regard highly.	(1.725)
A steady job, with little chance of being laid off.	(0.982)
Good chances of getting ahead.	(1.535)
	range = 5.24-20.97
	$\alpha = .649$

Family Self-Efficacy: What are the chances that . . .
you will have a happy family life?

1 = very low
2 = low
3 = about fifty-fifty
4 = high
5 = very high

Economic Self-Efficacy: same question as family self-efficacy; weighted sum of:	*Lambda coefficients from confirmatory factor analysis:*
You will have a job that pays well	(1.000)
You will be able to own your own home	(1.219)
You will have a job that you enjoy doing	(0.869)
	$\alpha = .820$
Annual Income:	$_____ (1994 before taxes)

(continued)

TABLE 8.1 Continued

Opportunity to be helpful: My job gives me a chance
to be helpful to others

1 = not at all true
2 = a little true
3 = somewhat true
4 = very true

Race:

0 = non-White
1 = White

Family Structure:

0 = other
1 = two-parent family

Parents' education: If both parents responded to
the Wave 1 survey, we averaged their educational
attainments.

1 = less than high school diploma
2 = high school graduate
3 = some college
4 = community/junior college
5 = 4-year college degree
6 = some graduate school
7 = master's degree
8 = Ph.D./professional

Family income: Reported by the father—reported
by mother if missing data on father's report.

1 = under $5,000
2 = $5,000 - 9,999
3 = $10,000 - 14,999
4 = $15,000 - 19,999
5 = $20,000 - 29,999
6 = $30,000 - 39,999
7 = $40,000 - 49,999
8 = $50,000 - 59,999
9 = $60,000 - 69,999
10 = $70,000 - 79,999
11 = $80,000 - 89,999
12 = $90,000 - 99,999
13 = $100,000 or more

coefficients derived from a confirmatory factor analysis. LISREL VII was
used to estimate the model, which demonstrated a good fit to the data. The
measurement structure for males and females is constrained to be the same
with no significant loss in fit to the model. In the same manner as family
plans, we asked about the anticipated importance of career.

Exploratory and confirmatory factor analyses of the job value items
showed that a two-factor model, with intrinsic and extrinsic dimensions, pro-

vided a good fit to the data. Again using LISREL VII, multiple group comparisons demonstrated that the measurement structure for males and females could be constrained to be the same with no significant loss in fit to the model. Extrinsic value items addressed income, advancement opportunity, security, and prestige. Intrinsic value items referred to the use of skills and abilities; learning opportunities; autonomy and responsibility; and the chance to work with, and be helpful to, other people.

We also considered the young people's sense of self-efficacy with respect to their future economic and family lives. The economic self-efficacy construct is a weighted sum of three items tapping the perceived chances of being paid well, owning a home, and having a job one enjoys in the future. Weights were again derived from a confirmatory factor analysis. Family self-efficacy was measured by a single item measuring the perceived chances of having a happy family life in the future.

In the 4 years following high school (1992-1995), respondents were mailed "life history calendars" (Freedman, Thornton, Camburn, Alwin, & Young-Demarco, 1988) on which they indicated activity and family status changes during the previous year, including school attendance, part- and full-time work, marriage, parenthood, and living arrangements in monthly units. To measure educational persistence, as well as investment in part- and full-time work, we added the number of months reported in each activity over the 4 years.[1] We similarly measured cohabitation as the number of months spent cohabiting over the 4 years. We measured marriage and parenthood by whether or not respondents had entered into marriage or parenthood by the Wave 8 survey in March 1995. To examine early occupational attainments, we asked respondents in Wave 8 for information about their current job, if they held one. We used measures of annual income and the opportunity to be helpful to others as characteristics of jobs that indicate early occupational accomplishments, highlighting a prominent extrinsic and intrinsic reward dimension.

FINDINGS

Comparing Males' and Females' Family and Achievement Orientations

We first compare the achievement and family orientations of males and females in the fourth year of the Youth Development Study, when most panel members were seniors in high school. Their achievement goals were found to be very much the same. As shown in Table 8.2, there were no significant differences in males' and females' level of educational aspirations, in their plans for educational attainment, or in the average prestige level of their aspired occupations. Educational aspirations were exceedingly high. Females and males both aspired, on the average, to achieve postgraduate levels of education (between 4-year college and master's degrees); more realistically, their plans for attainment were, on average, just below a 4-year college degree. Still, 59% of females and 61% of males planned to graduate from a 4-year college. Males and females also aspired to occupations of similar prestige, with their mean aspirations corresponding to occupations at managerial and lower-professional levels.[2]

Thus, in the attitudes of greatest interest to status attainment researchers, pertaining to future education and occupation, males and females in the Youth Development Study had substantially the same level of aspirations, both aiming quite high in terms of socioeconomic achievement. In this respect, Youth Development Study panel members are quite similar to youth described in other contemporary studies.

For both males and females, paid work was a major anticipated focus of adult life. Consistent with the dramatic rise in female labor force participation, especially among women with children, females were just about equally as likely to plan to be employed after having children as males (97% of the females and 98% of the males). There were also no significant differences between males' and females' scores on the economic self-efficacy scale.[3] Males and females were anticipating high work involvement and were equally likely to be confident of their ability to achieve their economic goals.

However, we find significant gender differences in adolescent family orientations, work values, and in attitudes concerning the compatibility of family and paid work. With respect to the work orientations, YDS females attached significantly *greater* importance to career than the males and expressed stronger occupational reward values in both the extrinsic and the intrinsic domains. Females also had stronger orientations to marriage and family life than did males. Females were more likely to plan to marry; they expected to marry at a younger age by about a year; and they attached greater importance to both marriage and to parenthood than did their male age peers. More than twice as many males (13%) as females (5%) expected to have no children at all. Females also had higher family self-efficacy, more confident of their chances of having a happy family life. Clearly, taken together, the females' value pattern suggests considerable engagement in paid work *in addition* to family roles, in support of the amalgamation hypothesis.

Table 8.2 Plans and Orientations Toward School, Work, and Family, Senior Year of High School (1991) and Postsecondary Activities

	Females (Mean)	Males (Mean)
During Senior Year of High School (W4):		
Educational aspirations	4.44	4.35
Educational plans	3.87	3.80
Prestige of occupational aspirations	53.74	53.38
Importance of career	3.51	3.42*
Extrinsic work values	17.56	16.95**
Intrinsic work values	17.59	16.40***
Plan to marry (% yes)	85.92	76.64**
Anticipated marriage age (years)	24.47	25.65***
Importance of marriage	3.52	3.27***
Importance of parenthood	3.61	3.20***
Interference of marriage with career (% yes)	9.66	5.75*
Interference of parenthood with career (% yes)	21.33	8.97***
Expect not to have children (%)	5.30	13.21***
Number of children	2.31	2.13
Expect to work after having children (% yes)	96.64	97.63
Expect spouse will work after marriage (% yes)	98.95	87.31***
Expect spouse will work after having children (% yes)	90.26	46.26***
Timing of return to work after having children	2.49	1.40***
Expect to be out of the labor force a year or more (% yes)	68.12	16.21***
Economic self-efficacy	12.16	12.19
Family self-efficacy	4.10	3.96*
Postsecondary:		
Attended school during W8 (%)	53.83	48.18
Mean months of school W5-W8	22.27	20.63
Mean months of part-time work W5-W8	23.55	19.81**
Mean months of full-time work W5-W8	15.02	18.09**
Mean months cohabiting W5-W8	6.35	3.78**
Married by W8 (%)	13.62	9.37[a]
Parents by W8 (%)	32.97	14.24***

a = $p < .10$; * $p < .05$; ** $p < .01$; *** $p < .001$

NOTE: Sample size ranges from 418 to 497 for females, and 327 to 435 for males, on senior year measures. The lower sample sizes are for questions asked of only a subset of the sample (e.g., anticipated marriage age was asked only of those who indicated they planned to marry). Sample size ranges from 365 to 464 for females, and 260 to 337 for males, on postsecondary measures.

Females' strong work and family values, and their high aspirations for achievement outside the family realm, are clearly not compatible with the persistent gender inequality in the family division of labor. It is therefore not surprising that females anticipated greater interference of marriage, and especially, parenthood, with their career goals than did males.

In prior research, both males and females have assigned *less* importance to work than to family roles (Herzog & Bachman, 1982). In accord with the amalgamation thesis, YDS females rated career and marriage, on average, as equivalent in importance. But when the demands of the two roles conflict, females expected to make sacrifices with respect to career. Females expected a longer delay after childbearing before returning to work. Such delay is consistent with social norms stressing greater female responsibility for parenting, particularly in the child's early years, as well as the greater importance they themselves attached to parenthood (in comparison to their male peers). In fact, two thirds of the females expected to be out of the labor force for a year or more after the birth of their last child.

Nearly all YDS females (99%) expected that their husbands would work outside the home after marriage. And, in keeping with traditional gender role expectations, almost all females (90%) expected that their husbands would work after the couple had children (9% are not sure).

Males displayed some elements of traditionalism mixed with anticipated change. Unlike the young men in Herzog and Bachman's (1982) study, YDS males attached *greater* importance to their careers than to their family lives ($p < .01$, for the evaluation of marriage vs. career; $p < .001$, for the evaluation of parenthood vs. career). Whereas the vast majority of YDS males (87%) did expect that their wives would work outside the home after marriage, only 46% of males expected their wives would be employed after they had children, and 44% expressed uncertainty about this prospect. In contrast, virtually all the females (97%), as noted above, planned to work after having children. Although in comparison to females, very few males expected an interruption of their work careers to care for young children, 16% also expected to be out of the labor force for a year or longer.

Comparing Male and Female Achievement and Family Formation

The young people's educational, work, and family-related activities in the 4 years after most had graduated from high school are also described in Table 8.2. Educational investment was a predominant activity for both genders; more than half the young women, and close to half the young men, were attending school in Wave 8. On the average, young women and men spent 22 and 21 months, respectively, in an educational program of one kind or another since they left high school; they spent a similar amount of time doing part-time work. Postsecondary education and part-time work go together ($r = .46$ for males; $r = .51$ for females; $p < .001$ for both), since most students find it necessary to support themselves at least partially while they are pursuing college, vocational training, or other educational programs.

Females, and to a lesser extent males, have spent fewer months doing full-time work than part-time work. Whereas the young women have spent somewhat more time doing part-time work than young men (23.6 vs. 20 months, respectively; $p < .01$), they spent less time in full-time employment than young men (15 vs. 18 months, respectively; $p < .01$).

With respect to family formation, young women appear to be acquiring family roles more quickly than young men. Females exceeded males in number of months spent in a cohabiting relationship during the 4 years following high school (6.4 vs. 3.8 months, for females and males, respectively; $p < .01$). Still, relatively little time in the cohabiting state was reported (given the period of observation was 4 years or approximately 48 months). About 14% of females had married by Wave 8, in comparison to 9% of males ($p < .10$). While almost one third of the females had become parents, only 14% of the males report having done so ($p < .001$).

Earlier analyses indicated that family formation had important implications for achievement-related activities (Mortimer & Johnson, 1999). Relatively early marriage limited young women's human capital investment in postsecondary education and part-time work, but had no significant implications for young men's corresponding investments. Early parenting was constraining to both men's and women's human capital development through schooling (and part-time work), and, for women only, through full-time labor force participation.

Comparing the Relations Among the Achievement and Family Orientations for Males and Females

Manifesting consistency on the part of both males and females, there were significant correlations *within* the achievement and family domains (see Table 8.3). That is, males and females who attached greater importance to career were also likely to have higher achievement aspirations (educational and occupational). With regard to job values, both males and females who attached greater importance to their future careers had stronger extrinsic and intrinsic occupational reward values. Seemingly, those with stronger preferences for each type of occupational reward realized that obtaining these rewards necessitates high levels of work involvement. Similarly, higher aspira-

Table 8.3 Interrelations of Achievement Orientations (School and Career), Family Orientations, and Work Values, Senior Year of High School (1991)

	Importance of Career	Achievement Aspirations	Importance of Family	Anticipated Interference	Marriage Age	Number of Children	Timing Return Work (F) /Spouse Work (M)	Extrinsic Work Values	Intrinsic Work Values	Economic Self-Efficacy	Family Self-Efficacy
Importance of career	1.00 (F) 1.00 (M)										
Achievement aspirations	.18*** .11*	1.00 1.00									
Importance of family	.17*** .29***	.10* .23***	1.00 1.00								
Anticipated interference	-.05 -.01	.02 -.08	.07 .04	1.00 1.00							
Marriage age	.03 .06	.33*** .05	-.16** -.15*	-.14** -.14*	1.00 1.00						
Number of children	-.07 -.07	.01 .09	.33*** .35***	.02 .01	-.08 -.10[a]	1.00 1.00					
Timing return work (F)/Spouse work (M)	-.15** .07	-.04 .18**	.06 .02	.05 .02	.01 -.02	.02 -.05	1.00 1.00				
Extrinsic work values	.39*** .46***	.04 .12*	.14** .30***	.02 .01	-.00 .11[a]	-.05 .09[a]	-.09* .04	1.00 1.00			
Intrinsic work values	.23*** .31***	.28*** .28***	.21*** .37***	-.00 -.02	.13** .11[a]	.10* .12*	-.05 .11*	.50*** .54***	1.00 1.00		
Economic self-efficacy	.31*** .23***	.38*** .36***	.17*** .33***	-.01 -.01	.15** .07	.16** .08[a]	-.05 .04	.32*** .28***	.36*** .36***	1.00 1.00	
Family self-efficacy	.11* .22***	.10[a] .21***	.32*** .44***	-.06 -.02	-.05 -.11*	.11* .24***	.06 .02	.18*** .23***	.22*** .38***	.44*** .57***	1.00 1.00

a = $p < .10$; * $p < .05$; ** $p < .01$; *** $p < .001$.

NOTE: Sample size ranges from 343 to 496 for females and 262 to 434 for males on senior year measures. The lower sample sizes are for questions asked of only a subset of the sample (e.g., anticipated marriage age was asked only of those who indicated they planned to marry).

tions were associated with stronger extrinsic and intrinsic reward values for males, and with stronger intrinsic values for females. Within the family domain, those who attached greater importance to family (the index of marriage and parenthood) wanted to marry at a younger age and planned to have a larger number of children.

More directly pertinent to the assessment of our hypotheses, Table 8.3 shows the interrelations of the senior year achievement and family orientations by gender. In support of the amalgamation hypothesis, females who attached greater importance to family also attached greater importance to career, had higher achievement aspirations, and placed greater importance on the intrinsic and extrinsic rewards of work. We find no evidence for the independence thesis among young women. Even though achievement in both roles may at times be incompatible for them, those young females who attached greater importance to careers did not appear to be withdrawing from family roles.

Instead, and consistent with the sequencing hypothesis, young women who planned to delay marriage anticipated less interference between family roles and their career plans (this pattern is also found among the young men). Consistent with a sequencing strategy, females with higher achievement aspirations also planned to delay marriage. Thus, while those females with high achievement aspirations did not attach less importance to their future family lives, they did plan to allocate more time to the nonmarried state, perhaps in the interest of human capital development.[4] Also manifesting a concern with the temporal patterning of their participation in work and family life, females who attached greater importance to their future careers planned to reenter the workforce more quickly than other females after having children, lessening time out of the labor force (and human capital depreciation).[5]

It is especially interesting to observe that marriage timing is linked to achievement aspirations (which include educational aspirations and plans), but not to the importance of career; and it is maternal leave time that is related to career salience, not to aspirations. This pattern is quite consistent with a temporal strategy. Because young women expect to marry first, before having children, they expect that early marriage would interfere with their educational attainment (as well as the prestige of their eventual occupations). Children are expected to come subsequently, perhaps after schooling is complete, so that an early return to work (a brief interruption) would support high career involvement. Marriage delay and a more rapid return to work may also be strategies needed to obtain high levels of intrinsic and extrinsic reward in work. Females with stronger intrinsic values anticipated an older age of marriage; those with stronger extrinsic values planned a shorter interruption for full-time parenting when their children are young.[6]

With respect to our indicators of self-confidence in the work and family domains, achievement aspirations, importance of career, extrinsic and intrinsic work values, and importance of family are positively related to both economic and family self-efficacy among females, demonstrating both within and across domain connections (the same is true for males). The fact that confidence in work and family spheres rise (and fall) together, supports an amalgamation hypothesis for those with high expectations in the economic domain. Females with greater economic self-efficacy also plan to delay marriage longer than their peers, and plan to have larger families. This link between young females' confidence in the economic realm and plans for larger families is consistent with our earlier discussion of women's increasing assumption of responsibility for family financial support. Higher family self-efficacy is positively associated with plans for larger families as well.

Positive correlations among variables indicating anticipated family and career involvement, and achievement aspirations, found in the male data, indicate a traditional orientation pattern. (Though the correlations for males were somewhat stronger, gender differences in these correlations were not statistically significant.) The magnitude of the correlations between economic and family self-efficacy for males ($r = .57$; $p < .001$) is particularly impressive, indicating a highly traditional orientation. Thus, for them, success in family and career clearly go together. Still, males with higher aspirations (educational and occupational), for whom the "two-person career" pattern (Papanek, 1973) is likely to be more prevalent, were *more* likely to expect that their spouses would work after taking on family roles as wife and mother. Clearly, they cannot expect the kind of supportive involvement, on the part of their wives, that professional and managerial men received in prior generations. Males with stronger intrinsic values were also more likely to expect that their spouses would work. It may be that just as they themselves seek self-fulfillment in employment, they anticipate that their spouses would want this as well, and would therefore want to be employed.

Though we had predicted that males with strong achievement orientations would want to delay marriage to enable pursuit of human capital investment, we found that males did not feel a need to postpone marriage to achieve their ambitions (for the gender difference between these correlations, $p < .01$). Like YDS females, males with greater family self-efficacy planned larger families. But unlike the females, family self-efficacy for males was also significantly related to plans for earlier marriage, indicating a more traditional orientation.

Effects of Adolescent Orientations on Education, Family, and Paid Work Behavior Four Years Following High School

Table 8.4 shows the zero-order correlations of prior orientations toward achievement and family measured in the senior year of high school, and the indicators of family formation, educational investment, and work experience during the 4 years after high school.[7] Consistent with status attainment research, early educational plans and occupational aspirations were positively related to months of schooling obtained after high school for both males and females. Educational plans and occupational aspirations were also positively associated with months of part-time work (which, as we have noted, often supports continuation in school), and negatively related to full-time work (which would more likely compete with the student role). For females, economic self-efficacy also predicted months of schooling and part-time work. Those with greater confidence in themselves spent more months in school and part-time work in the following 4 years. For females, the salience of career and earlier valuation of intrinsic job rewards were likewise positively related to months of part-time work and also to months of schooling (perhaps, for many, necessary to pursue the desired career). The negative linkage of the early achievement orientations with full-time work was especially pronounced for males. Consistently, young people with higher educational plans and occupational aspirations (males only) had lower annual incomes 4 years later.

Adolescents' job values were predictive of their job characteristics 4 years later. Early extrinsic reward values were linked to subsequent income attainment; early intrinsic reward values were associated with opportunities to help others on the job for both males and females.

Attitudes and behaviors in the family domain are also linked. Males and females who planned to marry earlier than their peers were more likely to have married and to have become parents by Wave 8.[8] Moreover, for females, anticipated marriage age and later cohabitation experience were significantly negatively related. This suggests that females who planned to delay marriage did not substitute cohabitation for marriage. Earlier analysis of these data likewise found a negative effect of anticipated marriage age on subsequent cohabiting behavior in the first 2 years after high school (Pimentel, 1996).

The relation of educational plans and occupational aspirations to the indicators of family formation are consistent with a sequencing strategy for both males and females. Educational plans and occupational aspirations were negatively related to months of cohabitation, for both. Earlier valuation of

TABLE 8.4 Interrelations of W4 Orientations With W8 Educational, Work, and Family Outcomes

Females	Months Schooling	Months Part-Time Work	Months Full-Time Work	Months Cohabiting	Annual Income	Opportunity to be Helpful.
Educational plans	.58***	.33***	−.16**	−.28***	−.16**	.09[a]
Occupational aspirations	.36***	.21***	−.17**	−.24***	−.09	−.02
Marriage age	.27***	.17**	−.07	−.30***	−.06	.02
Number of children	.02	.04	.05	.00	−.01	.01
Importance of family	.10[a]	.20***	−.13*	−.09[a]	−.07	.03
Timing of return to work	.04	.10[a]	−.09[a]	−.04	−.06	.05
Importance of career	.19***	.13*	.01	−.10[a]	.06	.07
Extrinsic work values	.01	.06	.08	−.08	.20***	−.01
Intrinsic work values	.22***	.18**	−.01	−.14**	−.02	.13*
Economic self-efficacy	.29***	.22***	.05	−.13*	.06	.09
Family self-efficacy	.09[a]	.16**	−.09[a]	−.01	.02	−.01

Males	Months Schooling	Months Part-Time Work	Months Full-Time Work	Months Cohabiting	Annual Income	Opportunity to be Helpful
Educational plans	.38***	.33***	−.40***	−.18**	−.33***	.10
Occupational aspirations	.58***	.27***	−.36***	−.20**	−.17**	.04
Marriage age	.13[a]	.10	−.21**	−.08	−.18**	.09
Number of children	.02	−.05	.07	.00	.11[a]	−.13*
Importance of family	.14*	.02	−.03	.04	.02	−.03
Spouse Work	.21**	.25***	−.24***	−.14*	−.13*	.11
Importance of career	.04	−.04	.07	−.08	.12[a]	.09
Extrinsic work values	.03	−.05	.06	−.06	.12*	−.01
Intrinsic work values	.08	.08	−.10	.01	−.07	.15*
Economic self-efficacy	.25***	.10[a]	−.06	−.03	−.01	−.04
Family self-efficacy	.09	.05	.02	.01	.14*	−.01

a = $p < .10$; * $p < .05$; ** $p < .01$; *** $p < .001$.
NOTE: Sample size ranges from 298 to 363 for females and 197 to 261 for males. The lower sample sizes are for questions asked of only a subset of the sample (e.g., anticipated marriage age was asked only of those who indicated they planned to marry).

intrinsic occupational rewards were likewise negatively related to months of cohabitation for females. The overall pattern of findings suggests that those who earlier had higher aspirations and plans invested in education and part-time work during the years immediately following high school, and avoided the potentially conflicting intimate role as cohabiting partner. Since cohabitation is often a prelude to marriage and/or parenthood, by forgoing cohabitation they would also avoid potential conflicts between schooling, on the one hand, and marriage and parenthood, on the other.

Contrary to popular images, researchers have found that cohabitation is not a college student phenomenon (Bumpass & Sweet, 1991). The correlation between months cohabiting and months of schooling in the 4 years following high school was negative for both males and females (–.40 and –.23, respectively; both $p < .001$). Earlier educational plans and occupational aspirations were also negatively related to subsequent parenthood, for both males and females, and to marriage, for males.[9]

Consistent with the amalgamation hypothesis, the importance females previously attached to family was positively, not negatively, related to subsequent schooling and part-time work. Similarly, it was negatively related to full-time work. Family self-efficacy, following the same pattern as the importance of family, was positively related to school (weakly) and part-time work, and negatively related to full-time work (weakly). This pattern is more suggestive of an amalgamation process than a retreat from marriage or a masculinization process. Greater commitment and confidence with respect to family life predicts extensive human capital investment through education and part-time employment. Supporting a sequencing strategy, later anticipated marriage age also predicted greater investments in schooling and part-time work. Those females who planned to marry at an older age when they were high school seniors achieved more months of schooling and more months of part-time work during the ensuing 4 years. Consistent with a desire to delay family formation on the part of women who expected to be successful in the economic realm, greater economic self-efficacy was associated with an avoidance of cohabitation. Both an orientation toward family life and a sequencing strategy, therefore, foster female attainment.

For males, consistent with a traditional "male breadwinner" orientation, we found that those who wished to delay marriage experienced fewer months of full-time work and had lower annual incomes 4 years later. Also reflective of a traditional breadwinner orientation, the importance males attached to family was positively related to months of schooling later obtained. Those with a greater sense of family efficacy while in high school had higher incomes 4 years later.

However, in light of gender role change, it is noteworthy that behaviors related to their own status attainment were related to males' prior expectation that their wives would similarly invest in work. Male adolescents' expectation that their wives would work was linked to subsequent investment in schooling and part-time work, and to the avoidance of full-time work (and lower earnings) and cohabitation. While this does not necessarily imply that males viewed their wives' achievement as equally important as their own, it at a minimum indicates movement away from traditional expectations.[10]

In order to determine whether the relationships between earlier orientations and later behaviors were spurious, due to their common associations with family background variables, we computed partial correlations, controlling race, family structure, parental education, and family income. We obtained very similar outcomes; in only four (of 132) instances did the findings change. In three cases, previously significant zero-order correlations were reduced to insignificance. In one, a nonsignificant correlation became statistically significant.[11] These results do not warrant change in our conclusions.

CONCLUSION

Summary and Implications for Future Research

This study, given its focus on a very recent cohort of young people, is indicative of both change and stability in males' and females' orientations toward achievement and family. It is clear from our study that adolescent females in St. Paul, Minnesota, in the 1990s had high educational and occupational aspirations, much like those of adolescent males. Unlike prior generations (Marini & Greenberger, 1978), they did not aspire, or plan, to have lower levels of educational and occupational achievement than males, nor were they less confident of their future economic prospects. Females, in fact, anticipated that career would be even more important than did males, and they expressed stronger intrinsic and extrinsic reward values. As adult women increasingly are entering the workforce and experiencing more continuous labor force participation, adolescent females considered work outside the home as a given. They almost universally expected to work, both after marriage and after having children.

But, at the same time, adolescent females are not withdrawing from anticipated family involvements. They expected to marry, to have children, and attached greater importance to their future familial roles than did their male peers. They were more confident than males that they would be able to have a happy family life as well. Clearly, a process of amalgamation, not substitution, is occurring with respect to females' anticipated work and family roles.

Young women in our study expected to attain high levels of educational attainment and occupational prestige, while being highly involved in their family roles.

From our data, it is apparent that young women were aware of the potential conflict between work and family roles. They anticipated greater interference of family and career than did the young men; they also expected to forgo labor force participation, at least for a period of time, to take care of infants or young children. We might conclude that high educational and occupational achievement orientations are being readily acquired by contemporary late adolescent women, while in terms of their anticipated family orientations and behaviors they remain ready to assume traditional "female" family responsibilities. It may be, as Machung (1989) found, that young women combine elements of traditional gender roles (expecting to remain out of the labor force with young children) with expectations for change in other traditionally "female" responsibilities (division of housework).

Adolescent males, in comparison to prior generations, were more likely to expect that their future wives would be employed after taking on family roles, especially if they themselves had high aspirations. But substantial proportions remained uncertain, or did not anticipate that their future wives would be in the labor force after children are born. This uncertainty may derive from not knowing their future spouses' intentions, and also from an understanding that supporting a family may require two earners. Given their ambivalence about their wives' working, and their own propensity to attach greater importance to career than family, it is likely that they will be quite receptive to their wives taking "time out" for child care, if it is financially feasible, while they themselves pursue more continuous careers. Few males in our panel expected to remove themselves very long from the labor force for the purpose of taking care of young children.

In terms of their post–high school behaviors, gender role distinctions remain clearly evident. Young women in the Youth Development Study have moved more quickly into marriage and parenthood than young men, as might be expected given their stronger earlier family orientations. Our earlier analysis (Mortimer & Johnson, 1999) found that those young women who married during the first 4 years after high school bore greater costs than married men with respect to schooling and part-time employment. While early parenthood was associated with less human capital investment in terms of part-time work and education, mothers also did less full-time work than women who had not become parents. In contrast, and in accord with the traditional notion of men as the economic providers, fathers did more full-time work.

For adolescents, anticipated involvement in work and in family go together. The positive correlations between these orientations suggest that the spheres are not seen as being mutually exclusive or constituting a zero-sum game, such that involvement in one sphere necessarily requires pulling back from the other. This pattern represents a continuing traditional work-family connection for males, but a new, amalgamation model for females.

Consistent with a sequencing strategy, females with higher educational and occupational aspirations, and stronger intrinsic job values, planned later marriages. Thus, while they may not have anticipated lesser involvement in family life once formed, greater anticipated involvement in work and education was associated with postponement of family life. Both males and females who planned later marriages also anticipated less interference between their family roles and their career plans. Females who attached greater importance to their future careers, and those who were more interested in the extrinsic rewards of work—income, prestige, security, and advancement—also expected to return to the labor market more quickly, devoting less time to full-time child care.

Adolescents' plans and orientations were predictive of later behaviors. Consistent with status attainment models, educational and occupational aspirations, commitment to work, and job values all predicted attainment 4 years later in terms of investments made in schooling, part-time work, full-time work, and job characteristics like income and the opportunity to help others. Achievement orientations were negatively related to family formation at this early life stage, including cohabitation, as well as marriage and parenthood.

Family plans and orientations were similarly predictive of family formation processes. Plans for earlier marriage and the importance of marriage were associated with entry into marriage and parenthood in the following 4 years.

This study demonstrates the importance of extending the social psychological study of attainment processes beyond a focus on aspirations and plans for achievement to include a broader set of orientations (Mortimer, 1996). For females, our findings indicate that the importance placed on family life is positively linked to investments in school and part-time work, and negatively linked to full-time work. Later anticipated marriage age also predicted investments in school and part-time work for females. Anticipated marriage age predicted lower investment in full-time work for males. These family orientations, including plans to sequence roles, thus influence early attainment for both genders.

Whereas it is customary for status attainment researchers to study achievement ambitions, and family researchers to focus on family attitudes (such as the anticipated age of marriage), a central contribution of this research is its demonstration that orientations to attainment and family role acquisition should be assessed in tandem. The interrelations of achievement and family orientations in late adolescence, as well as the predictive power of both achievement and family orientations for early adult behaviors in the "other" sphere, argues for a more integrative perspective.

Policy Considerations

The findings of this study should be of value to makers of family policy. Our findings indicate no evidence of a "retreat" from marriage; both males and females remain highly attached to future family roles and overwhelmingly anticipate getting married and having children. It does not appear that women's economic role is drawing them away from families. Instead, in the interest of human capital development, more young women are planning to delay family formation—but not to forgo it altogether. As indicated earlier, women's educational attainment and economic contributions to the family may also act as a stabilizing force in their future families.

This research suggests that adolescence is an optimal time for intervention efforts to promote educational and occupational attainment, as well as gender equity. The plans and goals of high school seniors with regard to their future employment and family roles do have important consequences for early adult attainment and family formation processes. And as prior research has shown, these early adult attainments and family transitions play a very important role in shaping life trajectories (Featherman, 1980). Young adults who delay family formation can more easily invest in postsecondary education that has life-long consequences. The timing of entry into family roles, especially parenthood, constrains or facilitates human capital investment through schooling and work. Shifts in attitudes and plans at this stage can have major implications for adult attainment.

Our results also indicate that a sequencing strategy fosters attainment. Some adolescents who aspire to a postsecondary educational degree may need help in separating the value they place on their role as spouse and parent from the desired timing of entry into those roles. Parents and counselors can encourage these young people's positive attitudes toward marriage and parenthood, while emphasizing that delaying these transitions will greatly facilitate their early educational and occupational achievements, as well as the welfare of their future families.

Information regarding employment practices (e.g., maternity and paternity leave), the implications for careers of taking time out of the labor force, and the constraining effects of early entry into family roles could be highly valuable at this life stage, given the effects of adolescent aspirations and orientations on educational and occupational attainment and family formation processes. Perhaps teachers and administrators can encourage exploration with regard to how employment and family life will be coordinated in programs designed for career exploration and preparedness. For example, when parents or other community members visit schools on "Career Day," they could be encouraged to speak to the issue of how choices they made, with respect to their jobs or careers and their families, shaped their investments in the other domain. In a similar manner, employers could describe policies with regard to parental leave and other family-related policies, in addition to the usual information on the educational and training requirements of their fields.

It may seem too early to address these topics, when the vast majority of adolescents have not yet begun to form their own families, but as this study shows, their perceptions of work and family life form the context in which many decisions of young adult life will be made. In other words, the work-family nexus should be dealt with explicitly so that adolescents can plan for their futures. Thoughtful consideration of work and family roles in the presence of this kind of information may clarify for adolescents the decisions they will need to make in early adulthood to achieve their desired goals. These steps, however, as they are aimed at the *social psychological* sources of attainment, will be of limited success without continued efforts to remove *structural* barriers to attainment and to design family-supportive workplace policies that ease the conflicts associated with balancing paid work and family roles.

NOTES

1. Because the Wave 8 survey was conducted in March, we were not able to discern whether a college degree was conferred within 4 years.

2. Male-typed occupations are concentrated at the top and bottom of the prestige scale. Female-typed occupations are concentrated at the center. Although mean prestige levels of occupational aspirations are similar, this does not indicate that males and females are aspiring to the same occupations.

3. In earlier waves of the Youth Development Study, females had significantly lower economic self-efficacy than males (Dennehy & Mortimer, 1993). Females' economic self-efficacy rose between the 11th and 12th grades to match that of males.

4. For females, the importance of career was not related to the anticipated timing of marriage, however. The desired number of children was unrelated to achievement aspirations for females and males, suggesting that adolescents did not perceive small families as particularly conducive to attainment. Clearly, adolescents were not planning to forgo having children or to limit family size in order to pursue careers.

5. Given the highly skewed distribution of the timing of return to work after children for males, we do not examine it with respect to the other achievement and family orientations. Similarly, because very few females expected that their spouses would remain out of the labor force after either marriage or parenthood, we do not further examine this variable.

6. It is noteworthy that extrinsic values were not related to the anticipated timing of marriage or to expected family size, since these both have implications for income attainment, especially for women.

7. While anticipated interference was initially considered in the analysis of the effects of high school plans and attitudes on later behaviors, the distribution of this measure was highly skewed and did not show any meaningful relationships with the outcomes.

8. Results were obtained from bivariate cross-tabulations of marital status and parenthood status with anticipated age of marriage (under 25 vs. 25 and older).

9. Results were obtained from bivariate cross-tabulations of marital status and parenthood status with plans to obtain a 4-year-college degree, and with occupational aspirations (above and below the median).

10. In contrast to the females', males' intrinsic values, extrinsic values, and anticipated work centrality were unrelated to subsequent education, work, and family-related investments.

11. For males, the relationship between the importance of family and months of schooling was reduced to .09 ($p > .10$) and the relationship between expecting that a spouse would work and months of cohabiting and annual income were reduced to $-.10$ ($p < .10$) and $-.09$ ($p < .10$), respectively. Also for males, the relationship between the importance of career and months of full-time work increased to .13 ($p < .05$).

REFERENCES

Ahlburg, D. A., & De Vita, C. J. (1992). New realities of the American family. *Population Bulletin, 47,* 1-44.

Baber, K. M., & Monaghan, P. (1988). College women's career and motherhood expectations: New options, old dilemmas. *Sex Roles, 19,* 189-203.

Bernard, J. (1981). The good-provider role: Its rise and fall. *American Psychologist, 36,* 1-12.

Bumpass, L. L. (1990). What's happening to the family: Interactions between demographic and institutional change. *Demography, 27,* 483-498.

Bumpass, L. L., & Sweet, J. A. (1991). The role of cohabitation in declining rates of marriage. *Journal of Marriage and the Family, 53,* 913-927.

Conger, R. D. (1996, August). *Social change in the lives of rural families: Marital response to economic decline.* Paper presented at the Annual Meeting of the American Sociological Association, New York City.

Crowley, J. E., & Shapiro, D. (1982). Aspirations and expectations of youth in the United States: Part 1. Education and fertility. *Youth and Society, 13,* 391-422.

Curry, C., Trew, K., Turner, I., & Hunter, J. (1994). The effects of life domains on girls' possible selves. *Adolescence, 29,* 133-150.

Danzinger, N. (1983). Sex-related differences in the aspirations of high school students. *Sex Roles, 9,* 683-695.

Dennehy, K., & Mortimer, J. T. (1993). Work and family orientations of contemporary adolescent boys and girls. In J. C. Hood (Ed.), *Men, work, and family* (Research on Men and Masculinities, Vol. 4, pp. 87-107). Newbury Park, CA: Sage.

Erwin, L. (1995, April). *"Having it all" in the nineties: The work and family aspirations of women undergraduates.* Paper presented at the conference, National Research and Policy Symposium: Research on Youth in Transition to Adulthood, Kananakis, Alberta.

Featherman, D. L. (1980). Schooling and occupational careers: Constancy and change in worldly success. In O. S. Brim, Jr., & J. Kagen (Eds.), *Constancy and change in human development* (pp. 675-738). Cambridge, MA: Harvard University Press.

Finch, M. D., Shanahan, M., Mortimer, J. T., & Ryu, S. (1991). Work experience and control orientation in adolescence. *American Sociological Review, 56,* 597-611.

Fiorentine, R. (1988). Increasing similarity in the values and life plans of male and female college students? Evidence and implications. *Sex Roles, 18,* 143-158.

Freedman, D., Thornton, A., Camburn, D., Alwin, D., & Young-Demarco, L. (1988). The life history calendar: A technique for collecting retrospective data. In C. C. Clogg (Ed.), *Sociological methodology* (Vol. 18). San Francisco: Jossey-Bass.

Gager, C. T. (1995). *Is love stronger than justice?: Perceptions of fairness in the division of household labor.* Unpublished doctoral dissertation, University of Pennsylvania.

Gerzon, M. (1992). *A choice of heroes: The changing faces of American manhood.* Boston: Houghton Mifflin.

Goldin, C. (1990). *Understanding the gender gap: An economic history of American women.* New York: Oxford University Press.

Greenhaus, J. H., & Beutel, N. J. (1985). Sources of conflict between work and family roles. *Academy of Management Review, 10,* 76-88.

Herzog, A. R., & Bachman, J. G. (1982). *Sex role attitudes among high school seniors: Views about work and family roles.* Ann Arbor: University of Michigan, Institute for Social Research.

Hochschild, A. R. (1989). *The second shift.* New York: Basic Books.

Huber, J., & Spitze, G. (1988). Trends in family sociology. In N. J. Smelser (Ed.), *Handbook of sociology.* Newbury Park, CA: Sage.

Johnson, M. K. (1996, August). *The effects of maternal employment in different stages of a child's life.* Paper presented at the Annual Meeting of the American Sociological Association, New York City.

Komarovsky, M. (1973). Cultural contradictions and sex roles: The masculine case. *American Journal of Sociology, 78,* 873-884.

Lambert, S. J. (1990). Processes linking work and family: A critical review and research agenda. *Human Relations, 43,* 239-257.

Lamphere, L., Zavella, P., & Gonzales, F., with Evans, P. B. (1993). *Sunbelt working mothers: Reconciling family and factory.* Ithaca, NY: Cornell University Press.

Lichter, D. T., McLaughlin, D. K., Kephart, G., & Landry, D. J. (1992). Race and the retreat from marriage: A shortage of marriageable men? *American Sociological Review, 57,* 781-799.

Machung, A. (1989). Talking career, thinking job: Gender differences in career and family expectations of Berkeley seniors. *Feminist Studies, 15,* 35-58.

Marini, M. M. (1978). Sex differences in the determination of adolescent aspirations: A review of research. *Sex Roles, 4,* 723-753.

Marini, M. M., Fan, P.-L., Finley, E., & Beutel, A. M. (1996). Gender and job values. *Sociology of Education, 69,* 49-65.

Marini, M. M., & Greenberger, E. (1978). Sex differences in occupational aspirations and expectations. *Sociology of Work and Occupations, 5,* 147-178.

Martin, T. C., & Bumpass, L. L. (1989). Recent trends in marital disruption. *Demography, 26,* 37-51.

Mortimer, J. T. (1996). Social psychological aspects of achievement. In A. C. Kerckhoff (Ed.), *Generating social stratification: Toward a new research agenda* (pp. 17-36). Boulder, CO: Westview.

Mortimer, J. T., Finch, M. D., Shanahan, M., & Ryu, S. (1992). Work experience, mental health, and behavioral adjustment in adolescence. *Journal of Research on Adolescence, 2,* 25-57.

Mortimer, J. T., & Johnson, M. K. (1998). New perspectives on adolescent work and the transition to adulthood. In R. Jessor (Ed.), *New perspectives on adolescent risk behavior* (pp. 425-496). New York: Cambridge University Press.

Mortimer, J. T., & Johnson, M. K. (1999). Part-time work and post-secondary transition pathways: A longitudinal study of youth in St. Paul, Minnesota (U.S.). In W. Heinz (Ed.), *From education to work: Cross national perspectives.* New York: Cambridge University Press.

Mortimer, J. T., & Lorence, J. (1979). Work experience and occupational value socialization: A longitudinal study. *American Journal of Sociology, 84,* 1361-1385.

Mortimer, J. T., & Lorence, J. (1995). Social psychology of work. In K. S. Cook, G. A. Fine, & J. S. House (Eds.), *Sociological perspectives on social psychology* (pp. 497-523). Boston: Allyn & Bacon.

Oppenheimer, V. K. (1994). Women's rising employment and the future of the family in industrial societies. *Population and Development Review, 20,* 293-342.

Oppenheimer, V. K. (1997). Women's employment and the gain to marriage: The specialization and trading model. *Annual Review of Sociology, 23,* 431-453.

Papanek, H. (1973). Men, women, and work: Reflections on the two-person career. *American Journal of Sociology, 78,* 852-872.

Pimentel, E. E. (1996). Effects of adolescent achievement and family goals on the early adult transition. In J. T. Mortimer & M. Finch (Eds.), *Adolescents, work, and family: An intergenerational developmental analysis* (pp. 191-220). Thousand Oaks, CA: Sage.

Schulenberg, J., Bachman, J. G., Johnston, L. D., & O'Malley, P. M. (1995). American adolescents' views on family and work: Historical trends from 1976-1992. In P. Noack, M. Hofer, & J. Youniss (Eds.), *Psychological responses to social change: Human development in changing environments.* New York: Walter de Gruyter.

Schuman, H. (1995). Attitudes, beliefs, and behavior. In K. S. Cook, G. A. Fine, & J. S. House (Eds.), *Sociological perspectives on social psychology* (pp. 68-89). Boston: Allyn & Bacon.

Sewell, W. H., & Hauser, R. M. (1975). *Education, occupation, and earnings: Achievement in the early career.* New York: Academic Press.

Shapiro, D., & Crowley, J. E. (1982). Aspirations and expectations of youth in the United States: Part 2. Employment activity. *Youth and Society, 14,* 33-58.

Spade, J. Z., & Reese, C. A. (1991). We've come a long way, maybe: College students' plans for work and family. *Sex Roles, 24,* 309-321.

Stevens, G., & Hoisington, E. (1987). Occupational prestige and the 1980 U.S. labor force. *Social Science Research, 16,* 74-105.

Willetts-Bloom, M. C., & Nock, S. L. (1994). The influence of maternal employment on gender role attitudes of men and women. *Sex Roles, 30,* 371-389.

CHAPTER 9

Transmission of Family Values, Work, and Welfare Among Poor Urban Black Women

ROBERTA REHNER IVERSEN

NAOMI B. FARBER

Young Black women from impoverished inner-city communities increasingly are expected to work and ultimately become financially self-sufficient. Yet, although their rates of high school completion and labor force involvement have risen in recent years (Gordon, 1994; Mishel & Bernstein, 1993), these young women are disproportionately likely to be poor, and those who work are disproportionately represented in low-wage, part-time, and contingent work (Harlan & Berheide, 1994; McLanahan & Sandefur, 1994; Polivka & Nardone, 1989). In 1990, 38.4% of Black women who were not living with a spouse were living in poverty (Danziger & Weinberg, 1994) and in 1991, 60.2% of employed Black women earned wages below 125% of the poverty level (Mishel & Bernstein, 1993). Some Black women in impoverished inner-city communities do attain "good jobs" with ample earnings and

AUTHORS' NOTE: From "Transmission of Family Values, Work, and Welfare Among Poor Urban Black Women," by Roberta Rehner Iversen and Naomi B. Farber, November 1996, *Work and Occupations, 23*(4), pp. 437-460. © Copyright 1996 Sage Publications, Inc.

nonwage benefits (Iversen, 1995; Jencks, Perman, & Rainwater, 1988), yet many more remain persistently poor (Edin, 1995; Mishel & Bernstein, 1993; Woody, 1989).

Scholars and policy makers have debated for several decades about how and why some poor urban Black women are able to achieve economic self-sufficiency through employment, whereas others experience or are at high risk of economic dependence through long-term welfare receipt. Some scholars attribute poorer economic status primarily to economic and social-structural elements such as inadequate networks for job information (Coleman, 1990), a paucity of inner-city jobs—particularly jobs that are not located in the secondary or contingent labor market (Wilson, 1991, 1996), and reduced returns to human capital investments for Black women (McCrate, 1989). Other scholars emphasize the negative impact of cultural and personal characteristics such as teenage childbearing and single-parent status (Hayes, 1987), "learned helplessness" and low levels of self-efficacy (Bane & Ellwood, 1994; Kane, 1987), and fear of family separation and anxieties associated with changing social status (Musick, 1993).

The relation of personal values to economic attainment remains a central focus in the long-standing debate over what factors maintain poverty among many Black inner-city residents. Since E. Franklin Frazier's early prediction that poor southern Black migrants to northern cities would assimilate steadily into the American social and economic mainstream, a substantial body of research has examined to what degree, if any, the persistence of poverty among a significant minority of the urban poor results from their holding deviant values (Frazier, 1939). One main theoretical focus has been on explaining the apparent divergence between holding dominant American ideal values and nonnormative conduct among many inner-city Black residents. For example, Liebow (1967) asserted that poor Black men held mainstream values about work but that, in part, because each succeeding generation was unable to attain meaningful employment, they developed a system of alternative "shadow values" that helped them cope with their frustration and failure. Rodman's (1971) analysis, intended primarily to explain lower-class, out-of-wedlock family formation, assumed also that poor Blacks held ideal normative values but resorted to "value stretch" in adapting to the "pressure of circumstances" (p. 191). These perspectives, like that of Stack's (1974) research about the adaptive nature of kinship-based exchange networks among poor Black women, emphasize the ways in which socioeconomic factors prevent poor people from acting on their ideal values about work and family life—how individuals adapt to the exigencies of poverty in ways that can become patterned over time. There remains no consensus, however, about whether these patterns are transmitted across generations or created anew, and very little information exists about how such behavior patterns and value systems actually may be transmitted.

Recent research focusing on personal values about work and welfare among ghetto residents examines more closely what is currently termed *economic dependency*. In the hauntingly familiar terms of the historic debate, some scholars maintain that poor urban residents hold values that deviate from those of the dominant culture and lead to economic dependence, such as a preference for immediate gratification over investments for the future (Wilson, 1994), a weak or inconsistent desire to work (Mead, 1992), and/or a preference for welfare over work (Mead, 1994). Other scholars hold that values among the urban poor are similar to those of the middle class, but that the connection between values and economic outcomes is not direct and also is highly complex and variable (Ellwood, 1989; Tienda & Stier, 1991). Although in some respects there is little new theoretically in the current debates, the confluence of recent economic structural changes and the continued poverty across several more generations creates new pieces of the complex puzzle of persistent urban poverty that must be analyzed in contemporary terms.

In this report, we present findings about the dynamic interaction among family values, family transmission processes, and young people's attitudes and behavior regarding both work and welfare, a dual focus that is seldom seen in research about occupational attainment. We examine the values about work and welfare and their transmission in relation to work status and perceptions of future work among a group of 50 poor Black women ages 15 to 23 from inner-city Milwaukee. Some of the women had children during their teen years, and some did not.

To examine if and how values and/or intrafamilial value transmission processes are associated with current and perceived future work- and welfare-related behaviors, we asked four questions. What values about work and welfare do the young women and their families hold? What are the intrafamilial processes through which these values are transmitted? How are the families' values about work and welfare and intrafamilial transmissions of these values associated with the young women's work and/or welfare statuses and to their perceptions about their economic futures? Do the women's work statuses, values, transmission processes, and ideas about the future differ according to their adolescent parent status?

Answers to these questions will contribute to theoretical knowledge about how values and family transmission processes are related to occupational attainment. Such knowledge is particularly needed now when the most basic assumptions about the purposes and nature of social welfare policies are being questioned and reformulated.

We begin with a general description of the study and the women in the study. We then present findings about values and value transmission processes, incorporating discussion about work statuses and perceptions about future economic status. We also discuss differences in these processes and perceived outcomes in relation to adolescent parent status. Policy and program implications are addressed in the concluding section.

FRAMEWORK

We view the entry of young women into the workforce and their continued participation as a process rather than an event or series of events (Rosenfeld, 1992). Our primary interest is in selected aspects of what influences the movement of the study women toward and into employment. We examine the values they and their families hold about work and welfare and the ways in which their families transmit these relevant values to influence their daughters' futures. In so doing, we do not adopt an individualistic perspective suggesting that these are determining factors over and above the structural characteristics of the local labor market or even their ability to overcome or circumvent external barriers to employment. Rather, we assume that multiple factors operating at many levels of individual experience and social organization influence outcomes. Therefore, especially insofar as research increasingly finds significant heterogeneity among residents of poor inner-city communities, it is important to examine in detail all aspects of individuals' lives to understand what factors might enhance or diminish individuals' sense of agency and influence their economic status.

The heart of our examination is what we term the *intrafamilial transmission of values*. We use Eagly and Chaiken's (1993) definition of values as "attitudes toward relatively abstract goals or end states of human existence (e.g., equality, freedom, salvation)" (p. 5). We consider work or "gainful occupation" an appropriate addition to this list of end states. Some of the values that are held traditionally in the United States, and generally are considered to be the values of the dominant majority, contribute to economic self-sufficiency; these include: respecting one's parents; being responsible for one's actions—for example, getting an education and being a good parent; earning a good living or getting a good job; and living up to one's full potential as an individual (Yankelovich, 1994). We assess the young women's values about work and welfare through their stated attitudes and descriptions of their families' views about both domains.

The process by which families transmit their values to children is defined by Baly (1989) as "the socialization of individuals to work attitudes, values, and behaviors of the dominant culture" (p. 247). Baly finds that parental influence on the career attitudes of adolescents is stronger among Blacks than Whites. That parents influence their children about work has formed the basis of much of the status attainment research from the earliest examples (Blau & Duncan, 1967; Otto & Haller, 1979). How parents transmit their values to their children, particularly those values about work and welfare, is less fully understood and is under scrutiny here.

Theory about social capital offers a useful way to conceptualize the transactional nature of intrafamilial value transmission processes as they relate to employment and perceptions of future economic status among young adults. Social capital "is the set of resources that inhere in family relations . . . that are useful for the cognitive or social development of a child or young person" (Coleman, 1990, p. 300). Coleman further asserts that social capital "inheres in the structure of relations between persons and among persons" (p. 302) and "is an important resource for individuals and can greatly affect their ability to act and their perceived quality of life" (p. 317).

Among families with limited external resources, aspects of social capital accumulation that may be particularly necessary to the creation of useful occupation-directed capital include the following: obligations and expectations between family members, including relations of authority and trust, and the potential for information transmission that inheres in social relations. Family characteristics that may enhance or limit the accumulation of social capital include the stability or instability of the social structure, ideologies of interdependence or disconnection, and whether the family social networks are closed or open. Families with closed intergenerational networks demonstrate maximum obligation to family members and provide numerous sources of information through mutually interdependent relations between adults. The impact of this authority and influence is potentially greater in closed networks than in open family networks, where obligations are diffused by interpersonal disruption or limited by isolation and, thereby, offer fewer authority and information resources, respectively. These family characteristics, as well as possibilities for the accumulation of social capital with organizations outside the family, will be examined.

In addition to describing family values and elucidating family transmission processes, we examine how these values and processes relate to the women's actual occupational behavior. Our explicitly emic or inside view of the values-behavior connection is based on the "assumption that the world of work is one actively constructed through the interpretive acts of agents involved" (Grint, 1991, p. 3). Similarly, attitude theorists posit the relevance of values or attitudes to behavior but also note the complexity and heterogeneity of the acquisition and realization processes (Eagly & Chaiken, 1993). We examine both objective behavior, such as occupational attainment, and subjective indicators of values, such as intentions, perceptions about future economic status, and perceived connections between school and work, school and welfare, and work and welfare.

METHOD

Sample

The data reported here are part of a set of focused life histories based on intensive interviews with 74 young Black women, ages 15 to 23, who reside in the inner city of Milwaukee, Wisconsin. Half of the respondents had a child before age 20; the remainder were nonparent peers from the same community. This article reports on data from a subset of 50 randomly selected participants—24 teen mothers and 26 nonparent peers.

Contacts were made initially with a few young women who previously participated in a survey of teenage parents on Aid to Families with Dependent Children (AFDC) (Danziger & Radin, 1990). From this core of teenage mothers, we used snowball sampling to get referrals to other potential participants. Snowball or chain referral sampling procedures are a particularly applicable methodology when the study focus is on sensitive topics such as personal values and economic behavior (Mead, 1994; Weiss, 1994). The majority of participants were recruited through personal referrals rather than through formal organizations to avoid any systematic bias introduced by professional intervention and to enhance the comparability of experience in the neighborhood and community-level environment. Thus, although there are problems with including younger teens in the nonparent peer category because they were still potentially teen mothers, that concern was weighed against an interest in environmental similarity and individual differences.

Data Collection and Analysis

One of the authors and two graduate research assistants from the University of Wisconsin-Madison School of Social Work conducted life-history interviews between 1987 and 1989. Nearly all the women participated in two intensive interviews in their homes. The open-ended interviews focused on the women's ideals and actual experiences in relation to their family, educational, occupational, peer, and community environments. Interviews were audiotaped and transcribed verbatim on the computer.

The data for this report were analyzed through a process of coding the interviews in terms of predefined categories that emerged from the participant's historical, current, and expected future educational, occupational, and welfare experiences; the experiences of her parents; her perceptions of her parents' values about these subjects; and the direct and indirect activities geared to transmit and reinforce those values.

We do not imply direct causal relations among teen parenting status, values, the processes of transmission, and occupational outcomes. However, insofar as becoming a teen parent is widely regarded, with some few exceptions, as being a critical, if not determining event in the life trajectory of a young woman, especially if she is poor and Black, such a comparison contributes to our understanding of how adolescents who do have children might differ from other teens, and how they differ from one another.

DESCRIPTION OF THE WOMEN

Many aspects of the young women's experiences are consistent with those reported through national and ethnographic data about their cohort in the following domains: marital status, childbearing, education, employment, family and personal welfare receipt, and parent marital status (Harris, 1993; Iversen, 1995; Jarrett, 1994). (See Table 9.1; some data are not shown.)

None of the study women is or has been married. Similarly, the study women's parents are unlikely to have intact marriages. Over half of the teens' parents were married at some point, but only a few were married at the time of the study and a sizable proportion had never married. Three quarters of the teen mothers had a single child.

Over half of the women completed high school, and over one third of the graduates pursued some postsecondary education or training. Seven women currently attended full-time postsecondary educational programs. Five peers and 11 teen mothers reported having significant learning problems in school, including repeating a grade. Nine women, all of whom were teen mothers, dropped out of high school before graduation, and all nine reported earlier academic difficulties. Four dropped out well before becoming pregnant, and five dropped out in conjunction with their pregnancies (see also Upchurch & McCarthy, 1990; Upchurch, McCarthy, & Ferguson, 1993). Fifteen women,

TABLE 9.1 Demographic Characteristics of the Women in the Study According to
Teen Childbearing Status

Characteristics	Nonparent Peers (n = 26)	Teen Mothers (n = 24)
Age		
Range	15 to 23	15 to 22
Mean ± SE	18.4 ± 0.36	19.1 ± 0.38
Number of children		
Range		1 to 4
Mean ± SD		1.3 ± 0.8
Age at first birth		
Range		14 to 20
Mean ± SD		16.8 ± 1.7
Educational attainment		
School dropout	0	9 (38%)
In school (pre–high school graduation)	10 (38%)	5 (21%)
Completed 12th grade	9 (35%)	8 (33%)
More than 12th grade	7 (27%)	4 (17%)
Occupational status		
Unemployed	3 (12%)	9 (38%)
Employed part-time	0	4 (17%)
Employed full-time	7 (27%)	6 (21%)
Postsecondary + part-time work	6 (23%)	1 (4%)
In high school	10 (38%)	5 (21%)
In high school + part-time work	5 (50%)	1 (20%)
Family history of government financial assistance (n, percent)		
Never	5 (24%)	5 (22%)
Ever	16 (76%)	18 (78%)
Current family receipt of government financial assistance		
None	9 (39%)	13 (59%)
AFDC	9 (39%)	7 (32%)
SSI	5 (22%)	2 (9%)
Parental marital status		
Never married	7 (28%)	12 (50%)
Separated/divorced	11 (44%)	10 (42%)
Married	7 (28%)	2 (8%)

NOTE: AFDC = Aid to Families with Dependent Children; SSI = Supplemental Security Income.

including two teen mothers who dropped out previously, attended high
school full-time.

All but one of the teens had some kind of job history, which began, on average, at age 15. The simplest job history was the 15-year-old mother with a single job at age 10 selling fruits from a fruit stand. The most complex job history was that of the nonparent peer in her senior year of college who plans a graduate business degree and worked part-time with her own creative arts business. In addition, half of the peers and teen mothers participated in high-school-connected work programs, co-ops, or programs for low-income youth that linked them with jobs, particularly during summers.

The women's occupational status comprised five categories: unemployed, employed full-time, employed part-time, attending a full-time postsecondary educational program and part-time work, and attending high school full-time with and without part-time work. One quarter of the women were unemployed, some "temporarily," some more permanently. The remainder of the women were gainfully occupied in school or work pursuits. The jobs for virtually all the study women, both part- and full-time, were located in the secondary labor market or service sector. Typical jobs included housekeeper, nursing aide at a nursing home, fast-food worker, and retail cashier. Aspirations for future work, however, for 8 of the teen parents and 15 of the nonparent peers, were in labor market sectors that offer the potential for economic self-sufficiency. Aspirations for jobs in the professional sector included accountant, lawyer, teacher, nurse, and social worker. Aspirations for jobs in the high-skill sector included hotel management and military officer.

The families generally had backgrounds of AFDC receipt but relatively low levels of long-term dependence. Three quarters of the families received governmental financial assistance at some time in the past, but slightly less than half the families received such assistance at the time of the study. The families of 1 in 4 peers and 1 in 5 teen mothers received AFDC for the respondents' entire lives.

Twenty of the 24 teen mothers received some income from AFDC, and for half, AFDC was the only income source. None of the peers received AFDC directly, per program definition.

VALUES

Values About Work

Overall, the women expressed and perceived that their families hold values about or relevant to work that are consistent with those of the dominant society, as outlined above. Values such as respecting one's parents and being responsible for one's actions, were expressed by teen mothers and nonparent peers alike.

A nonparent peer in high school who held two part-time jobs and linked her work future with her respect for her mother's wishes was typical: "I'll be in Job Corps and going into the Navy or the Army or the Marines. It's cuz my mama want me to. Because she said she wants me to make something out of myself. She want to be proud of me."

The importance of education was the value almost universally expressed by the women, either for itself (Farber & Iversen, 1998) or for its instrumental purpose. Half of the nonparent peers and two thirds of the teen mothers associated education with work achievement, evident in the peer who stated that "Education is gonna be needed to get a job, and your skills. And so, I'm all for it." However, although peers and teen mothers valued education, the level of education they discussed was different. All the peers and some of the teen mothers focused on the need for postsecondary education, expressed by one peer's goal to "finish college and get a good job and settle down." In contrast, most of the teen mothers who dropped out of school, whether before or after their child's birth, focused on the need to complete high school or get a general equivalency diploma (GED) to achieve their goals in the workplace.

Many teen mothers were motivated to achieve by their responsibility to their children, exemplified by one 11th-grade dropout: "I'm ready to go out and work. My head is on straight now. My son. Since I had him, I need more responsibilities. Need my high school diploma, really. If I really want to do something. I want him to grow up to do something too."

Consistent with the literature that notes the complexity of the values-work connection, a number of the women held mainstream values that conflict with one another. Some teen mothers experienced conflict between the value of being a good parent and the value of earning a living. Despite having histories of work, some of these teen mothers currently were full-time at-home mothers: "Three years at the day care center when I got out of high school. But now like if I work, I want to wait until he get older."

Another conflict was described by a 17-year-old nonparent in high school who was interested in a career in law enforcement but whose religion discouraged higher education: "Because they don't pressure their kids to go to college. Well, they feel that, it's a long story behind it, this world wouldn't stay that long for us to get involved with a career or anything."

A number of women's comments explicitly demonstrated the disparities between personal values about work and occupational opportunities. A teen mother who worked part-time and also received AFDC benefits described the difficulty encountered in attempting to act on her desire for education and employment:

> I hate being on welfare, OK. I don't, I want to be independent, I want to be on my own, I want to have a good job. I did go to school but, I went to MBTI, and I graduated but it just didn't turn out, I didn't find a job in that field. People wanted experience, they didn't want training. After I graduated I went on a thousand interviews, but all of them wanted more experience.

Values About Welfare

As with work, both nonparent peers and teen mothers generally reported mainstream values about receiving AFDC: most "hate it," "don't want it," "hope I never have to be on it," and "want to get off it." Most of the women regarded work as the desired means of avoiding dependence on welfare.

One 21-year-old teen mother, employed after high school graduation but unemployed since her child's birth a year earlier, expressed respect for her own mother's ability to exit AFDC through hard work:

> She works at, um, this laundry hospital cleaning place doing the laundry for the hospital. And on her night job, she just cleans; you know, the night-time maintenance downtown. She's struggling and everything, but she's making it; she don't get it no more.

Another teen mother, employed full-time, expressed pride in obtaining a better job that obviated the need for welfare: "I got me a job and starting a better job Wednesday, and you know, I'm doing good for myself, taking care of my baby. I don't get any welfare, so I must be doing something good."

A nonparent peer who held two jobs associated the values of bettering herself and living up to her potential with her desire to be an accountant and to be notably different from her family, which received welfare:

> I work at the nursing home as a nurse's aide, almost every day from 6 till 2:30. When I get off that job, I go to my second job, work in the box office from like, 3 till 9. The only thing I can say that I guess I want a better life. I would rather work any day, I would rather work for $3.35 than to be on welfare. Everybody in my family was on welfare. I don't want to be on welfare. I want to be different. I want to show them that what I can do. . . . I like to be on top.

Most peers and teen mothers also think education and welfare are closely connected, as one peer in high school said:

> But just look in the future and say "well, a couple of years from now, I'm almost grown. I'm gonna have to have to have, go to college, or do something. I don't want to be on welfare. I want to make something of myself."

A teen mother high school graduate's comments are typical of the many mothers who believed that education would allow them to be financially self-supporting:

> I pray that as soon as C. gets old enough, I'm going back to school. And then have me a job. I want a job that's going to get me completely off you know where I can pay for my own doctor bills or my insurance.

Some women equate being responsible parents with avoiding welfare. Peers still in high school typically expressed this position, as demonstrated by one 17-year-old in her discussion about avoiding pregnancy: "When I have my kids, I don't want to be on welfare. I want to take care of my work and take care of my kids on my own. That's probably why—one reason—why I haven't got pregnant."

Similarly, one teen mother stated,

> Because it was hard for me working until I put her in the day care center. One day, I just said I wanted to work, I don't want any welfare. I don't want more kids. And I just all of the sudden one day said I'm going to do it. And I did it, for like 10, 11 months now.

A small minority of the women did not express such strong disapproval of welfare, although only one of the women's comments could be classified as approving. This teen mother dropped out of school in eighth grade and considered her current job "a mother."

> It will always be available because G [baby's father] he has diabetes, so I don't think he'd be able for you know for him to get a job and then. It's always there available for me. [see as long term?] Yeah. I really don't like, but it's a source of income for the baby and me, a way to eat, a place to sleep. I can't get a job because of the baby, the baby's there and anyways I wouldn't want to get a job, it's too hard.

While this woman's statement that work is "too hard" could be considered deviating from a traditional work ethic, her comments about participation in a work-training program for low-income students also demonstrated a paucity of knowledge about how to maneuver in the labor market: "I went and applied the year after I had the job, but they didn't call me. They didn't do nothing. And I didn't miss hardly no work. I was there like almost every day."

Although nearly all women in the study valued and hoped to achieve long-term economic self-sufficiency, many also expressed some doubt about their abilities to act on those values. Some nonparent peers reported a kind of generalized uncertainty about the future, evident in comments such as "If I can help it, I just don't want to be on it, period," or uncertainty about labor market opportunities with views such as "If I can get a good job, I don't want to be on welfare all my life," and "I know I don't want to get on welfare. I know there's not too many jobs out there, but at least you got to try."

Some teen mothers, in addition to having similar uncertainties to those of peers, also believed that they might not be able to avoid welfare in the future because of their own or their child's health needs, as this mother with cerebral palsy noted: "But if I have to be on it till D. is 18, then I'll just have to be on it, as much as I go to the hospital."

These women's resigned acceptance of AFDC for health needs was frequently linked with experiences of jobs that do not offer health insurance, a situation found typically in part-time and secondary labor market jobs attained by poor Black women in general. A teen mother who was employed part-time as a school bus driver expressed this typical dilemma: "I don't want to be on AFDC. I'd rather work for my own money and make more than what I get on AFDC [medical card is important] because I don't have no insurance from the bus company."

VALUE TRANSMISSION PROCESSES

There was general agreement among most of the poor young women and their families in the study that education and work are, in principle, desirable and that receiving welfare is not a valued state. However, there was much more diversity among the women in terms of the ways in which their families transmitted those values and in the current and anticipated statuses of the women themselves.

Three central processes of value transmission emerged from the interviews. We discuss findings about these processes in conjunction both with adolescent parent status and with work status and perceptions about future employment. We assess the potential for accumulation of social capital within the family by examining the content of the particular transmission processes that the women describe.

Direct Verbal Messages. The first type of value transmission is through messages about work from parent(s) and/or other family members directly to the teen. These messages are verbal communications, and they often are repeated frequently. Such reinforcement is thought to be a crucial contributing element in the socialization and inculcation of values (Wilson, 1994).

Some direct messages are encouraging and motivational—potential builders of social capital through positive obligations and expectations between family members. The nonparent peers and teen mothers in high school and postsecondary educational pursuits most frequently reported receiving encouraging messages, ones based on ideologies of family interdependence. One nonparent peer, who was employed full-time and wanted to attend business college, received from her grandmother, her primary parent, a typical encouraging message:

> She would just always say, "yeah, I want you to finish high school and go to college, so you can have a good job." Just, you know, really encourage me to do these things, you know. "You'll be the first one. I want you to do this and do that," you know.

Conversely, research findings suggest that youths experience frustration in making career decisions when they receive conflicting messages from significant others (Otto & Haller, 1979). In this study, the women who were unemployed most frequently reported receiving mixed or discouraging direct messages. A teen mother who was unemployed and dropped out of school several years before she had her child suggested that the critical way in which the message is conveyed may influence its impact:

> They just tell me that I'm going to need my education one day. I should go to school. And they saying to think about it, and it's something I should want to do it, 'cause I'm going to regret it when I get older. And you find yourself wanting to work here and work there. And you ain't going to be able to do it 'cause you don't have an education. And then they'd really rubbing it in real good.

Tangible Actions. The second type of value transmission process is tangible, step-by-step actions directed at the teen's efforts toward education and work. One way that these actions potentiate social capital accumulation is through enhancing relations of authority and trust. Conversely, capital accumulation is limited where trust is abrogated, as occurs in three-generational family units that do not function as effective child care systems (Furstenberg, 1991). In addition, such assistance helps the young women have experiences that are investments in future achievement and are self-reinforcing in developing confidence and self-esteem.

Typical tangible support is in the form of child care, transportation, parental supervision, and financial help specific to the job, such as the purchase of materials, supplies, or clothes. Perhaps the most graphic example of the potential of such support is the teen parent who signed over temporary custody of her child to her mother to pursue her lifelong goal of military service:

> I'm gonna go into the reserves. I go to basic training in the summer of '89.
> And then, come back for college, and I'll be in the reserves, and then after
> then I plan on going in as an officer. It's really like a job, the Army . . . ever
> since I was in the sixth grade I always thought of going. Now I'm trying to
> get a ROTC scholarship.

In a few cases, the tangible help of an extended family member is an attempt to compensate for disruptive effects of family violence and neglect, illustrated by the comments of this teen mother who remained in high school and wanted to be a secretary:

> My mother drank occasionally 'cause she had problems. My stepfather, he
> did drugs. And I was pregnant. My grades were dropping. I was just de-
> pressed, that's all. I didn't completely cut school off. My auntie made sure I
> got my homework. She's a teacher. She made sure I got my homework,
> made sure I did it.

Outside of family support, school-based and city-based low-income work programs provide considerable tangible support to the teens for their work efforts—a supplemental or, in many cases, a substitute source of social capital. Cooperative programs aimed at school and employment and summer work opportunities for low-income families are the two main sources of this extra-familial support. Half the peers and teen mothers alike reported participating in such programs. A nonparent peer who was temporarily unemployed but had firm plans for 4-year college attendance for child care education, illustrated the information potential in tangible support from combined family and outside-family sources:

I got into a program called DECA—Distributive Education Clubs of America. And that helps you find jobs, and so my mother was proud of me. My mother taught us, in case something happens to her, we all know about how to go about getting things. I know how to drive; we know how to pay bills. She teaches us all that. We know how to provide for ourselves. She encouraged all of my sisters you know, "Whatever you're going to do, be your best at it," and that's what we did, and so, we're making it right now.

Examples/Indirect Messages. The third and most commonly reported type of value transmission is through examples of parents' and other family members' jobs and job histories. The potential for occupational information and the openness or closedness of social networks, in conjunction with ideologies of family interdependence, are elements of social capital accumulation that are particularly relevant to this mode of values transmission.

Although most of the women reported familial examples of work, the strength of the messages varied. Strength is assessed by the level of detail the teens related about the parent's tenure at a work site, about the content of the parent's job, and about the course of employment for the parent, as well as by the number of family members about whom job information is known.

The reports of nonparent peers tended to be more detailed than those of the teen parents. In addition, even though the marital histories of the peers' parents were similar to those of the teen mothers' parents, the peers were more likely to know details about their fathers' work histories, regardless of the frequency or quality of the contact with him. The nonparent peers also knew more about the jobs of other family members than did the teen mothers.

This peer, one of 14 children of married parents, who was about to finish a 4-year college program in social welfare and also worked part-time, displayed very detailed knowledge:

He [father] works for the LMN bus company. He used to drive the bus, but now he's a mechanic for the bus department. He used to do construction, and then he, I don't know how, what happened, why he changed, but he was running for alderman, and then he broke his hip, and then he was laid off for a while, so it was like a gap in between. As far as I know, he's never been unemployed. She [mother] works for the government, the [XXX] Department in Milwaukee. And she was a caseworker, but now she's, she'll be a caseworker investigator. Before she worked for the welfare department, she used to do hair, so she had to go to school to do, to get her beauty's license, but I think she's been with [XXX] Department, 15, 16 years.

The teen mothers generally provided less detailed information about their parents' and family members' work histories. A typical example is the more vague description by a teen mother, who was currently in high school with no declared work goals, of her mother's experience after moving to Milwaukee to improve opportunities for work:

> She thought that we needed a new environment, and that basically, if she lived in a bigger city, she could find a better job. She found a job but it's not paying very much, making hair combs, and she's working for a job service.

Another teen mother, who had never worked and had no future work aspirations "because I was just too busy taking care of my brothers and sisters," described a situation suggesting the diffuse obligations of a more open family network and a family ideology characterized by intergenerational disconnection:

> Well, she's [mother] working when she had me but then um my grandma pushed her into getting welfare because she couldn't, it was only a part-time job, and she couldn't get a whole job being pregnant with me, so she stopped working and went on welfare. Well, her boyfriend owns a bar. My mom works there sometimes; she don't, but they got a room upstairs. Not supposed to say anything to anybody.

Multiple Transmission Processes. Each of the three transactional processes of transmitting values about work and welfare within a family is important and potentially influential to the accumulation of social capital. There is variation by parent status in how many of the three processes operate within any one family. More peers than teen mothers reported the presence of all three processes in their family interactions—direct messages, tangible support, and examples—resulting in greater potential for the accumulation of social capital, as seen by the teens' occupational attitudes and pathways.

These multifaceted transmissions were described most uniformly among the women who attended full-time postsecondary educational programs and worked also at supplementary jobs, and only slightly less uniformly among the women who were employed full-time or who were in high school with part-time jobs. These women also were more likely to have definite, knowledgeable plans for educational and occupational attainment, which they connected with futures of economic self-sufficiency.

When intrafamilial transmission processes consisted of only one of the above dimensions, were seldom repeated or absent, showed little or no tangible help, and consisted of limited work attachment or success among family members, the women were likely to be less gainfully occupied. Such women were unemployed for longer periods, were employed part-time, or were in high school with no outside employment. They also were more likely to anticipate futures of economic dependency than futures of self-sufficiency.

One nonparent peer highlighted the potential for accumulation of social capital in families in which all three value transmission processes were active. She worked at two part-time jobs while attending a postsecondary program and was preparing to transfer to the local university for a 4-year business education program. After receiving her B.A. and her master's degree, the young woman intended to complete a hotel and restaurant program, anticipating about 8 to 10 years of part-time education. This peer associated her direction, focus, and success with family members' messages of encouragement, tangible help through step-by-step teaching, and the informative, motivational examples of many family members' work histories. The following excerpts illustrate the strength of social capital accumulation in closed family networks:

> I always watched Julia Child cook. Every Saturday I was watching Julia Child, I was not watching *Sesame Street*. I went over there [grandmother's], we started making cookies, cakes, and pies for Christmas around 10:00. And she let me do everything. I was doing everything. I was only around 6 or 7 or something like that. She would just tell me, I would ask her was it OK? She say, "Yeah, I was doing it fine." And it was just like, from that day on, I just had this motivation to cook or to run something of my own.
>
> To the growing up. I always had this. My grandfather was a cook for the railroad, and my grandmother, she always cooked, and that's where, like, me wanting to run my own hotel. I had money to go places instead of having to ask my mother. I was my own independent person. Mother told me "I want you to see that pay, that's what I try to show you. Be your own independent."

Fewer in number, some teen mothers reported similarly rich value transmission processes, although their aspirations and accomplishment levels generally were lower than those of the peers. The history of one 21-year-old teen mother, who dropped out of school in eighth grade and had her sole child at age 18, suggests how strong family and external support combined with her own desires for occupational achievement can mitigate the worst consequences of early motherhood and school failure. She attended Job Corps for a year and finished training for a cook's certificate before she was able to complete her GED, but she only found work as a salad bar assistant thereafter. Recently, the young woman began working in a nursing home, first as a bed maker and feeder. She then took a class at the home and had become a nurse's aide. She planned to pursue nursing as a career because she didn't "want to be nurse's aide all my life." She received AFDC for 2½ years but did not receive any at the time of the interview. This young woman associated her aspirations and accomplishments with family messages of encouragement, examples of parental work attachment, and tangible help:

> I didn't like going down there [to get AFDC], standing in no line, trying to wait to be seen. That's one thing I said I won't do. I'll get to work the best way I can, I don't care. You feel good that you doing it yourself. You know, not sitting around month after month waiting on a check to come.
>
> [Father worked] at [XXX] company. I think they make cars there, and they laid him off. So, he's been laid off for a while. But the plant is opening back up and now they're calling back all the people who worked there before. And in all that time, he opened up a bar, so we own a bar now. [Mother] came up here and I think she worked, she was a resident nurse at um, uh, I can't remember the name of the hospital up there. It's one of them homes. And she was a resident nurse, and she sometimes she used to have to take care of the wing without aides and everything. And um, then she used to teach uh, it's like dancing or drill team. And then she teached that for a while and then she went into business of her own. Started selling you know, selling, opening up stores and stuff. She uh five stores so far. So she's just really been going at it, you know, over the years ever since she's been in business of her own, she always tell me she don't really want to work for anybody, you know, she like working for herself. I worked with my mother. She have like resale shops and we had stores, you know, grocery stores. I helped out in there, working on the cash register and stuff. Yes, we had to go with her. Every time she opened up, you know, she took at least one of us with her and we helped out around.

In both peer and teen mother groups, all but two women who reported these multiple transmission processes were gainfully occupied in school or work, even though some of the teen mothers received reduced AFDC benefits also. The two unemployed teen mothers reporting the same strong level of value transmissions received only AFDC income and indicated that they were only temporarily unemployed.

DISCUSSION

Despite coming from impoverished inner-city backgrounds, most of the young Black women in our study were or planned to be gainfully occupied in educational and/or employment pursuits. Most of the teen mothers currently received some income from AFDC, yet almost half received work income as well. None of the women wanted to be on welfare forever. At the same time, they had varying degrees of confidence that they could become financially self-sufficient. They were acutely aware of the external barriers to success that abound in their community as well as the challenges of their own personal circumstances.

All but one of the women expressed normative values about work and perceived that their families value work. They believed that work is important for self-sufficiency, survival, and self-esteem and is strongly preferable to relying on welfare. These findings counter the characterization of all poor urban residents as holding nonnormative values about work as the desired means of economic support. Yet, if their ideal values suggest acceptance of mainstream norms of economic self-support through work, what accounts for the variation in their pursuit and achievement of education and jobs? Our findings support Ellwood's (1989) view that the values-behavior connection is complex.

Our study elucidates some of this complexity in focusing on selected intrafamilial processes that are an integral aspect of the development of social capital for poor young Black women. Such processes that contribute to the accumulation of social capital directed toward a young woman's future educational and occupational achievement vary widely among the families and are associated with differential current status as well as perceptions of future status by the young women in the study. The processes we describe suggest how values about work and welfare become, or fail to become, investments in the development of social capital resources for the young women's economic futures. In general, the young women who described multidimensional processes of value transmission within their families had higher levels of educational attainment and stronger work histories and perceive futures of continued productivity. The women who described more limited transmission processes were more likely to be less gainfully occupied and to anticipate futures of economic dependency on AFDC rather than work.

This study also supports other research showing that teenage childbearing is not an automatic road to a future of welfare dependency (Furstenberg, Brooks-Gunn, & Morgan, 1987). All women in our study who did not experience a mix of types of value transmissions perceived less certain economic futures, regardless of teen parent status. Conversely, strong family resources directed toward educational and occupational achievement can mitigate the extra burdens of being a young parent, evident in those teen mothers who remained in school and work. However, teen mothers do face particular challenges in achieving their commonly desired futures of self-sufficiency. Fewer teen mothers than peers reported rich transmissions of values about education and work. Because the families of peers and teen mothers had similar histories of work or welfare receipt, these factors alone cannot be presumed to account for the differences in value transmission processes. Teen mothers may have family-based demands that limit their ongoing exposure to sources of job market information, particularly those who have no school affiliation, or they may have less rich social capital interactions through family and school sources, independent of childbearing. A larger-scale replication of this study is needed to more fully disentangle the aspects of what, if anything, differentiates the value transmission processes in families of young women who bear children early from the processes in families where teen childbearing does not occur.

Policy and Program Implications

Our findings indicate both *that* and *how* the intrafamilial value transmission processes are important to the economic lives of young adults. Multifaceted transmissions are associated with stronger occupational efforts and can mediate other economic disadvantages that may or may not be related to teenage childbearing. These findings provide direct support for the expansion rather than reduction of economic and social welfare policies and related programs that will maximize the abilities of all family members to contribute to social capital development. Our particular suggestions are: comprehensive work-enhancement programs with intensive case management services for all family members, expanded middle and high school academic and vocational guidance services that are closely associated with local employers and job markets, and community-based centers for ongoing job information and training.

First, that interpersonal processes within families are of critical importance to young women's work pathways has pointed implications for the scope of programs designed to enhance the economic self-sufficiency of poor young women. To date, such programs typically are directed at welfare recipients only, with limited long-term success in moving the participants into financial self-sufficiency (Nightingale, 1995). Recent research finds that programs whose objectives include enhancement of poor mothers' work activity and reduction of welfare receipt are more effective when they are comprehensive in scope and include intensive case management services (Bloom, Fellerath, Lons, & Wood, 1993; Rangarajan, Meckstroth, & Novak, 1998). Such services recognize the variability of each woman's route to welfare receipt and address her particular needs accordingly, such as child care, transportation, job network information, health and mental health issues, and parenting information. Moreover, because many women who are employed in low-wage jobs have similar difficulty achieving above-poverty level incomes, work-enhancement programs should be expanded to include them as well.

Our findings suggest, in addition, that a family-based component could be included productively in case management, to work toward addressing the occupational, income, and support needs of other family members to facilitate value transmission. The importance of value transmissions from fathers to children is documented in other recent research (Parcel & Menaghan, 1994). Our findings indicate that the influence of work and welfare value transmissions of nonresident, sometimes completely absent, fathers is extremely important. Programs, then, must address the needs of all family members.

Second, in instances in which families cannot provide the social capital that their youngsters need to develop the capacity for self-support, the needs of individual youths should be addressed not only through traditional social service agencies but through high school educational and vocational guidance programs that are closely involved with local labor markets. To supplement or substitute for family resources, such programs should provide ongoing assessment of young women's academic abilities, provide help to those with performance problems because 25% to 40% of AFDC recipients are estimated to have generally unaddressed learning disabilities (Maynard, 1995), and maximize opportunities for vocational guidance. Currently, high school counselors in poor urban areas typically are overloaded; thus they are limited in their ability to provide adequate information about jobs and job networks. The importance of multiple work examples to youth work efforts supports the expansion of the few programs in which local professionals and employers develop scholarship and mentor programs and encourage on-site student participation in work. However, the aim of contemporary welfare-to-work policy is "any job" rather than a "good job," making eventual self-sufficiency unlikely (Glazer, 1995). Ultimately, to move both welfare recipients and low-wage workers toward good jobs, planned articulation between education, job skills training, and actual, available jobs is essential.

Third, our findings also argue against assuming a lockstep, intergenerational pattern of welfare receipt, even among families where teenage childbearing takes place. Many of the families in the study received welfare for some time but avoided long-term reliance. Significantly, there is every indication that the teens preferred work to receiving welfare. The greater success in transmitting work values among families where two parents, regardless of marital status, hold steady jobs suggests that social-structural factors such as job availability and strong value transmissions are related. Among the children in such families, work, rather than welfare receipt, can be a result. The development of centers for ongoing job training and consultation for all adults who experience periods of layoff, underemployment, or unemployment would help to alleviate periods of economic disadvantage that are experienced by families increasingly in our changing economy and would facilitate intergenerational social capital development in the process. In addition, expansion rather than curtailment of the Earned Income Tax Credit program and other related policy initiatives would address families' needs in changing labor market conditions.

In sum, although the above policy and program suggestions cannot alter characteristics in the labor market that contribute to unemployment, they can support poor families' attempts to provide resources for their children's work efforts. A philosophical and political orientation that recognizes the inextricable and mutually influential connection between family processes and work is a must for all work-related policy and program action as the 21st century nears.

REFERENCES

Baly, I. (1989). Career and vocational development of Black youth. In R. L. Jones (Ed.), *Black adolescents* (pp. 247-265). Berkeley, CA: Cobb & Henry.

Bane, M. J., & Ellwood, D. (1994). *Welfare realities: From rhetoric to reform.* Cambridge, MA: Harvard University Press.

Blau, P., & Duncan, O. D. (1967). *The American occupational structure.* New York: John Wiley.

Bloom, D., Fellerath, V., Lons, D., & Wood, R. (1993). *LEAP: Interim findings on a welfare initiative to improve school attendance among teenage parents.* New York: Manpower Demonstration Research Corporation.

Coleman, J. S. (1990). *Foundations of social theory.* Cambridge, MA: Harvard University Press.

Danziger, S. H., & Radin, N. (1990). Absent does not equal uninvolved: Predictors of fathering in teen mother families. *Journal of Marriage and the Family, 52,* 636-642.

Danziger, S. H., & Weinberg, D. H. (1994). The historical record: Trends in family income, inequality, and poverty. In S. H. Danziger, G. D. Sandefur, & D. H. Weinberg (Eds.), *Confronting poverty* (pp. 18-50). Cambridge, MA: Harvard University Press.

Eagly, A. H., & Chaiken, S. (1993). *The psychology of attitudes.* Fort Worth, TX: Harcourt Brace Jovanovich.

Edin, K. J. (1995). The myths of dependence and self-sufficiency: Women, welfare, and low-wage work. *Focus, 17,* 1-9.

Ellwood, D. T. (1989). The origins of "dependency": Choices, confidence, or culture? *Focus, 12,* 6-13.

Farber, N. B., & Iversen, R. R. (1998). Family values about education and their transmission among Black inner-city young women. In A. Colby, J. James, & D. Hart
(Eds.), *Competence and character through life* (pp. 141-167). Chicago: University
of Chicago Press.

Frazier, E. F. (1939). *The Negro family in the United States.* Chicago: University of
Chicago Press.

Furstenberg, F. F., Jr. (1991). As the pendulum swings: Teenage childbearing and social concern. *Family Relations, 40,* 127-138.

Furstenberg, F. F., Jr., Brooks-Gunn, J., & Morgan, S. P. (1987). *Adolescent mothers
in later life.* New York: Cambridge University Press.

Glazer, N. (1995). Making work work: Welfare reform in the 1990s. In D. S. Nightingale & R. H. Haveman (Eds.), *The work alternative: Welfare reform and the realities of the job market* (pp. 17-32). Washington, DC: Urban Institute.

Gordon, L. (1994). *Pitied but not entitled: Single mothers and the history of welfare.*
New York: Free Press.

Grint, K. (1991). *The sociology of work.* Cambridge, England: Polity.

Harlan, S. L., & Berheide, C. W. (1994). *Barriers to workplace advancement experienced by women in low-paying occupations.* Washington, DC: U.S. Department of
Labor, Glass Ceiling Commission.

Harris, K. M. (1993). Work and welfare among single mothers in poverty. *American
Journal of Sociology, 99,* 317-352.

Hayes, C. (1987). *Risking the future: Adolescent sexuality, pregnancy, and childbearing* (Vol. 1). Washington, DC: National Academy.

Iversen, R. R. (1995). Poor African-American women and work: The occupational attainment process. *Social Problems, 42,* 554-573.

Jarrett, R. L. (1994). Living poor: Family life among single-parent, African-
American women. *Social Problems, 41,* 30-49.

Jencks, C., Perman, L., & Rainwater, L. (1988). What is a good job? A new measure of
labor-market success. *American Journal of Sociology, 93,* 1322-1357.

Kane, T. J. (1987). Giving back control: Long-term poverty and motivation. *Social
Service Review, 61,* 405-419.

Liebow, E. (1967). *Tally's corner.* Boston: Little, Brown.

Maynard, R. A. (1995). Subsidized employment and nonlabor market alternatives for
welfare recipients. In D. S. Nightingale & R. H. Haveman (Eds.), *The work alternative: Welfare reform and the realities of the job market* (pp. 109-136). Washington, DC: Urban Institute.

McCrate, E. (1989). *Discrimination, returns to education, and teenage childbearing.*
Manuscript for the Middlebury College Conference on Discrimination Policies
and Research in the Post-Reagan Era, Middlebury, VT.

McLanahan, S., & Sandefur, G. (1994). *Growing up with a single parent: What hurts,
what helps.* Cambridge, MA: Harvard University Press.

Mead, L. M. (1992). *The new politics of poverty.* New York: Basic Books.

Mead, L. M. (1994). Poverty: How little we know. *Social Service Review, 68,* 322-350.

Mishel, L., & Bernstein, J. (1993). *The state of working America: 1992-93* (Economic Policy Institute Series). Armonk, NY: M. E. Sharpe.

Musick, J. (1993). *Young, poor, and pregnant: The psychology of teenage motherhood.* New Haven, CT: Yale University Press.

Nightingale, D. S. (1995). Welfare reform: Historical context and current issues. In D. S. Nightingale & R. H. Haveman (Eds.), *The work alternative: Welfare reform and the realities of the job market* (pp. 1-13). Washington, DC: Urban Institute.

Otto, L. B., & Haller, A. O. (1979). Evidence for a social psychological view of the status attainment process: Four studies compared. *Social Forces, 57,* 887-914.

Parcel, T. L., & Menaghan, E. G. (1994). Early parental work, family social capital, and early childhood outcomes. *American Journal of Sociology, 99,* 972-1009.

Polivka, A. E., & Nardone, T. (1989). On the definition of "contingent" work. *Monthly Labor Review, 112,* 9-15.

Rangarajan, A., Meckstroth, A., & Novak, T. (1998). *The effectiveness of the postemployment services demonstration: Preliminary findings.* Princeton, NJ: Mathematica Policy Research.

Rodman, H. (1971). *Lower-class families: The culture of poverty in Negro Trinidad.* Oxford: Oxford University Press.

Rosenfeld, R. A. (1992). Job mobility and career processes. *Annual Review of Sociology, 18,* 39-61.

Stack, C. B. (1974). *All our kin.* New York: Harper & Row.

Tienda, M., & Stier, H. (1991). Joblessness and shiftlessness: Labor force activity in Chicago's inner city. In C. Jencks & P. E. Peterson (Eds.), *The urban underclass* (pp. 135-154). Washington, DC: Brookings Institution.

Upchurch, D. M., & McCarthy, J. (1990). The timing of a first birth and high school completion. *American Sociological Review, 55,* 224-234.

Upchurch, D. M., McCarthy, J., & Ferguson, L. R. (1993). Childbearing and schooling: Disentangling temporal and causal mechanisms. *American Sociological Review, 58,* 738-740.

Weiss, R. S. (1994). *Learning from strangers: The art and method of qualitative interview studies.* New York: Free Press.

Wilson, J. Q. (1994). Culture, incentives, and the underclass. In H. J. Aaron, T. E. Mann, & T. Taylor (Eds.), *Values and public policy* (pp. 54-80). Washington, DC: Brookings Institution.

Wilson, W. J. (1991). Studying inner-city social dislocations: The challenge of public agenda research. *American Sociological Review, 56,* 1-14.

Wilson, W. J. (1996). *When work disappears.* New York: Alfred A. Knopf.

Woody, B. (1989). *Black women in the new services economy: Help or hindrance in economic self-sufficiency?* (Working Paper No. 196). Welsley, MA: Wellesley College Center for Research on Women.

Yankelovich, D. (1994). How changes in the economy are reshaping American values. In H. J. Aaron, T. E. Mann, & T. Taylor (Eds.), *Values and public policy* (pp. 16-53). Washington, DC: Brookings Institution.

Index

About the Editors

Toby L. Parcel is Professor of Sociology and Associate Dean, College of Social and Behavioral Sciences at The Ohio State University. She is coauthor of *Parents' Jobs and Children's Lives* (1994), which was awarded the Goode Book Award from the Family Section of the American Sociological Association in 1996. She is also editor of *Research in the Sociology of Work: Work and Family* (1999), as well as numerous articles and chapters concerning earnings inequality, work and technology, and work and family. Her current research interests include analyses of the effects of social capital, financial capital and human capital at home and at school on child outcomes, and regional differences in child academic achievement. She is also studying the effects of occupational labor market conditions on earnings attainment of men and women.

Daniel B. Cornfield is Professor and Chair of the Department of Sociology at Vanderbilt University and editor of *Work and Occupations*. His research on the changing workplace, employment relationship, and work and family has appeared in numerous scholarly journals and books. Among his recent publications are "Institutional Constraints on Social Movement 'Frame Extension': Shifts in the Legislative Agenda of the American Federation of Labor, 1881-1955," with Bill Fletcher in *Social Forces,* (June 1998), and "In the Community or in the Union? The Impact of Community Involvement on Non-Union Worker Attitudes About Unionizing," with others in Bronfenbrenner et al. (eds.), *Organizing to Win* (1998). A former member of the sociology panel of the National Science Foundation and past chair of the Section on Organizations, Occupations and Work of the American Sociological Association, he is researching the international evolution of the sociology of work and the social implications of workplace restructuring.

About the Contributors

Paul Burstein is Professor of Sociology and Adjunct Professor of Political Science at the University of Washington. His major interests are political sociology, social movements, social stratification, and the sociology of law. Among his publications on work and family issues are "Work, Family, and Gender on the Congressional Agenda" (*American Sociological Review* (1995), with Marie Bricher and Rachel Einwohner) and "Problem Definition and Public Policy" (*Social Forces* (1997), with Marie Bricher).

Amy G. Cox is an associate social scientist at RAND. She earned her Ph.D. in sociology from the University of Maryland in the fall of 1997 and spent two years as a postdoctoral fellow in RAND's Labor and Population Program. Her areas of interest are social inequality, labor markets, and families, and her research addresses how gender, racial-ethnic, and class systems interact with economic context to affect individuals' well-being. In addition to employment schedules, she has studied the relationship between female labor demand and the dynamics of women's poverty, the importance of economic opportunity for the likelihood that women will marry, the use of public assistance by grandparent-grandchild families, and the role of caseworkers in the implementation of welfare reform.

Mikaela J. Dufur is a Ph.D. candidate in sociology at The Ohio State University. Her research interests include stratification in major institutions, including the U.S. labor market, the U.S. educational system, families, and sport. Her current research includes a series of papers examining the ways families and schools work together to promote child achievement and social development (with Toby Parcel). Her dissertation focuses on mobility processes across institutions within occupational internal labor markets. Her previous work has appeared in *Work and Occupations, Journal of Marriage and the Family,* and the *Handbook of the Sociology of Gender* (1999), edited by Janet Saltzman Chafetz.

Naomi B. Farber, Ph.D., M.S.W., is Associate Professor of Social Work at the University of South Carolina. Her research has focused on the areas of adolescent pregnancy and parenting and of family life in the context of urban poverty with an emphasis on how class and race intersect to influence family development. Her current research interests include state policies of adolescent pregnancy prevention and the return migration of African Americans from northern to southern communities. Dr. Farber is currently the managing editor of the journal *Arete.*

Kathleen Gerson is Professor of Sociology at New York University and the author of several books on gender, work, and family issues, including *No Man's Land: Men's Changing Commitments to Family and Work* (1993) and *Hard Choices: How Women Decide About Work, Career, and Motherhood* (1985). She is currently collaborating with Jerry Jacobs on a project sponsored by the Sloan Foundation to examine trends in working time and their consequences for work-family conflict and gender equity in the modern workplace. In another ongoing project, she is writing a book on how the children of the gender revolution are responding to their experiences growing up in nontraditional families. A member of several policy forums on gender, work, and family issues, she also recently served as the 1998 Feminist Lecturer on Women and Social Change for the Sociologists for Women in Society.

Sandra L. Hofferth is Senior Research Scientist at the Institute for Social Research, University of Michigan, and Research Associate of the Population Studies Center. She directs the Child Development Supplement to the Panel Study of Income Dynamics. Her current research focuses on public policy and public assistance receipt, children's time, and parental employment, child care, and child well-being. She is on the Board of Directors of the Population Association of America, a member of the National Institute of Child Health and Human Development Family and Child Well-being Research Network, and past Chair of the Sociology of Children Section of the American Sociological Association.

Roberta Rehner Iversen, Ph.D., MSS, is Assistant Professor and Clinician Educator at the University of Pennsylvania School of Social Work. Recent publications in *Work & Occupations* and *Social Work* reflect her research focus on occupational attainment among poor women, including related issues of adolescent childbearing, family relations, race and ethnicity, and mental health. A recent article in *Demography* highlighted connections between literacy, interpretive issues, and error-making in the 1990 Census. Dr. Iversen is currently conducting an ethnographic examination of job retention supports and outcomes among constituents of welfare-to-work programs, including participants, program staff, and employers. She also develops and provides training in work-focused assessment materials for TANF programs.

Jerry A. Jacobs, Ph.D., is Professor of Sociology and Chair of the Graduate Program in Sociology at the University of Pennsylvania, where he has taught since earning his doctorate in sociology from Harvard University in 1983. He has studied a number of aspects of women's employment, including authority, earnings, working conditions, part-time work, and entry into male-dominated occupations. His current research projects include a study of women in higher education, funded by the Spencer Foundation, and a study of working time and work-family conflict, funded by the Sloan Foundation.

Monica Kirkpatrick Johnson, Ph.D., recently completed her graduate studies at the University of Minnesota and currently holds a postdoctoral research position through the Carolina Population Center at the University of North Carolina-Chapel Hill. Her fields of interest are work and family, race, gender, and quantitative methods. Her dissertation focused on the influences of work and family experiences on values during young adulthood. Other current projects include research on adolescents' anticipations of work-family conflict (with Sabrina Oesterle and Jeylan T. Mortimer); inheritance and property arrangements of adults in unmarried committed relationships (with Jennifer K. Robbennolt); and volunteerism during the transition to adulthood (with Sabrina Oesterle and Jeylan T. Mortimer).

Jeylan T. Mortimer is Professor of Sociology at the University of Minnesota and Director of the Life Course Center. She has conducted a series of longitudinal research projects related to the social psychology of work, including studies of occupational choice, vocational development in the family and work settings, psychological change in response to work, job satisfaction, work involvement, and the link between work and family life. Since 1987 she has directed the Youth Development Study, an ongoing longitudinal examination of the effects of early work experience on students and its implications for mental health, adjustment, and achievement as they mature. The interrelations of adolescent work and family life are examined in her book, *Adolescents, Work, and Families: An Intergenerational Development Analysis* (1996), coauthored with M. Finch. She is now studying the effects of adolescent work on the timing and patterning of markers of transition to adulthood. She is past chair of the Social Psychology Section and current chair of the Sociology of Children Section of the American Sociological Association and a fellow of the American Association for the Advancement of Science. She holds a B.A. degree from Tufts University and M.A. and Ph.D. degrees from the University of Michigan.

Rebecca A. Nickoll holds master's degrees in labor and human resources and in sociology, both from The Ohio State University. Her master's thesis, "The Effects of Parental Work and Maternal Nonemployment on Children's Reading and Math Achievement," was published with Toby Parcel and Mikaela Dufur in 1996. She received her B.A. in sociology from Indiana University. She is currently employed with Nationwide Insurance in Columbus, Ohio, as a performance improvement consultant. This role allows her to combine her sociology and human resources background to work on organizational development initiatives.

Harriet B. Presser (Ph.D. 1969, University of California, Berkeley) is Distinguished University Professor in the Department of Sociology and Director, Center on Population, Gender, and Social Inequality at the University of Maryland, College Park. She is past president of the Population Association of America (1989), and was named George Washington University's 1992 Distinguished Alumni Scholar, having received her B.A. from there in 1959. She has been a fellow at the Center for Advanced Study in the Behavioral Sciences at Stanford (both in 1986-87 and 1991-92), a fellow at the Netherlands Institute for Advanced Study in the Humanities and Social Sciences (1994-95), and a visiting scholar at the Russell Sage Foundation (1998-99). She has held faculty positions at the University of Sussex (England) and Columbia University's School of Public Health, and was also on the staff of the Population Council, the Institute of Life Insurance, and the U.S. Bureau of the Census. Her research expertise is in the areas of social demography and issues relating to gender, work, and the family, both domestically and internationally.

Joanne C. Sandberg is a doctoral candidate in sociology at Vanderbilt University and Assistant Professor of Sociology at Tennessee Technological

University. Her areas of interest include gender, work and family, and social stratification. She is currently researching the effects of family demands and employment-related resources on men's and women's decisions to take family leaves.

Heike Trappe (Ph.D.) is a sociologist and scientific researcher at the Max Planck Institute for Human Development in Berlin. Her research interests are in the areas of gender stratification, labor market research, and family sociology. She is author of *Emanzipation oder Zwang? Frauen in der DDR zwischen Beruf, Familie und Sozialpolitik* [Emancipation or Coercion? Women in the GDR between Employment, Family, and Social Policy] (Berlin: Akademie Verlag). As well as continuing her collaboration with Rachel Rosenfeld on occupational sex segregation in Germany, she is currently involved in a research project on young people's transition to employment and early work histories in Germany.

Susan Wierzbicki is a Ph.D. candidate in sociology at the University of Washington. Her other published work looks at differences in socializing inside and outside of neighborhoods. Her dissertation examines immigrants' residential patterns and networks.